Rottweilers For Dummies®

Your Puppy Shopping List

Before you bring your Rottweiler pup home, have the following items on hand. Refer to Chapter 5 for more information on welcoming home your puppy.

- Paneled fence partition or pen to cordon off a living area for the puppy
- Fiberglass kennel crate or metal wire cage
- Feeding bowls and water dishes
- Food prescribed by the breeder
- Brushes, combs, and nail clippers
- Doggy quick bath
- Special dog shampoo
- Collars and leashes
- Toys
- Household odor neutralizer and cleaners
- Chewing deterrents

What to Keep in Your Rottweiler First Aid Kit

Keep the following items in a first aid kit for your dog. Refer to Chapter 13 for more information on responding to emergencies.

- Activated charcoal tablets
- Adhesive tape (1- and 2-inch widths)
- Antibacterial ointment (for skin and eyes)
- Antihistamine (approved by your vet for allergic reactions)
- Athletic sock (to slip over an injured paw)
- Bandages and dressing pads (gauze rolls, 1- and 2-inch widths)
- Blanket (for moving an injured dog or warming)
- Cotton balls
- Diarrhea medicine
- Dosing syringe
- Eyewash
- Emergency phone numbers (taped on the cover of the first aid kit)
- Hydrogen peroxide (3 percent solution)
- Ipecac syrup (to induce vomiting)
- Nylon stocking (to use as a muzzle)
- Petroleum jelly
- Pliers or tweezers (for removing stings, barbs, and quills)
- Rectal thermometer
- Rubber gloves
- Rubbing alcohol
- Scissors (preferably with rounded tips)
- Tourniquet kit
- Syringe (without needle, for administering oral medications)
- Towel
- Tweezers

For Dummies: Bestselling Book Series for Beginners

Rottweilers For Dummies®

When to Call the Vet

If your Rottweiler has any of the following symptoms, call your vet immediately:

- Blood in the stool
- Limping, trembling, or shaking
- Abscesses, lumps, or swellings
- Dark or cloudy urine
- Difficulty urinating
- Loss of bowel or bladder control
- Deep red or white gums
- Persistent coughing or sneezing
- Loss or impairment of motor control
- Gasping for breath
- Chronic vomiting
- Chronic diarrhea
- Continued listlessness
- Loss of appetite
- Excessive thirst
- Runny nose
- Discharge from eyes or ears

Cheat Sheet $2.95 value. Item 5271-6.
For more information about Hungry Minds, call 1-800-762-2974.

References for the Rest of Us!®

BESTSELLING BOOK SERIES

Do you find that traditional reference books are overloaded with technical details and advice you'll never use? Do you postpone important life decisions because you just don't want to deal with them? Then our *For Dummies®* business and general reference book series is for you.

For Dummies business and general reference books are written for those frustrated and hard-working souls who know they aren't dumb, but find that the myriad of personal and business issues and the accompanying horror stories make them feel helpless. *For Dummies* books use a lighthearted approach, a down-to-earth style, and even cartoons and humorous icons to dispel fears and build confidence. Lighthearted but not lightweight, these books are perfect survival guides to solve your everyday personal and business problems.

"More than a publishing phenomenon, 'Dummies' is a sign of the times."

— The New York Times

"A world of detailed and authoritative information is packed into them. . ."

— U.S. News and World Report

". . .you won't go wrong buying them."

— Walter Mossberg, Wall Street Journal, on For Dummies books

Already, millions of satisfied readers agree. They have made For Dummies the #1 introductory level computer book series and a best-selling business book series. They have written asking for more. So, if you're looking for the best and easiest way to learn about business and other general reference topics, look to *For Dummies* to give you a helping hand.

1/01

Rottweilers FOR DUMMIES®

by Richard Beauchamp

Best-Selling Books • Digital Downloads • e-Books • Answer Networks • e-Newsletters • Branded Web Sites • e-Learning

New York, NY ◆ Cleveland, OH ◆ Indianapolis, IN

Rottweilers For Dummies®

Published by
Hungry Minds, Inc.
909 Third Avenue
New York, NY 10022
www.hungryminds.com
www.dummies.com

Library of Congress Control Number: 00-108201

ISBN: 0-7645-5271-6

Printed in the United States of America

10 9 8 7

1B/SX/QT/QS/IN

Distributed in the United States by Hungry Minds, Inc.

Distributed by CDG Books Canada Inc. for Canada; by Transworld Publishers Limited in the United Kingdom; by IDG Norge Books for Norway; by IDG Sweden Books for Sweden; by IDG Books Australia Publishing Corporation Pty. Ltd. for Australia and New Zealand; by TransQuest Publishers Pte Ltd. for Singapore, Malaysia, Thailand, Indonesia, and Hong Kong; by Gotop Information Inc. for Taiwan; by ICG Muse, Inc. for Japan; by Intersoft for South Africa; by Eyrolles for France; by International Thomson Publishing for Germany, Austria and Switzerland; by Distribuidora Cuspide for Argentina; by LR International for Brazil; by Galileo Libros for Chile; by Ediciones ZETA S.C.R. Ltda. for Peru; by WS Computer Publishing Corporation, Inc., for the Philippines; by Contemporanea de Ediciones for Venezuela; by Express Computer Distributors for the Caribbean and West Indies; by Micronesia Media Distributor, Inc. for Micronesia; by Chips Computadoras S.A. de C.V. for Mexico; by Editorial Norma de Panama S.A. for Panama; by American Bookshops for Finland.

For general information on Hungry Minds' products and services please contact our Customer Care Department within the U.S. at 800-762-2974, outside the U.S. at 317-572-3993 or fax 317-572-4002.

For sales inquiries and reseller information, including discounts, premium and bulk quantity sales, and foreign-language translations, please contact our Customer Care Department at 800-434-3422, fax 317-572-4002, or write to Hungry Minds, Inc., Attn: Customer Care Department, 10475 Crosspoint Boulevard, Indianapolis, IN 46256.

For information on licensing foreign or domestic rights, please contact our Sub-Rights Customer Care Department at 212-884-5000.

For information on using Hungry Minds' products and services in the classroom or for ordering examination copies, please contact our Educational Sales Department at 800-434-2086 or fax 317-572-4005.

Please contact our Public Relations Department at 212-884-5163 for press review copies or 212-884-5000 for author interviews and other publicity information or fax 212-884-5400.

For authorization to photocopy items for corporate, personal, or educational use, please contact Copyright Clearance Center, 222 Rosewood Drive, Danvers, MA 01923, or fax 978-750-4470.

About the Author

Richard G. ("Rick") Beauchamp has been successfully involved in practically every facet of purebred dogs. He has bred them as well as trained and handled them professionally in the show ring. For many years, he owned and managed a publishing house devoted almost entirely to books and periodicals about purebred dogs. He is a published author of numerous breed and all-breed dog books and has lectured extensively on purebred dogs throughout the world.

As a breeder-exhibitor, Rick has been actively involved in breeds of nearly all the Variety Groups, including top winning Chow Chows, Dachshunds, Salukis, and Irish Setters. His Beau Monde Kennel has produced outstanding Boxers, Cocker Spaniels, Poodles, Wire Fox Terriers, Bull Terriers, Pembroke Welsh Corgis, Cavalier King Charles Spaniels, and Chinese Shar-Pei.

As a judge of all breeds with the Federacion Cynologique Internationale, Rick has had the distinct pleasure of judging Rottweilers at championship events many times in Mexico, throughout the United Kingdom, Scandinavia, Europe, Australia, New Zealand, South Africa, the Orient, Central America, and South America. Rick now judges throughout North America for the American Kennel Club, the Canadian Kennel Club, and the United Kennel Club.

In his *other* life, Rick has had a lifelong interest in film and theater and spent several years as a copy editor and reporter for the television and film industry's bible, *Daily Variety.* He lives in Cambria, California, which is situated midway between Los Angeles and San Francisco.

Dedication

This book is dedicated to the Rottweiler breeders, exhibitors, and owners who, through the years, have worked hard to preserve and enhance the great qualities the breed was created to possess — bravery, loyalty, and devotion. It goes without question that there are other breeds who may possess any one or perhaps even all of these same characteristics, but I am quite confident that none could possibly combine them so well and so uniquely as does the Rottweiler.

Author's Acknowledgments

No words will ever be able to express my appreciation for those wonderful books with dog heroes in them written by the late Albert Payson Terhune. His books not only inspired a love of all nature but a fascination with the magic of the written word.

The enthusiastic and supportive people at Hungry Minds have helped tremendously in translating my fascination with purebred dogs and the words we use to describe them into what I sincerely hope is a helpful guide to understanding and appreciating the many fine qualities of the Rottweiler breed.

I particularly wish to thank my editor, Elizabeth Kuball, who assisted me so well in consolidating all the bits and pieces of my experience with dogs in general and the Rottweiler in particular into this book.

About Howell Book House
Committed to the Human/Companion Animal Bond

Thank you for choosing a book brought to you by the pet experts at Howell Book House, a division of Hungry Minds. And welcome to the family of pet owners who've put their trust in Howell books for nearly 40 years!

Pet ownership is about relationships — the bonds people form with their dogs, cats, horses, birds, fish, small mammals, reptiles, and other animals. Howell Book House/Hungry Minds understands that these are some of the most important relationships in life, and that it's vital to nurture them through enjoyment and education. The happiest pet owners are those who know they're taking the best care of their pets — and with Howell books owners have this satisfaction. They're happy, educated owners, and as a result, they have happy pets, and that enriches the bond they share.

Howell Book House was established in 1961 by Mr. Elsworth S. Howell, an active and proactive dog fancier who showed English Setters and judged at the prestigious Westminster Kennel Club show in New York. Mr. Howell based his publishing program on strength of content, and his passion for books written by experienced and knowledgeable owners defined Howell Book House and has remained true over the years. Howell's reputation as the premier pet book publisher is supported by the distinction of having won more awards from the Dog Writers Association of America than any other publisher. Howell Book House/Hungry Minds has over 400 titles in publication, including such classics as The American Kennel Club's *Complete Dog Book,* the *Dog Owner's Home Veterinary Handbook, Blessed Are the Brood Mares,* and *Mother Knows Best: The Natural Way to Train Your Dog.*

When you need answers to questions you have about any aspect of raising or training your companion animals, trust that Howell Book House/Hungry Minds has the answers. We welcome your comments and suggestions, and we look forward to helping you maximize your relationships with your pets throughout the years.

The Howell Book House Staff

Publisher's Acknowledgments

We're proud of this book; please send us your comments through our Online Registration Form located at www.dummies.com.

Some of the people who helped bring this book to market include the following:

Acquisitions, Editorial, and Media Development

Project Editor: Elizabeth Netedu Kuball

Acquisitions Editor: Scott Prentzas

Technical Editor: Gwen Chaney

Editorial Manager: Pamela Mourouzis

Editorial Assistant: Carol Strickland

Cover Photo: The Image Bank © Stephen Deer

Production

Project Coordinator: Maridee Ennis

Layout and Graphics: Jacque Schneider, Julie Trippetti, Jeremey Unger

Special Art: Barbara Frake

Proofreaders: Corey Bowen, David Faust, Susan Moritz, York Production Services, Inc.

Indexer: John Sleeva

Hungry Minds Consumer Reference Group

Business: Kathleen A. Welton, Vice President and Publisher; Kevin Thornton, Acquisitions Manager

Cooking/Gardening: Jennifer Feldman, Associate Vice President and Publisher

Education/Reference: Diane Graves Steele, Vice President and Publisher

Lifestyles/Pets: Kathleen Nebenhaus, Vice President and Publisher; Tracy Boggier, Managing Editor

Travel: Michael Spring, Vice President and Publisher; Suzanne Jannetta, Editorial Director; Brice Gosnell, Publishing Director

Hungry Minds Consumer Editorial Services: Kathleen Nebenhaus, Vice President and Publisher; Kristin A. Cocks, Editorial Director; Cindy Kitchel, Editorial Director

Hungry Minds Consumer Production: Debbie Stailey, Production Director

Contents at a Glance

Cartoons at a Glance

By Rich Tennant

"We enjoy our Rottweiler's protection and companionship. His herding instinct also comes in handy when I'm at the Mall with the kids."

page 5

"No, it's not normal to dress a Rottweiler this way, but it puts the Vet at ease when I bring him in for a checkup."

page 29

"OK, I'LL LET HIM PLAY AS LONG AS YOU STOP SAYING, 'YOU CAN'T TAKE AN OLD DOG'S NEW TRICKS'."

page 57

page 137

page 199

Fax: 978-546-7747
E-mail: richtennant@the5thwave.com
World Wide Web: www.the5thwave.com

Table of Contents

Introduction

In *Rottweilers For Dummies,* you'll be introduced to all the good, the bad, and the ugly that surrounds the breed. Too many books written about purebred dogs do nothing but try to convince you that the breed is not only faultless but suitable for every household in America (or anywhere else in the world for that matter). I seldom find this to be true of any breed, and I know this doesn't describe the Rottweiler. So you won't find me twisting your arm and trying to convince you that a Rottweiler is right for you. In fact, if anything, I'm as honest as possible about this challenging breed. That way, if you're still eager to get one of these wonderful dogs, you'll be prepared for any drawbacks and able to handle them well.

Rottweilers are one of the smartest, most trainable breeds I have ever known. Not only is the Rottweiler capable of learning just about everything any other breed can master, the Rottie also has the energy, the strength, and the enthusiasm to carry it all off. A Rottie is smart, affectionate, protective, and easy-going around those he loves.

Along with all those perfect dog qualities I've attributed to the Rottweiler, there are a few drawbacks. Among them is the fact that those same qualities have made the Rottweiler one of the most popular breeds in the world. The breed's popularity, as well as population, have soared over the past decade. This popularity puts the breed into the hands of people who are completely incapable of providing the training and care a Rottweiler needs.

The Rottweiler whose owner has neglected training is nothing but a big nuisance. Without the proper training, a Rottweiler can become an unruly brute. A Rottweiler wants — and needs — a leader in his life. If an owner doesn't provide that leadership, the Rottie assumes the role himself, and a Rottweiler acting on his own volition can be difficult — if not downright dangerous.

The information in *Rottweilers For Dummies* will help you decide if you should even consider taking on the responsibility of Rottweiler ownership. If the answer is yes, you'll find plenty of valuable information, tips, and suggestions that will assist you and your Rottie along the road to a mutually delightful relationship.

So Who Am I?

Nothing in this book came by way of divine inspiration. Everything in *Rottweilers For Dummies* is the result of my own years of trial and error with purebred dogs or through the kind intervention of my many mentors through the years.

My interest in purebred dogs goes back as far as I can remember and has led me through practically every facet of these wonderful animals: breeding, exhibiting, professional handling, publishing, writing, and judging. All that experience has also assisted me in presenting lectures to dog fanciers around the world.

For over 30 years, I owned and published *Kennel Review Magazine,* and doing so associated me with some of the most learned dog men and women the world over. As a breeder/exhibitor, using the Beau Monde kennel prefix, I have bred nearly 100 American Kennel Club champions in a number of different breeds.

My judging assignments have taken me to practically every major dog showing country in the world, which has given me the opportunity to judge Rottweilers in almost every instance. I now judge for the American Kennel Club, the Canadian Kennel Club, and the United Kennel Club in North America.

How This Book Is Organized

Rottweilers For Dummies is divided into five parts. If you're just starting to think about getting a Rottweiler, try starting out with Chapter 1. If you already own a Rottweiler and have a specific question or problem, dive into the chapter that best suits your needs right now.

Part I: Getting to Know Rottweilers

In this part, you'll get a feel for Rottweilers as a breed. Then you'll set about to determine whether a Rottweiler is right for you. Everyone's needs and personalities are different, and before you head out to the nearest breeder to find a Rottweiler pup, you owe it to yourself and the dog you may bring home to do some serious soul-searching.

Part II: Searching for Your Soul Mate

The chapters in this part are geared toward helping you figure out what you actually want in a Rottweiler. You may be sure a Rottweiler is right for you.

But Rotties vary just like people do. So knowing your lifestyle and priorities is just as important at this stage in the game as it is in determining what breed you want.

You also need to know where to look for your new best friend. So I guide you through the process of finding a reputable breeder and tell you which ones to steer clear of altogether.

Finally, you get to the fun stuff: picking out a puppy. Sometimes looking at the pups in a litter makes you want to bring them *all* home. So in this part I let you know which traits to look for in a puppy, physically and emotionally.

Part III: Living with a Rottweiler

In this part, you plan ahead so that you have all the toys and tools you'll need before that plump little pup arrives. And you also get tips on introducing your Rottweiler pup to his new home. Finally, no puppy would be a puppy without the need for training. So you'll figure out which behaviors to start working on with your Rottweiler from the very first day. And you'll also get tips on which behaviors your dog should know as he grows into adulthood. You even get suggestions for going the extra mile with your dog and going through more formal obedience training with a professional trainer.

Living with a Rottweiler? Here I make it one of life's greatest joys.

Part IV: Keeping Your Rottweiler Healthy

Many dog owners accept as fact the stories they've heard for generations, when the stories are, in reality, pure fiction. Knowing what makes your Rottweiler tick and how to keep that well-functioning clock in perfect order are important if you want your pal to live a long and healthy life. This includes knowing what to feed your dog and how much exercise to give her. In the chapters in this part, you get information on anything and everything that pertains to your Rottie's health.

An ounce of prevention is most definitely worth a pound of cure. So I let you know how to prevent your dog from getting sick by taking care of him along the way.

Accidents and illnesses are not always avoidable, so being fully prepared for these events is always wise. In this part, you'll find instructions for dealing with emergencies involving your dog. And you'll know what chronic health problems sometimes affect Rotties as they age and how best to handle them.

Part V: The Part of Tens

In this part you'll get lots of useful information in a small amount of space. Whether you're trying to figure out whether to get a Rottweiler, or you want to find ways to train the one you already have, there's something in this part for you. I offer some useful tips on traveling with your pet as well. In a time crunch? Turn to the chapters in this part.

Icons Used in This Book

Icons are those eye-catching little pictures in the margins of this book. They're meant to grab your attention as you flip the pages, and they steer you to specific bits of information you need. Here's a list of the icons in this book and what I use them for:

If you're looking for information on how to do something better, look for the Tip icon.

Whenever something could harm your Rottweiler or someone else, I flag it with this icon.

This icon is the place to turn for information that you can use to impress your friends at the dog park. But you probably don't *need* to know it. If you just want the basics, pass these paragraphs by.

Some pieces of information are so important that they're worth repeating. So when you see this icon, pay attention. Because the information nearby includes things you'll want to remember.

Throughout this book, you'll find interesting Rottweiler anecdotes or funny stories that are great to know for fun but probably aren't critical to know. I flag them with this icon.

Occasionally, I toss in products or services that are useful for Rottweiler owners, and I highlight them with this wagging tail.

Part I

Getting to Know Rottweilers

The 5th Wave By Rich Tennant

©RICHTENNANT

"We enjoy our Rottweiler's protection and companionship. His herding instinct also comes in handy when I'm at the Mall with the kids."

In this part . . .

In this part, I let you know all the basics you need on Rottweilers as a breed. I also guide you through the process of figuring out whether a Rottweiler is the right dog for you. If you're just starting to think about getting a Rottweiler, this is the place to begin.

Chapter 1

So What Exactly Is a Rottweiler?

In This Chapter

- Taking a look at what makes the Rottweiler unique
- Knowing the breed standards for the Rottweiler
- Figuring out which of the breed standards your Rottweiler must meet
- Getting a primer on the Rottweiler's history and what it means to you today

If you're taking the time to read this book, you've probably either seen a Rottweiler in the flesh or at least have seen pictures of the breed. You know what Rottweilers look like. But the Rottweiler is much more than his looks. So in this chapter, I take you through the basics of the breed. I help you understand not only why the Rottweiler looks the way he does, but also why he is able to perform in the many capacities that he's bred for. How a Rottweiler behaves and his high level of trainability are as important as, if not more important than, what the individual dog looks like.

In this chapter, I take you through everything from the German breed standard and American Kennel Club (AKC) breed standard to what you can and should expect from a Rottweiler and why. You get a good picture here of what the Rottweiler is all about, which can help you in your quest to get to know this wonderful and challenging breed.

Understanding What Sets the Rottweiler Apart

The Rottweiler has a reputation for being tough, and deservedly so. But that doesn't mean the breed is, or ever should be, mindlessly mean. The ideal Rottweiler's character and temperament are the result of generations of controlled breeding and rigorous testing by the breed's German developers.

Although the Germans who framed the Rottweiler breed wanted a dog who was courageous and protective, the last thing they had in mind was a dog who couldn't be controlled or one who went off half-cocked.

Mature Rottweilers can be as strong as most men, and probably a lot more agile. In the right hands, a Rottweiler can be the best security system in town and, at the same time, he can be a good friend the entire family can rely on for fun and games. The well-bred, well-trained Rottweiler, like the one shown in Figure 1-1, has the courage of a lion and is as willing to obey as the best-behaved child. In the wrong hands, the very same dog could just as easily be a complete menace. The Rottweiler has an amazing capacity to learn, but he also requires a capable teacher.

Everything in the Rottweiler's history, including the guys in Germany who formulated the first breed standard, demands that the breed be bold, courageous and protective. Yet standing right alongside those requirements are demands that the breed be peaceable and of a good nature — cooperative and possessed of a willingness to learn and to abide by a master's wishes. If the scale tips more to one side or the other, the essence of the Rottweiler is lost. However, if balance is achieved, you have Rottweiler perfection.

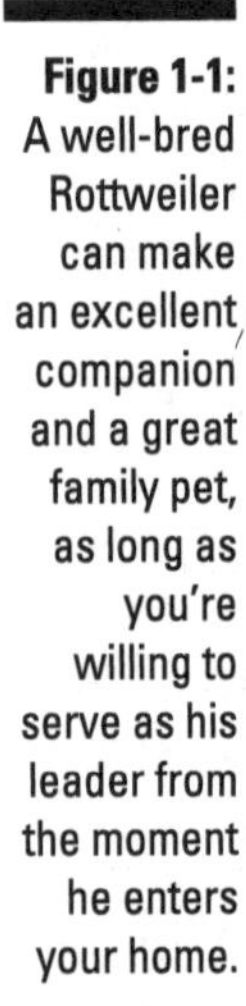

Figure 1-1: A well-bred Rottweiler can make an excellent companion and a great family pet, as long as you're willing to serve as his leader from the moment he enters your home.

Photograph courtesy of Judith E. Strom

Looking at the Purpose of Breed Standards

With all of this talk about what the Rottweiler should and shouldn't be and how he should and shouldn't act, you may be wondering, "Who says so?" The presiding kennel club of each country in the world has a system for registering the purebred dogs that are born and bred in that country. The American Kennel Club (AKC) is the recognized authority here in the United States. These clubs issue certificates of registration that are probably best described as canine birth certificates. These canine birth certificates are just as important as ours. The only way a dog can be considered a purebred and be registered is if the dog's father and mother (*sire* and *dam* in dog parlance) are registered, and the only way they could have been registered is if their parents were registered, and so on.

For a breed to be accepted by one of the registering sources in the first place, the supporters of the breed must form a club and provide credentials certifying that their dogs were bred true to form and free of *outcrosses* (the introduction of other breeds) for at least five generations. Before a breed is given official recognition, the sponsoring club is also required to submit a written description of the breed that gives a word picture of both what the breed should look like and how it should interact with humans. This written description is called the *breed standard.* Rottweilers were granted recognition by the AKC in 1936.

The AKC currently offers the prospective dog owner 148 breeds to choose from, and there are probably upwards of 400 breeds recognized worldwide. They range from Chihuahuas — one of the tiniest toy breeds, weighing in under 6 pounds — to the giant breeds that include man-sized Great Danes and Irish Wolfhounds. Practically every one of these breeds was developed with a specific purpose in mind. Chihuahuas may have been developed for different reasons than Great Danes, but there was a reason for the development of each breed.

The toy breeds were meant to be companions, in most cases for the ladies who wanted a dog small enough and light enough to be carried around easily. Canine duties for larger dogs range from hunting small game to hauling large loads. The size, shape, and temperament of each breed has been carefully manipulated though many generations to conform to an ideal. To this day, in order for a purebred dog to be a good example of his breed, the dog must not only have a specific look, but must also *behave* in a manner typical of the breed.

Let's face it, if you went out to buy a laid back kind of a dog like a Basset Hound and the dog behaved like a Jack Russell Terrier, you would understandably be somewhat upset. On the other hand, if you brought home a dog to guard the family jewels and it met intruders at the door with his tail wagging and a road map to the safe in his mouth — well, I think you see the point I'm trying to make.

Most breed standards explain how tall the average dog of the breed you are considering will grow by giving a height at the *withers.* That measurement is taken from the top of the shoulder to the ground. Some standards also give the average weight of full-grown dogs and bitches.

Many breeds have changed so drastically in both form and temperament from the original concept that they are barely recognizable today. Rottweiler breeders in the United States and throughout the world have made every effort to maintain the essence of the breed. A truly outstanding Rottweiler is respected and appreciated anywhere he goes — truly an international citizen.

The German standard

In Germany, dog breeding was never a case of taking your female dog down the street to get her hitched to the neighborhood male. As new breeds were created, German fanciers organized clubs to improve and protect their respective breeds. If people wanted to breed dogs, they had to join the club dedicated to the breed and abide by the club's rules and regulations.

The club that was organized to oversee the breeding of Rottweilers was the *Allgemeiner Deutscher Rottweiler Klub* (the General German Rottweiler Club, or ADRK). The ADRK wrote a standard of perfection for the Rottweiler upon which all other standards, including the American and British, are based.

The ADRK has never had any qualms about amending or adding to its standard and has created a great deal of supplementary material to accompany the original standard. The information in the following sections is the basic standard advocated by the ADRK. The American (AKC) standard follows the original ADRK standard in essence.

Few titles earned by dogs in foreign countries engender as much respect as those earned by the Rottweiler in Germany, the breed's country of origin. This is largely due to Germany's great reputation for breeding highly intelligent working dogs, and the training ability of the people who work with those breeds.

Read through both the German and AKC standards of the Rottweiler (in "The AKC standard," later in this chapter), and you will begin to see that the Rottweiler is described as a dog of great power and grace. Sheer bulk alone does not give a Rottweiler the strength and agility to perform as the breed was intended.

Size and appearance

According to the German standard, "The Rottweiler is a medium-large, robust dog neither gross nor slight, nor spindly. In correct proportion he is compactly and powerfully built indicating great strength, maneuverability, and endurance." In other words, don't judge your Rottweiler puppy by the pound. The Rottweiler is a medium-large breed, not a giant breed. Huge Rottweilers are often far more prone to joint diseases and other ailments than their smaller counterparts.

"Medium-large" means that the standard is 24 to 27 inches high and 100 pounds for dogs and 22 to 25 inches high and 92 pounds for bitches.

The head

The head is medium-long and broad in the back. The dog should have pronounced cheekbones and strong jaws, and the upper incisors should close like scissors over the lower teeth. Rottweilers should have a full complement of 42 teeth. Each eye should be dark and shaped like an almond. The ears should be triangular and set high on the skull.

The head sits atop a powerful, moderately long, well-muscled neck that is slightly arched.

The body

The Rottweiler should have a straight and strong back, a broad chest, and a short *docked* (artificially cut) tail.

Both front and rear legs are straight and not set close together. The feet should be round and hard, with black nails and no *dewclaws* (an extra claw on the inside of the front leg — a kind of rudimentary fifth toe). The thighs are powerful and heavily muscled.

The coat actually consists of an outer coat and under coat. The outer coat is medium-long, coarse, thick, and straight. The under coat must not show through the outer coat. A Rottweiler should be black with sharply defined, dark reddish-brown markings on the cheeks, muzzle, under the neck, on the chest and legs, over the eyes, and under the tail.

When the Rottweiler moves, the back remains firm and relatively motionless. The gait is harmonious, positive, powerful, and free, with long strides.

Faults

A dog with no faults simply doesn't exist. Every dog deviates from the ideal in some way. Still, the breed standard has a long list of faults that judges and breeders are asked to take note of. These include having a narrow or long head; light eyes; a back that dips down or humps up; crooked legs; a coat that is too long, too short, too soft or of the wrong color; and various faults of the ears, eyes, nose, cheeks, lips, feet, legs, tail, back, chest, and just about every other part of the body. A Rottweiler who looks less than solid and strong is also considered to have faults. These faults should be weighed carefully when a dog is being judged, either in the show ring or in a breeding program, but they don't eliminate a dog from contention.

However, some faults do eliminate a Rottweiler from contention in dog shows. These more serious faults are called *disqualifying faults.* Disqualifying faults include dogs that look like bitches (and vice versa), having yellow eyes or various eye conditions, missing molars, missing testicles, a long and curly coat, white markings, or grossly incorrect colors.

A dog who is nervous, shy, or vicious also has a disqualifying fault. According to the German standard, the Rottweiler "is descended from friendly and peaceful stock and by nature loves children, is affectionate, obedient, trainable, and enjoys working. His rough appearance belies his ancestry. His demeanor is self-reliant, with strong nerves and fearless character. He is keenly alert to, and aware of, his surroundings."

Although not all breed disqualifications (flaws that eliminate a dog from being shown) necessarily eliminate a Rottweiler from being a happy, healthy companion, there is one that does. Any Rottweiler of unsound temperament should not be shown, bred from, or *ever* owned as a pet.

The AKC standard

The AKC standard for the Rottweiler is much more detailed than the German standard, because the German standard is accompanied by official statements of requirements that are not necessarily contained in the standard. The German standard and the accompanying statements are far more likely to be amended or changed over time than is the AKC standard. Changing an American standard requires serious consideration by both the AKC and the American Rottweiler Club (ARC); the membership of the ARC must put any change to a vote.

Size and appearance

According to the AKC standard, "The ideal Rottweiler is a medium large, robust, and powerful dog, black with clearly defined rust markings. His compact and substantial build denotes great strength, agility, and endurance. Dogs are characteristically more massive throughout with larger frame and heavier bones than bitches. Bitches are distinctly feminine, but without weakness of substance or structure." Sound familiar?

Height is the same as the German standard for dogs and bitches (24 to 27 inches for dogs; 22 to 25 inches for bitches), but no weights are given in the AKC standard. The standard then goes on to say, "Correct proportion is of primary importance, as long as size is within the standard's range." The formula for figuring correct proportion is that the ratio of height to length should be 9 to 10.

The head and body

In the AKC standard, the Rottweiler's head and neck are described with much of the same language as in the German standard. However, the AKC standard makes two additional points:

- The underline of a mature Rottweiler has a slight *tuck-up,* which means there is an upward arch to his belly.
- "The back remains horizontal to the ground while the dog is moving or standing," which provides a lot of information about proper structure.

The AKC's descriptions of a Rottweiler's coat and markings are pretty much the same as the German standard as well. But the AKC standard tells us that the Rottweiler is to be exhibited in the natural condition with no trimming — in others words, there's no fudging a coat that's a little too long.

Faults, both disqualifying and not, are also much the same.

A long-coated Rottweiler cannot be shown at AKC shows, but they are born into some litters. This does not change the character of the dog, and as long as the pet owner has no intention of showing or breeding a long-coated Rottweiler, he makes just as good a pet as his short-coated littermates.

Temperament

The AKC standard has this to say about the Rottweiler's temperament:

> The Rottweiler is basically a calm, confident, and courageous dog with a self-assured aloofness that does not lend itself to immediate and indiscriminate friendships. A Rottweiler is self-confident and responds quietly and with a wait-and-see attitude to influences in his environment. He has an inherent desire to protect home and family and is an intelligent dog of extreme hardness and adaptability, with a strong willingness to work, making him especially suited as a companion, guardian, and general all-purpose dog. The behavior of the Rottweiler in the show ring should be controlled, willing, and adaptable, trained to submit to examination of mouth, testicles, etc. An aloof or reserved dog should not be penalized, as this reflects the accepted character of the breed. An aggressive or belligerent attitude towards other dogs should not be faulted. A judge shall excuse from the ring any shy Rottweiler.

Most established breeders anticipate that at least 95 percent of the Rottweilers they breed will spend their lives in homes as family companions. Therefore, the one thing they will not make concessions on is temperament — and that applies to not only the dogs they keep to show and breed but also to the majority of their dogs, who will be household pets. However, temperament is a two-way street. A well-bred Rottweiler puppy comes to you with a sound and stable temperament, but you must return the efforts of the breeder by making sure your puppy is properly socialized and given the proper amount and kind of training. Otherwise, the best efforts of the breeder will fail.

Knowing Whether Your Rottweiler Has to Fit the Standard

The standards I cover in this chapter are guidelines. Because nothing in nature is ever perfect, these guidelines act like carrots in front of a good breeder's nose — perfection is always just out of reach. The best of a breeder's efforts are what he or she uses to perpetuate the line and what often becomes show stock — the dogs who are campaigned to achieve Championship status.

Some dogs do, of course, fall just a bit too short of this elusive perfection to be either show stock or breeding stock. They are the Rottweilers, both male and female, who are intelligently bred and of sterling temperament but who just don't have what it takes to come home with all the blue ribbons.

A highly recommended breeder will give you the assurance that the puppy or young adult you buy will meet the highest physical and temperamental standards of the breed. That must be your top priority in the purchase of a Rottweiler. Minor cosmetic shortcomings will not change the breed's compatibility or temperament. When you are going to live with a dog for many years, a tiny blemish here or there is not going to make one iota of difference.

If you are looking for a Rottweiler that you want to show or breed, you must discuss your plans with the breeder so that he or she can help you choose a puppy that qualifies both temperamentally and physically.

Taking a Quick Tour of Rottweiler History

By the time Romans were attending games in the amphitheaters, humans had developed a level of sophistication that was reflected in many ways. Classes of society had developed so that there were those who did the work and those who sat around and thought up all kinds of work for everyone else to do. One of the things thought up was how to further meddle with nature and make more breeds of dogs out of those that already existed.

The noble ladies of Rome had tiny dogs to sit on their laps and keep them company, but real men (the ones who didn't eat quiche) had dogs that were large enough and fierce enough to fight lions, tigers, and assorted other wild beasts in the arena. Only the largest, strongest, and fiercest of these dogs were allowed to fight in the Roman arenas. These brawny beasts were known as the *Mollosus,* and although there were undoubtedly many candidates for the honor of tearing everything in sight limb from limb, not all the dogs qualified. From the same litters that produced the arena dogs came the dogs that became guards, protectors, and *draft* (hauling) dogs for the Roman legions. Ancient writings that describe these military dogs reveal dogs that were similar to the Rottweiler as we know the breed today.

Bravery and protectiveness have been selected for throughout the Rottweiler's history, and they are qualities the breed is respected for to this day. The great efforts that those who love the breed have expended in developing a dog that uses these qualities wisely is something worthy of your respect.

The Roman legions that set off to conquer the world as they knew it were veritable moving cities. Because they were often gone for years at a time, everything that was needed became a portable part of the troop movements: livestock, harvested crops, shoe repair shops, pottery makers, blacksmiths, shop keepers, servants for the officers, and sometimes even their wives.

Because the Roman armies were constantly on the move, their dogs had to serve a more diversified purpose than the fighting dogs of the arenas. Their great courage was employed to ward off wild animals that threatened the livestock that accompanied the legions, but the dogs had many other duties as well. The speed and agility of the dogs made them excellent drovers for the cattle that accompanied the troops. Their large size and great strength made them capable of hauling carts loaded with weight that often far exceeded their own.

The Rottweiler's German roots

There is no recorded proof that these Mollosus dogs were, in fact, the ancestors of today's Rottweiler. However, dogs of this type existed throughout every region of Europe where the Roman legions traveled — including Germany. As early as 2000 B.C. the Romans occupied a town in Southern Germany that they called Arae Flavia. It was an isolated but strategic town militarily and politically. For this reason, Arae Flavia became a highly developed administration and social center. The town had a large enough population and sufficient activity to encourage setting up the fun-and-games facilities the Romans were accustomed to back home. Baths and brothels proliferated, along with the more serious aspects of the Roman lifestyle such as temples and aqueducts.

All this activity called for building administration centers. The more important of these centers had red tiled roofs, and the town eventually became known as *Rottwil* (translated, it means "red villa").

Through the ages, Rottwil (later Rottweil) endured invasions and occupations that decimated the Roman populations, and their dogs along with them. The surviving dogs found mates among the local breeds, and, as time passed, two distinct types of dog emerged. One type was very large and was used primarily for draft work. Those dogs also doubled as guards to ensure the safe arrival of the contents of the carts they pulled.

The other type of dog that developed in Rottwil was a more moderate but versatile variety. No less courageous an animal, the smaller dogs were initially used for herding, but as time passed they became known as the *Metzgerhunde,* or butcher's dog, because so many of the people who made their living as butchers kept the dogs. Eventually, though, the two types of dogs merged and became known simply as Rottweilers.

According to folklore, in the Middle Ages Rottweilers were known as the butchers' dogs of Rottweil. The name developed from the fact that butchers of the area tied the money they would use to buy cattle around the dogs' necks for safekeeping. What thief would dare take the money off the neck of a Rottweiler?

The changing role of the Rottweiler

In spite of the unique adaptability of these dogs, they were not exempt from the social changes of the following years. With the arrival of the 20th century, many of the jobs that had been performed by the Rottweiler were eliminated. Industrialization began to make the existence of the dogs an expense rather than an asset. By 1905, breed history discloses, there was only one dog, a female, of this type left in Rottweil.

Elsewhere, because of the German fondness for the Rottweiler, efforts began to save the breed from extinction. A short-lived International Club for Leonberger and Rottweiler Dogs was established. The first written standard for the breed was published by that organization in 1901. This standard was followed in 1907 by the organization of The German Rottweiler Club in Heidelberg, and, through that club's efforts, the breed prospered and was recognized as a service dog for use with the police and the military. With this formal recognition, the breed's situation really started to improve.

By 1920, the *Allgemeiner Deutscher Rottweiler Klub* (the General German Rottweiler Club, or ADRK) was formed to protect the Rottweiler's physical and mental health. Strict codes of conduct were established for Rottweiler owners, including making sure all dogs had hip x-rays performed to prevent *hip dysplasia* (a degenerative joint disease that is prevalent in the breed). Only the very best dogs were allowed to be bred.

The members of the ADRK were dedicated to preserving and enhancing the health and welfare of the Rottweiler. Their purpose was to eliminate from the gene pool any dog who did not mentally, physically, and genetically live up to the extremely high standards of the organization. The ADRK was highly successful in its efforts to preserve the best qualities of the breed, and it was not long before the rest of the world began to take an interest in this rugged protector.

The transplanting of Rottweilers to the United States

The first Rottweilers were imported into the United States in the 1930s, and the breed was given full recognition by the American Kennel Club in 1936. The breed was also registered with The Kennel Club in England in 1936.

The first American-born Rottweiler litter recorded was bred in 1930 by Otto Denny, a German immigrant who had already established himself as a breeder before he left his homeland. Denny's litter was not registered with the AKC, but instead with a German-based breed club — not an unusual occurrence at the time.

Stina v Felsenmeer was the first Rottweiler to be registered with the AKC, and when she was bred to Arras v Gerbermuhle, Stina's was the first AKC-registered litter. From that point on, interest in the breed began to grow in America — very slowly at first. But over the next 60 years, the popularity of the breed grew to what dedicated fanciers saw as alarming proportions.

When World War II came to a close, America began to forget its anti-German sentiments and Americans had more money to spend than many knew what to do with. Sports and hobbies like dog breeding and dog showing began to attract interest. In 1960, the AKC registered 77 Rottweilers. Thirty-seven years later the tally was nearly 77,000!

Amazingly, for a breed that was to soar to such heights of popularity finding American supporters in the early days of the breed was difficult. Not until the 1960s was the first failed attempt made to organize a national club for the breed. After several stops and starts, in 1973 the American Rottweiler Club found enough support to become the first national club for Rottweilers in the United States.

Initially, the Rottweiler earned itself a place of respect with American dog trainers and in obedience circles. It was only a matter of time, however, before the breed also began to catch the eye of those who were showing dogs in the conformation rings.

The breed's first American conformation Champion was Zero, a male belonging to Paul Jones. Zero's sister, Zola, became the first female Rottweiler champion. Jones became a founding member of the American Rottweiler Club. Jones also handled the first Rottweiler to win a Working Group first in this country. The first all-breed Best in Show was won by Ch. Kato v Donnaj, CD, TD, owned by Jan Marshall.

A lot of credit for maintaining the level of quality that had been established in the Rottweiler's homeland can be attributed to the efforts of Clara Hurley and her Powderhorn Press in California. Hurley translated and published the many important books written by the breed masters in Germany, giving Americans the benefit of all the work that had already been done on the breed's behalf. Hurley was also instrumental in establishing the Rottweiler Registry to chart the status of hip dysplasia.

The Rottweiler's role in modern day

If you have no immediate plans to cross the Alps, send your dog off to gladiator school, or tie your life savings around your Rottweiler's neck, you may be wondering what you can give your talented, energetic dog to do.

The size, agility, and intelligence level of your Rottweiler open doors to both of you that you may never even have considered. The following list barely scratches the surface of areas in which the Rottweiler has excelled:

- Obedience programs
- Hospital therapy volunteer programs
- Search and rescue work
- Herding trials
- Carting trials
- Watchdog work
- Schutzhund training
- Tracking tests
- Agility competition

If you want more information on these and other fun activities you and your Rottweiler can do together, check out Chapter 9.

Chapter 2

Is a Rottweiler Right for You?

In This Chapter

- Understanding what's entailed in dog ownership
- Figuring out whether you and a Rottweiler would make a good match
- Taking a look at the resources you need to be a responsible Rottweiler owner

Today it seems like everyone wants a Rottweiler. When the American Kennel Club (AKC) issued its most recent official count (in 1999), more than 41,000 Rottweilers were registered in that year alone, giving the Rottweiler the number eight spot out of the 148 breeds the AKC registered that year. Check out Table 2-1 for a list of the top ten most popular breeds registered with the AKC in 1999.

Table 2-1 The Top Ten AKC-Registered Breeds of 1999

Breed	*Number of Dogs Registered*
Labrador Retriever	154,897
Golden Retriever	62,652
German Shepherd	57,256
Dachshund	50,772
Beagle	49,080
Poodle	45,852
Chihuahua	42,013
Rottweiler	41,776
Yorkshire Terrier	40,684
Boxer	34,998

Just a few decades back, hardly anyone had even heard of Rottweilers. And then, all of a sudden — pow! — up the popularity ladder they shot. Rottweilers are not just popular in the United States; they have become one of the most popular breeds in the entire world.

Rottweiler ownership has become a status symbol, an ego boost, a style trend, and an outward symbol of a macho attitude. All of these are reasons that people have decided to bring Rottweilers into their lives, but none of them are *good* reasons. Nor, would any of the people who were inspired by those reasons provide a suitable home for a Rottweiler. So if you're thinking of owning a Rottweiler because you think it'll make you look macho or because you think it's a sign of status, buy a new car or some other inanimate object instead. Rottweilers are living, breathing creatures — not objects to acquire in the pursuit of a certain image.

The well-bred and well-trained Rottweiler has qualities that have made the breed one of most highly admired in the world. What too many would-be Rottweiler owners don't stop to consider is how difficult life can be when you have to cope with a Rottweiler who hasn't had the benefit of an owner committed to giving the dog the care and training it requires.

If more prospective owners took the time to investigate the breed's history and understood the kind of owner a dog of this character requires, they might reconsider bringing a Rottweiler into their homes. On the other hand, for the person who does the research and understands the Rottweiler's temperament and needs, there could be no better choice. Few breeds have a greater capacity to learn or to be better pals to their owners and their owners' families than the Rottweiler.

Before dashing out to buy yourself a Rottweiler, you have to take a number of important steps. First, be very honest with yourself about how you deal with responsibility. Think back on your past experiences with pets. How those characteristics and experiences interact with the Rottweiler's needs and behavior will determine whether yours will be a match made in heaven. Having a 100-pound-plus problem child on your hands is not exactly fun and games, and the best way to avoid that situation is to be sure — very sure — that the Rottweiler is the right dog for you and that you are the right owner for the breed.

In this chapter, I help you do exactly that. Here, you get a feel for what dog ownership is all about — the good, the bad, and the ugly. You get the chance to assess yourself, to see if you really have what it takes to own and care for this special breed. And you get real about important elements like time, space, and money — all of which are required if you're going to give a good home to a Rottweiler.

Being Honest with Yourself about What You Have to Give

Owning a dog is a big responsibility, and many people enter into dog ownership with all kinds of misconceptions about what it's all about. Your first job when you start to consider owning any pet, but especially a Rottweiler, is to be honest with yourself about what you're willing and able to give.

A Rottweiler will give back to you in love, friendship, and loyalty, but you have to be willing to put in a lot of time and effort to have that kind of rewarding relationship. If you're not, consider another option instead.

Knowing the kind of time and energy dog ownership requires

Pets come in as many different shapes and sizes as people do. I have friends who seem determined to have at least one representative of every animal species in the world. What's more, they seem to thrive on all the work required to maintain the menagerie. I have other friends who find having to feed a goldfish once a day or throw a handful of cedar shavings into the hamster cage too much work. Know which end of this spectrum you call home.

If feeding the goldfish or buying liner paper for the birdcage seems like drudgery, dog care is going to be a monumental task. You'd better think twice (or four times?) about this one!

After a pet enters your household, she will be there all day, every day. She will rely entirely on you for care and comfort, and that's not even counting the training necessary for some pets, including dogs — that is, if you want to protect your sanity and the sanity of those you live with. If the pet was your idea in the first place, don't rely on someone else in the household to step in and help. Unless the other person has already volunteered to do so (and *meant* it), you may end up very disappointed.

If the kids in your family promise, promise, promise not a day will go by without the pet taking first priority, don't believe it! It's not that your kids are lying — they believe every word they say when they promise they'll care for a pet. They don't intend to mislead you (well, not always), but to kids, first priority means one thing today and another thing tomorrow. Just as your puppy is needing the most time and attention, your kids are likely to have moved on to another interest or activity, and you'll be left to assume all the responsibility. So don't get a dog with the idea that your kids will help out in the time and responsibility department. If you can get them to, that's great. But be prepared to do it all yourself.

Pets can't grab a snack out of the refrigerator when they're hungry. They don't clean up their own messes, and when they require exercise, they can't hire a personal trainer. All that is up to you, you, and only you. If your plan is to hire someone to do all those things for you just so you can have some ears to scratch, save yourself the time, the aggravation, and the money — get a stuffed toy instead.

Understanding that Rottweilers aren't perfect

If you believe what you read in some of the "I Love My Dog" kinds of books written today, you would swear some breeds can do it all. Many dog-lovers (especially those enamored with Rottweilers) would have you believe that a Rottie is the one breed that can do everything, plus eliminate your need for a security system and help your kids with their algebra homework on the side.

Don't have unrealistic expectations of your dog. Your puppy will arrive with a blank slate; the only writing that will appear on it is what *you* write or what the puppy writes herself. And keep in mind that puppies can't spell.

No Rottweiler — no breed of dog, for that matter — can do everything. In fact, your brain-trust Rottie is not going to be inclined to do anything outside of misbehave without the benefit of a leader who can teach the dog what to do and when to do it. Rottie puppies have a great *capacity* to learn, but they do not come preprogrammed. Guess who needs to help the dog fully realize that capacity? You!

As puppies begin to venture out of the little nest their mother made for them, they are looking for two things:

- A pack leader.
- The pack rules and regulations that let them know what they can and cannot do.

In nature, mama wolf and her relatives provide what the pup seeks without thinking twice. Because your Rottweiler puppy is not living in the great North Woods but in your home, you're the one who is elected to perform all the duties of the pack leader. If you do it, you'll have a great companion. If you don't, you could have more headaches than you could ever have imagined.

Knowing Whether You Have What It Takes to Own a Rottweiler

Buying a dog, especially a Rottweiler, before you are absolutely sure you are ready to make such a major commitment can be a serious mistake. A new dog owner must clearly understand the amount of time and work involved in the project. If feeding the goldfish or watering the philodendron proved to be something you did grudgingly and only because you had to, a Rottweiler is going to make you feel like you're responsible for the national debt.

In the following sections, I guide you through the painstaking process of evaluating yourself and your own abilities when it comes to raising a Rottie. ***Remember:*** Be honest with yourself. If you aren't, you and your dog will suffer.

Seeing how ready you are to own a Rottie

Grab a pencil and a sheet of paper, and answer the following questions as honestly as you possibly can. The final results will tell you a lot.

- Does the person who will actually care for your Rottweiler really want a dog?
- Is *everyone* you live with as anxious as you are to have a Rottweiler in the home?
- Does your lifestyle allow time for a Rottweiler's care and training?
- Is your living environment suitable for a dog of this size?
- Do you have the endless patience required for your Rottweiler's training regimen?
- Are you physically strong enough to handle a fully grown Rottweiler?
- Is your own character and personality strong enough to establish the proper relationship with a Rottweiler?
- Can you afford the cost (purchase, upkeep, veterinary care, food) of Rottweiler ownership?

If you answer "no" to any of these questions, a Rottweiler is *not* for you. Other dog breeds may not require a "yes" to every single question, and there are other pets for which hardly *any* of the questions require an answer in the affirmative. But for a Rottweiler owner, all eight points need an emphatic "yes!"

Think about each of the points in this questionnaire carefully. Your dog will need a primary caretaker. Is that person you? Is that your significant other? If you live alone, the answer is simplified; naturally, *you* will be the caregiver. On the other hand, if you live alone, you probably have to trudge off to work every day so you can earn the money to keep your Rottweiler in dog biscuits. So who will sit and hold your growing giant's paw all day long?

Leaving this bundle of curiosity home alone all day will do nothing for her personality and less for your household goods. You may think worrying about the personality and friendliness of the dog you obtained to guard you and your belongings is irrelevant, but think again. A guard dog is one thing; an uncontrollable beast is another. Young Rotties left home alone day after day will begin to see life on their own terms — and *solely* their own terms. This mindset can include how strangers will be dealt with and whom the dog decides she should protect you from.

Rottweiler pups have a huge storehouse of energy that they must expend in the course of day. They can do this constructively with exercise and games or destructively by snacking on your shoes or excavating for a lost treasure in the middle of your antique Persian rug.

If you live alone, you need to make sure you have a strong enough desire to make the necessary commitment dog ownership entails. If you share your life with a significant other or an entire family, you have to consider other opinions as well. Your significant other may not be interested in having your twosome become a threesome, and if that's the case, don't think you're going to change that person's mind.

In many households, mothers — even working mothers — are the automatic winners of the daily drawing in the who-will-take-care-of-the-dog-when-we're-all-away contest. Regardless of whether mom works away from home, all too often she's saddled with the additional chores of feeding and trips to the veterinary hospital. She may not be entirely keen about adopting yet another needy child — especially if it was not her idea in the first place.

Looking at the specifics of what dog ownership requires

Owning a Rottweiler requires *time* (for feeding, exercising, and training), *space* (a fenced yard, dog run, and/or indoor private space), and *money* (there's no such thing as a bargain Rottweiler, and you can't skimp on care).

In the following sections, I look at all three of these basic requirements.

Time

Rottweiler puppies need lots of training. And training takes time and patience (with a very strong emphasis on the latter). You need to train your puppy every day. Not feeling up to it isn't a good excuse. Not only must you *feel* up to it, you must *be* up to it, because your state of mind has a great deal to do with how well your training sessions go.

Losing patience and taking it out on your Rottweiler doesn't work. A properly raised and educated Rottweiler understands and accepts correction, but the breed does not tolerate abuse. If a Rottweiler is continually subjected to abusive treatment, even the most amiable and temperamentally sound dog can become neurotic and unpredictable.

On the other hand, don't be passive in raising and training your Rottie. A Rottweiler puppy has to start learning the house rules on the very first day she comes to your home. If the puppy is to believe you and learn to avoid certain behavior, the "no" command must mean no all the time, not just most of the time or when the dog decides she wants to respond.

Climbing up on the sofa will never be a forbidden zone for your Rottie if you relent and allow the dog to climb up and cuddle with you on the days you feel in need of comfort. Rottweilers have a great deal of difficulty relating to the very human concept of changing minds. If mama wild dog were teaching her offspring to stay down in the den while she was gone, she would enforce the rule *all* the time, not just on rainy days or days when she felt up to correcting the little ones.

Rule enforcement is one of the important reasons to have a safe, secure enclosure in which to keep your Rottweiler when you're too busy to insist the rules be obeyed or when you're not home. A securely fenced yard, a fenced and gated outdoor run, or a secure indoor crate will keep your dog contained and out of mischief when you are involved in activities that take your attention elsewhere.

Space

Training is one thing, exercise is another. For your Rottie to grow and develop both mentally and physically, she needs plenty of space in which to exercise. Think about human children and the never-ending fountain of energy they all seem to be blessed with. Now multiply that by about five and you have the activity level of the average Rottweiler pup.

A securely fenced yard is not only a great place to keep your dog when you don't have the time to make sure she's not getting into mischief, it's also a great place for her to burn off some of that extra energy. Consider the space of your home and yard and how much space your Rottweiler will have to run and play before you bring her home. If you live in a small space without a yard, and you can't see yourself making daily trips to a nearby park to play with your dog, a Rottweiler is not for you.

Not only do Rottweiler pups have an amazing energy capacity, they use it! Pups either unload all those energy molecules under your supervision in some acceptable activity, or they devise activities of their own. And believe me, what these little guys can think up on their own will make you wonder why on earth you decided to bring a dog into your life in the first place. Fashioning hideouts in the new sofa cushions, removing baseboards from the walls, digesting the contents of your most prized literary masterpieces — these are activities any self-respecting Rottweiler puppy has all the energy in the world for and she needs no training at all to do it well.

The basics of good breeding

The only way a breeder can earn a reputation for producing quality dogs through the years is by maintaining a well-thought-out breeding program. Responsible breeders rigidly select the individual dogs they will use in their breeding programs. Selective breeding is aimed at maintaining the virtues of a breed and eliminating genetic weaknesses. Effectively conducting a breeding operation of this kind takes a great deal of time, space, and testing, and all this is extremely costly. So responsible Rottweiler breeders protect their investment by providing the utmost in prenatal care for their brood matrons (the female dogs breeders use in their breeding programs) and maximum care and nutrition for the resulting offspring.

When the puppies arrive, the knowledgeable breeder initiates a well-planned socialization program. Only when these breeders feel the puppies have been given the benefit of the best care, nutrition, and sufficient human contact do they even begin to look for the proper homes for each and every puppy in the litter. This may mean keeping one or even all the puppies in a litter until they are four, five, or even six or seven months of age.

The only way a breeder can continue to breed and raise Rottweilers in this responsible way is to charge a realistic price for his puppies. Naturally, a puppy with all these advantages is going to cost more than a puppy from a litter whose mother was never tested for any of the breed's genetic weaknesses or who was bred to a male of unknown mental stability. Some people are always ready and willing to jump on the bandwagon and exploit a breed for financial gain. These people give no thought to the breed's health or welfare, or to the homes in which the dogs will be living. But could you even consider bringing into your home a Rottweiler who was not given these important advantages? A well-bred Rottweiler may cost more initially, but in the end that sound investment could save you thousands of dollars in veterinary bills and professional training to cope with inherited health and temperament problems. As with anything else in life, you get what you pay for when it comes to buying a Rottweiler pup.

Money

Even a Rottweiler pup with all the space in the world may suddenly decide the time has come to redecorate the family room or help you get rid of all those shoes in your closet. (You can only wear one pair at a time — why keep so many?) Until the two of you have gone through all these activities together and you have convinced your young friend that they will not be tolerated, you may need more than just a dollar or two to repair the damage your dog does.

The cost of repairing and replacing damaged items must be added to fencing the yard or building a secure run so that your little Rottie doesn't wander off down the street. Then there are those costly trips to the vet for shots, breaks, and bruises. Add to that the cost of enrollment in puppy kindergarten and on and on. . . .

And we haven't even discussed how much it will cost to get a Rottweiler in the first place. You must purchase your Rottweiler from a breeder who has earned a reputation over the years for consistently producing dogs who are mentally and physically sound — and those dogs don't come cheap.

Beware a breeder who offers a bargain-basement price for a Rottweiler. Highly recommended breeders usually have waiting lists for their puppies. Don't allow someone to unload their problems onto you. Expect to pay at least $800 to $1,000 for a companion-quality Rottweiler puppy.

Weighing Your Decision Carefully

Have I discouraged you from owning a Rottweiler? Good!

No one who isn't at least 110 percent sure a Rottweiler is what he or she wants should think about the venture. The Rottweiler is not a breed for just anyone, and it is never a breed that should be purchased on a whim. But if you've thought through all the pros and cons and you're still with me, we can get on to the great joy, challenge, companionship, and devotion Rottweiler ownership entails.

Part II
Searching for Your Soul Mate

"No, it's not normal to dress a Rottweiler this way, but it puts the Vet at ease when I bring him in for a checkup."

In this part . . .

If you've already decided to get a Rottweiler, the chapters in this part are the place to start. Here you'll find great information on knowing what to look for in a breeder, because getting your pup from a reputable breeder makes all the difference. And I also let you know what to look for in a Rottie pup. They all look cute, but here you'll get the information you need to pick the right one for you.

Chapter 3

Knowing What You Want in a Rottweiler

In This Chapter

- Knowing what to expect from the breed
- Making room for individual differences
- Seeing how gender plays a role in a Rottweiler's personality
- Knowing what to expect from a Rottweiler no matter what his age

After you've determined that a Rottweiler is right for you and you're right for a Rottweiler, you need to consider what kind of Rottweiler you want. Although Rottweilers as a breed share certain specific characteristics, factors like personality, gender, and age all play an important part as well. In this chapter, I point out issues of personality as well as remind you of some basic traits to expect from any well-bred Rottweiler. I also highlight some important gender differences in Rottweilers to help you figure out which one is right for you. And I take you on a quick tour through the stages of a Rottweiler's life, so you know what to expect from birth through adulthood.

Remembering That Each Dog Is Unique

Keep in mind that each dog has a different and distinct personality. Some of the differences are the direct result of which end of the gene pool a pup emerged from, and some are influenced by the other dogs and the humans the pup interacts with. But the nature/nurture argument is really moot. What is important to know is that all dogs are different and they are different in many ways — even dogs in the same breed.

Still, purebred dogs perform and behave the way they do because of generation upon generation of selective breeding. Expecting a purebred dog to behave *against* his basic nature leads to frustration for both dog and owner.

Despite their distinct individual personalities, all Rottweilers share certain breed characteristics. You can be fairly certain, barring unforeseen accidents or unfortunate treatment, that each Rottweiler pup in a litter will grow up with some pretty similar characteristics, including the following:

- All the pups will grow up to be on the medium-large end of the canine size scale.
- Your pup will be the same color and same general shape when he grows up as he is on the day you bring the little fellow home. (Check out Figure 3-1 for a size comparison of a Rottweiler at 8 weeks, 6 months, and 3 years.)
- As an adult, the dog will have a relatively strong inclination to protect you and your family.
- Your Rottie will be territorial and will not welcome trespassers.

Figure 3-1: Rottweilers maintain the same general shape as they grow, but the difference in size between the pup you bring home and the dog you end up with years down the road is considerable — and something to keep in mind.

What most people don't stop to consider is that all of those characteristics fall on a continuum. Your Rottweiler pup may grow up to be big, or he may grow up to be a giant. All Rottweiler adults may maintain the same basic proportions, but some dogs pack a little muscle in that package, and others pack a lot. Even more important, one dog may be reasonably protective and territorial, whereas another may grow up to protect you from situations and people you haven't the least desire to be protected from!

The breeder of a litter is most apt to know at which end of the temperament scale an individual puppy stands. There is always a range, even within a breed known for its courage and aggressiveness. Each individual dog manifests these characteristics in his own way.

Sit down and talk to the person who bred the litter. He or she has been observing the pups since they were born. If the breeder you are visiting is an experienced person, he knows best how to mix and match the pups from the litter with the right owners. One pup may need a Marine drill sergeant for an owner, while the next may be just the ticket for a 90-pound weakling who just needs a good canine friend to lean on.

Deciding Between a Male and a Female Rottie

There are many breeds in which the sex of the dog makes little difference when it comes to pet ownership. But this may *not* be the case with the Rottweiler.

Although both the male and female Rottweiler are capable of becoming excellent companions and are equally trainable, do keep in mind the fact that a male Rottie will be larger and heavier than his sister, and he will have all the muscle power to go with that extra weight. Give serious consideration to your own strength and stature when you decide between a male and a female Rottweiler.

Sexual differences totally apart from size and weight are also a factor. The maternal instincts of the females serve to make them a bit sweeter and gentler, and they are inclined to be less boisterous. Boys will be boys, on the other hand, and most of them grow bigger and faster than they are aware of themselves, which can make for some clumsy fellows! When those hormones start raging, the males are inclined to be somewhat challenging, too — not unlike most male teenagers.

Although the Rottweiler is a clean breed and relatively easy to housebreak, the male dog of any breed has a natural instinct to lift his leg to mark his territory with urine. The amount of effort involved in training the male not to do this varies with the individual dog, but remember that a male considers everything in the household to be a part of his territory and he has an innate urge to establish this fact. Unfortunately, this may include your designer drapery or newly upholstered sofa.

Rottweilers are not beyond getting into arguments with other dogs, and the tendency in males may be considerably stronger. A male Rottweiler is all male and has no qualms about making a point of this.

Granted, there are smaller, very docile males and larger, considerably dominant females, but generally speaking, the male Rottweiler is larger, stronger, and of a more dominant personality. Dominance ranges from the "I prefer not to do that" kind of dog on up to the "just you try and make me!" attitude.

You can deal with variations on the personality scale. The secret is knowing what kind of personality a pup has and knowing yourself well enough to know if you are able to provide that particular Rottweiler with the care and training he will require.

Female dogs have their own set of problems. Their semiannual heat cycles begin at about one year of age if the dog is not spayed. These heat cycles last about 21 days, and during this time the female has to be confined to avoid soiling her surroundings with the bloody discharge that accompanies estrus. At pet supply stores, you can buy special *britches,* which assist in keeping the female in heat from soiling the area in which she lives. If you have a female dog in heat, you must also carefully watch her in order to prevent males from gaining access to her, or she will become pregnant. Do not expect the marauding male to be deterred by the britches either!

A good many of these sexually related problems can be avoided or at least reduced by having your pet Rottweiler altered. Spaying the female and neutering the male saves the pet owner all the headaches of sexually related problems without changing the basic character of your dog. If there is any change at all in the altered Rottweiler, it is only in making the dog an even more amiable companion. Above all, altering your pet precludes the possibility of his adding to the unwanted pet problem that exists worldwide.

Considering the Age of Your Dog When You Bring Him Home

Your Rottweiler's age when he first enters your household determines how you will handle the arrival and what you'll have to deal with in the following weeks and months. You may decide that a very young puppy will not work under your particular circumstances. A young adult, a mature dog, or even an old-timer may be your best choice instead.

Don't discount the older dog. Sometimes an older fellow loses his loving owners and needs another good home to finish out those golden years. These dogs can make great pets.

Dispelling myths about spaying and neutering

All too often, people who have purchased purebred pets will say, "We're only going to breed our dog once and then have her spayed," or "Bruno needs a girlfriend to relieve his frustration."

I assure you, neither dog needs sex to make their lives complete. Actually, in Bruno's case, breeding will only *increase* his frustration rather than relieve it.

Like all living things, Rottweilers have different needs at different stages of their lives. They react to their new environment accordingly, and you should be prepared for this. In the following sections, I let you know what to expect from your Rottweiler every step of the way.

Birth to 7 weeks

During these first few weeks of life, a Rottweiler pup needs nothing more than he needs his mother and littermates. They provide sustenance, comfort, and warmth for a puppy. During this period, the pups find out other creatures exist and they have to be coped with. At first, a pup is just aware of mom and her milk bar, but soon the pup finds he must compete with the other pups for what he needs.

Rottweiler moms also teach their offspring a great deal during these first weeks of life. Having this time with his mother and littermates is extremely important to a pup's development.

Seven to eight weeks

When a Rottweiler pup is in this stage of life, it's the perfect time to introduce him to his new home. At this age, he is mature enough to readjust easily, but not old enough to have developed strong attachments to his mother, littermates, and breeder. Puppies that remain too long as part of a litter, instead of getting on to their individual homes, learn to identify with their siblings instead of transferring this relationship to humans.

When you have decided upon the breeder your Rottie will come from, discuss your lifestyle. You know best what you will be able to do for the new dog and what you won't be able to do. Then, the breeder can best decide the best age for you to take home your puppy or young adult.

8 weeks to 6 months

As with children, this stage stretches on for a bit. It's not only the *stage* that is stretched — you'll wonder how elastic your patience can be! From eight weeks to almost six months of age, you may wonder at times whether your pup has taken leave of his senses with his nonsensical behavior and arbitrary balkiness.

Everything in life is an experiment at this stage, and there is no end to a pup's curiosity. This is the time when all electrical wires must be pulled, all fences climbed, and all objects tested to determine their chewability.

At the same time, your Rottweiler pup is pretty much dependent on you and wants to be with you all the time, wherever you go. This is the proper time for the puppy to learn good puppy basics. Confidence begins building at this stage, and the early dependency that was so typical may diminish almost overnight.

6 to 12 months

In this stage of a dog's life, anything you can do he can do better, or at least he likes to think so. Large breeds, including Rottweilers, grow quickly and mature slowly. Maturity seems to manifest itself spontaneously and in awkward stabs at independence. What were cute puppy antics become obnoxious behavior if you haven't corrected them by this time.

If those early bad habits haven't been curbed, you may have to deal with variable degrees of rebellion. This stage can be hardest on the males and their owners because of raging hormones, so these young rebels must understand clearly that you're in charge.

The adult Rottweiler

The well-adjusted adult Rottweiler is confident and devoted, protective without being rash. If you get an adult Rottie who hasn't had the benefit of good training, you have some serious work to do. However, a well-trained adult can adjust to a new home and will make a great pet.

Chapter 4

Finding and Choosing Your New Friend

In This Chapter

- Being able to recognize a responsible breeder when you see one
- Knowing what to expect from a responsible breeder
- Looking at the possibility of rescuing an adult Rottweiler
- Selecting the best bundle of joy for you and your family
- Taking home all the paperwork you need when you get your puppy

So you've decided the time and commitment involved in owning a dog, especially a Rottweiler, is worth the effort. You've been honest with yourself about what you're willing to give to a dog, and you're confident that you are an ideal candidate for Rottweiler ownership. The breed's history and origin are firmly implanted in your repertoire of canine knowledge. You are practically an expert in how a Rottie should and shouldn't look and act. So, you're done — out the door and get that puppy, right? Wrong!

You've done your homework, and this makes you a potential candidate for Rottweiler ownership. But trust me, many of the people who own the breed, and even many of the people who profess to be breeders, couldn't tell a Rottie's left foot from her right. You can find responsible breeders and not-so-responsible breeders. And no matter how much you know about Rottweilers, you have to find a reputable breeder, one who will help you choose a dog and be a resource as you raise the dog in the coming years.

Unfortunately, Rottweiler puppies are born every year who should never have seen the light of day. Hidden recessive traits in pedigrees can produce health and temperament problems that make dog ownership an incredibly expensive and complicated experience, to say nothing of the toll it can take on your emotions. If you have ever lived through the recuperation of a seriously ill dog, you know what a helpless and frustrating feeling it can be. The dog cannot tell you what the problem is, and you are seldom able to guess. You only know your buddy is sick and there doesn't seem to be much you can do to help. Rottweilers are also prone to some very debilitating and painful skeletal diseases that would bring tears to the eyes of even a stoic.

You have no way of predicting these problems when all you have to look at is a litter of very young puppies. Unless the breeder can show you that the parents of the litter have been proven clear of potential problems, it is all a case of caveat emptor (let the buyer beware)! No one can predict the future, but the fact that the breeder has taken pains to guard against potential disasters is at least some insurance that the puppy you take home has a better than average chance of being healthy as an adult.

In this chapter, I guide you through the process of finding a good breeder, telling you some signs to look for and questions to ask along the way. I also help you choose the right puppy for you and let you know what kind of paperwork you should take with you when you bring your pup home.

Knowing the Difference between Responsible Breeders and Backyard Breeders

Rottweilers are a popular breed, so you're likely to find ads in the newspapers, puppies at the pet store, even litters at a friend's or neighbor's home. As hard as it is to believe, I have even seen what are supposedly purebred Rottweiler puppies being sold by a forlorn-looking little youngster standing outside the supermarket.

If you've read anything at all about buying a puppy, you have undoubtedly come across a couple of warning statements published by the AKC or by concerned owners and breeders of purebred dogs. The advice is sound and is not to be taken lightly:

- **Buy from an experienced and recommended breeder.** A *recommended breeder* is a person who is a member of the American Rottweiler Club and has agreed to abide by its Mandatory Practices. The AKC can put you in touch with recommended breeders in your area.
- **Beware the backyard breeder or the mass producer.** Actually, the name *backyard breeder* was invented to save dog buyers a lot of head- and heartaches — and, in the case of Rottweiler buyers, to save them from bringing a 100-pound wrecking ball into their home. The term refers not so much to a place (the backyard), as to an experience level and an attitude about breeding.

You need to know how to tell the difference between a responsible breeder and a backyard breeder. So, here's a list to help you decide whether the person you are talking to or visiting is the real thing or someone to be avoided at all costs:

- **Responsible breeders belong to Rottweiler or all-breed dog clubs and participate in many activities that support the breed.** In the case of Rotties, just about every breeder I know is involved in training organizations of some kind. The Rottweiler is a breed that has such a great capacity to learn that dedicated owners would feel as though they were negligent in not providing an opportunity for the dog to develop. Participating on this level also provides the Rottie with the socialization and discipline the breed must have.
- **Backyard breeders do nothing with their dogs except breed and sell.** Their dogs have no special titles or accomplishments and the owners do no training, nor do they participate in activities designed to protect and preserve the breed.
- **Responsible breeders are delighted to set up an appointment so that you can visit their home or kennel and meet their dogs.** They want you to see their puppies and their puppies' parents and have a look at the environment in which the dogs are raised.
- **Backyard breeders may offer excuses why you can't see the mother or father of the puppies, perhaps because "they don't like strangers."** They hesitate to take you into the area where the puppies and grown dogs spend their time.
- **Responsible breeders know a great deal about the dogs they have bred and their pedigrees, and they are ready and willing to discuss any of the problems that could conceivably exist in any Rottweiler pedigree.**
- **Backyard breeders are quick to assure you that their dogs have no problems.** They seldom know much about anything in the genetic makeup of their dogs.
- **Responsible breeders show you certificates that certify the health tests that have been performed on the puppies' parents before the breeding took place.**
- **Backyard breeders do not perform health tests on the puppies' parents.** If you ask about them, they'll assure you that the puppies are "perfectly healthy."
- **Responsible breeders ask you so many questions that you'll think you are being investigated for top secret clearance.** They ask questions about your home, your family, and the conditions under which the puppy will be living.

- **Backyard breeders are willing to sell you a puppy with no questions asked.**

The amount of time a breeder spends interrogating you as a potential owner of one of his puppies and the degree of his involvement in outside activities with the breed are strong indicators of the health and stability of their breeding stock.

Working with a Responsible Breeder

When you work with a responsible breeder, you should feel like you're being interviewed for a job — because you are. Responsible breeders aren't invading your privacy with all their questions, but they are extremely discerning about where their puppies go. Expect to answer a lot of questions about why you want a Rottweiler and how you intend to care for the puppy. Get over the idea that you are doing a responsible breeder a favor by taking a puppy off his hands. If you do get that impression from a breeder, walk out the door and find another one.

The following questions are ones most breeders ask. And you should be asking yourself these same questions, because they are all important for anyone who wants to own a Rottweiler.

- **Why do you want a Rottweiler?** A good breeder wants to know what experience with the breed made you decide that a Rottie is right for you.
- **Do you have a home with a fenced yard?** If you don't, a good breeder may ask whether you or someone in your family will be there to take the dog outdoors on a leash as many times as her age and circumstances require.
- **Are you prepared to have the pet Rottweiler you buy spayed or neutered?** Most breeders either require this before releasing registration papers to you or sell the pet-quality puppy with a *Limited Registration,* which means the AKC can't register any puppies your dog may produce.
- **Do you have children in your family and, if so, how old are they?** Most breeders want to meet the children who will be living with the puppy, to get a sense of how well behaved the children are. Households with children who do not mind well are not good environments for a Rottweiler to grow up in.
- **Do you have other pets?** Breeders want to know what other kinds of pets are already living in your home and if these other pets can adjust easily to a new dog or puppy.

Understanding which health tests and guarantees the breeder provides

Before you even ask, a responsible breeder will usually tell you what kind of testing has been done and what kind of guarantees he offers with any dog or puppy he sells. But these are issues that you should check against your own list, just to make sure that nothing has been missed or that you haven't misunderstood what the breeder is responsible for.

Testing for health and temperament are, of course, extremely important to everyone concerned with Rottweiler breeding and ownership. Guarantees provided by the breeder will also help assure you of a happy transition for your new Rottweiler, regardless of her age.

Health tests

When you're working with a breeder, check for results from the following health-related tests and exams:

- **Tests and certification that the parents of the litter are free of hip and elbow disorders.**
- **Appropriate eye and heart checks to establish that the parents are regularly tested and are clear of problems.**
- **A veterinary examination revealing the current state of health of the puppy or adult being considered, and a complete list, by date, of all inoculations given and due.**

Temperament testing

Just as important as physical health is your Rottweiler's temperament. So make sure that:

- **The parents of the litter are certified as having passed character tests for stability of temperament.**
- **You have been allowed to meet and handle both parents if they are on the premises.** If the parents are not present, make sure their whereabouts have been established.

Guarantees

A responsible breeder provides certain guarantees with every puppy he sells. Make sure you understand:

- **The conditions under which you may return the dog or puppy for a full refund.**

- **The conditions under which you may ask the seller to replace the dog or puppy with another dog or puppy.**
- **The kind of continuing care, advice, and assistance the breeder offers.**

Asking the breeder which puppy he would choose for you

You may have done your homework and consider yourself something of an authority on all things Rottweiler. And an authority you may be. However, no one knows more about the individual Rottweiler you are considering than the dog's breeder. A good breeder has not only observed each puppy in the litter since they were as little as the 1-week-old pups shown in Figure 4-1, but he also knows each puppy's characteristics and knows which of these characteristics should be given special attention. Breeders know the bullies, they know the crybabies, and they know which of the puppies will require an exceptionally stout heart and a firm hand.

Figure 4-1: The breeder has the advantage of observing the pups in a litter from the time they are born and can offer excellent advice when it comes to choosing the right pup for you and your family.

Photograph courtesy of Judith E. Strom

When you honestly answer all the questions the breeder asks about you and your family, you're giving the breeder valuable information that will help him know which of the puppies in the litter would be the best choice for you. The bravest and boldest of the litter may come bounding out to greet you and may even be secure enough to give you a cute little "woof" to let you know your presence is being questioned. A winning personality? Perhaps. But this behavior may also indicate early aggressive tendencies that should be handled in a special way in order to produce good temperament.

This information even applies to grown dogs. People experienced in the breed know what to look for when it comes to character, and although your first impression may be entirely positive or entirely negative, the longtime breed authority may know things about the dog you would never think to question.

If you put your trust in what the breeder feels would be the right puppy for you, he could easily lead you to that absolutely perfect canine friend and companion you have been hoping for.

Considering the Rescue Option

You may be able to find the Rottweiler of your dreams and help a deserving dog find the home of *her* dreams in the process. There are all kinds of reasons why so many Rottweilers around the country need new homes. Chief among them is the buyer who sees one of these magnificent creatures and thinks how protected or how fashionable life would be with a dog like that. What they don't stop to do is exactly what you have been doing — trying to find out if a Rottweiler is right for them and if they are right for a Rottie.

Most dogs wind up in shelters because the former owner says he is moving and cannot take the dog with him. Sometimes this is so, and sometimes it's just an excuse. Be sure to find out what reasons the former owner gave for abandoning his dog, particularly if the Rottie will be around young children.

A Rottweiler with an owner who has not been able to provide the leadership this breed needs can become a terrible nuisance — if not a menace. Usually, no one is willing to accept responsibility or blame, and the neglected Rottie is the one who must pay the price.

Irresponsible owners are not the only reason Rottweilers sometimes find themselves homeless. What otherwise was a perfect home can be disrupted by divorce or serious illness, and maintaining and properly caring for a dog the size of a Rottweiler can become impossible for some people. As unfortunate as these scenarios are, it is far better that a new home be found for the dog than that a loved companion is neglected.

If you're looking for a Rottweiler, a *rescue organization* or animal shelter may be just the place to find one. rescue organizations locate and care for dogs in need, saving as many as possible from euthanasia and placing those dogs in responsible, permanent homes. Often, they focus on a single breed of dog;

sometimes they only have adult dogs rather than puppies (but adult dogs can make super pets). Shelters, of course, will not always have Rotties, but you can put your name on a waiting list.

American Rottweiler Club rescue

Nicely bred Rottweilers who can become treasured members of a second home are often available through the many rescue agencies throughout the country. The American Rottweiler Club (ARC) has a Web site (`www.amrottclub.org`) that will guide you to the National Rescue Coordinator, who will be able to put you in touch with the rescue chapter groups that are affiliated with the club throughout the United States.

If you don't have access to the Internet, you can call the American Kennel Club (AKC) at 919-233-9767 and ask for the name and contact information for the Rottweiler National Rescue Coordinator.

Independent rescue groups

Many independent Rottweiler rescue organizations are maintained by people who simply love the breed. These individuals cannot stand by and allow a Rottie to be euthanized in an animal shelter because no one has taken the time to find a good home for the dog.

Most of these bona fide Rottweiler rescue organizations or individuals have resources to trace the background of the abandoned dogs and observe and test character and temperament. Naturally, knowing the background, character, and temperament of the dog is an extremely important consideration when adopting an adult Rottie.

When you're working with an independent rescue group, ask for references. Many, many groups of goodhearted souls are out there, but there are a few not-so-good groups. Expect to pay a fee to help defray the costs of rescue, but if the group seems more interested in making money than in the quality of home you can provide for the dog, beware!

Humane societies and animal shelters

Countless numbers of healthy, well-bred Rottweilers end their lives in our nation's animal shelters. (For this reason, responsible breeders will insist that all dogs they sell be returned to them if the buyer is unable to keep the dog.) If you're considering adopting a dog from a shelter, be sure to investigate the background of the dog and find out just why she wound up in the shelter in the first place.

Background information on the dog you're considering adopting may be readily available at the shelter, or it may take a bit of private investigating on your part. Regardless of how much time it takes, it is time well spent. You are looking for a mentally and physically sound friend and companion, not someone else's problem pooch. Often, local Rottweiler organizations can assist you in your search for information. Taking the time to investigate the dog's circumstances and history could easily result in your finding an outstanding dog who desperately needs a new home.

Choosing a Puppy

When you've found a responsible breeder, you're a long way toward finding the right dog, because a responsible breeder can help you determine which puppy is right for you. But that doesn't mean you aren't responsible for checking out each pup you consider. So in this section I let you know what to look for in a Rottweiler puppy.

Don't bring the entire neighborhood with you when you visit a breeder. A big crowd of people only creates confusion and is a distraction for the breeder, who has a great deal to discuss with you. Even if you have a very large family, you're much better off making several visits with just two or three members of the family in attendance each time.

Pay attention to the puppy's health

No matter what kind of a future you have planned for your Rottweiler, chief on your list of considerations must be mental and physical health. The Rottweiler was bred to be an asset to her owners, and you shouldn't settle for anything less.

Above all, the Rottweiler puppy you buy should be a happy, playful extrovert. Don't even think about taking a puppy who appears sickly because you feel sorry for her and just know you'll be able to nurse her back to good health. You'll find nothing but heartache in a situation like that. Besides, responsible breeders would never dream of letting a sickly puppy go, so if a breeder tries to get you to take an unhealthy dog, move on to another breeder.

Well-bred Rottweiler puppies with positive temperaments are not afraid of strangers. In fact, they love the world. Do not settle for anything less. Under normal circumstances you will have the whole litter in your lap if you kneel and call them to you.

Other (not so great) places to get a Rottweiler

On more occasions than I care to remember, I have received phone calls from friends who want me to help them search for a Rottweiler puppy. Before I can even begin my search among responsible breeders, I often get a follow-up call from the same person, telling me the "perfect" puppy has been found! Without even asking, I know the pup has come from a litter bred by the fellow down the street or by a friend of a friend. That is all well and good if the neighbor or the friend knew what he was doing when he planned the breeding and if he is knowledgeable enough to help you select the right puppy.

The same rule applies to classified ads in the newspapers and sweet-looking little puppies you may see staring out the window of a mall pet shop. Only there the unknowns are even greater. Classified ads can state what they want to state, but you don't even have the recommendation of friends and neighbors to rely upon.

Sincere and responsible pet shop owners who sell live animals are undoubtedly out there, but you can rest assured that of those who qualify in reliability and integrity, very few (if any) would prove to be Rottweiler breeders. More often than not, the dogs offered for sale in pet shops come from a source that the pet shop owner knows nothing about. You have absolutely no way to determine the character of the pet shop puppy's parents. You have no way to check what kind of care the puppy had from the time she was born until she reached the pet shop. Even with a guarantee of the puppy's current state of health, how could you possibly know what the genetic makeup of the pup will bring in the future when it comes to health issues?

And health is not the only issue in a large, powerful breed like the Rottweiler. Unreliable temperament in miniature and toy breeds can prove to be a nuisance. In a Rottweiler, unreliable temperament can result in danger to you or your family and even to lawsuits from those outside your home. So be sure when you're looking for a breeder that, even if a friend recommends someone, you check the breeder out as stringently as you would a complete stranger.

Even if your puppy is eventually going to be entrusted with guarding the crown jewels, never consider a puppy who acts shy or suspicious of you. Nor should the pup act threatening or aggressive. The protective nature of the Rottweiler establishes itself with maturity. If a puppy shows any signs of an aggressive nature, something is definitely wrong. Puppies are babies, and properly socialized babies do not threaten — ever!

One quick look at the conditions the puppy is living in will tell you a great deal about the puppy's health. The puppy you select may smell perfumed and sweet, but if the environment in which she is living is dirty and unsanitary, all the perfume in the world will not be able to cover up the stench of neglect.

If one puppy in particular appeals to you, pick her up and ask the breeder if you can carry her off to an area nearby where the three of you can spend some time away from the puppy's littermates. As long as a puppy is still in a fairly familiar environment where scents and sounds are not entirely strange, the pup should remain relaxed and happy in your arms. Avoid any puppy who becomes tense and struggles to escape.

Inspecting the puppy

Do not be afraid of offending the breeder by thoroughly inspecting your prospective puppy. Good breeders want you to be as pleased with the puppy you select as they are with the home their puppy is going to. If you know what to look for to get a sense of the pup's overall health, this will assure the breeder that the puppy will get the care she deserves.

When you have the puppy away from the rest of the pack, here's what to look for:

- **Body:** In body, Rottweiler puppies should feel compact and substantial to the touch. A puppy is a bit more *cobby,* or square, in appearance than an adult; therefore, she should never be short-legged or long in the body. Don't mistake puppy clumsiness for unsoundness though. Rottweiler pups aren't the most graceful creatures in the world — they need a while to become accustomed to those big feet and chubby bodies.
- **Coat:** The coat should be clean and soft — jet black with tan markings.
- **Conformation to the breed standard:** Conformation is important even at an early age, and you want to be sure to find a puppy who represents the breed well. Rottweiler puppies should have a fair amount of skeletal substance and strength, and their legs should be straight. The back should be strong and level. The well-made Rottie's head is powerful looking, even as a puppy, with a broad skull and strong muzzle. (Do realize, though, that female puppies will be finer in structure than their male counterparts.) Movement should be free and easy. All in all, the Rottweiler puppy does not go through the extreme metamorphosis that some other breeds do. You can expect the Rottie puppy to look much like a miniature version of the adult.
- **Ears:** The puppy's ears should be pink and clean, and there should be no odor. Lift the ear flaps and check inside.
- **Eyes:** The eyes should be dark, but clear and bright. Even very young Rottweiler puppies have a distinctly intelligent expression.
- **Lips:** The lips should be black and should not droop, allowing the puppy to drool.
- **Nose:** The nose of a Rottweiler puppy is black and should not be runny.

- **Teeth:** The puppy's teeth should be clean and white. They should meet in a *scissors bite,* in which the lower incisors touch the inside of the upper incisors. If you have any questions at all about the alignment of the teeth, discuss them with the breeder.

An adult dog has 42 teeth (22 in the lower jaw, 20 in the upper jaw). However, until a puppy is about 3 months old, she has only 28 temporary or baby teeth. With this first set of teeth come 12 incisors in the puppy's mouth. The incisors are the six small teeth at the front of both the upper and lower jaws. These are the teeth that should mesh in a scissors bite.

Knowing what danger signs to look for

Avoid a puppy who seems bony and undernourished or one who is bloated; a taut and bloated abdomen is usually a sign of worms. However, a rounded puppy belly is normal. Check the belly button for lumps, which could indicate a hernia.

Coughing or signs of diarrhea are danger signals, as are skin eruptions. Flaky or sparse coats can be signs of both internal and external parasites. Although the puppy coat is softer and finer than the adult's, the hair should not be long or fluffy.

Any odor or dark discharge from the ears could indicate ear mites, which in turn suggests poor general care. A crusted or running nose is another sign of possible serious problems. There should be no malformation of the mouth or jaws.

Running eyes can indicate any number of problems. Check to see if the eyelids are turned inward, as well. Inward-turned eyelids create a condition called *entropion,* where the lid brushes against the cornea. *Ectropion* is another eye abnormality, in which the eyelid droops down and outward, exposing the eyeball and subjecting it to irritation and damage. Both conditions are damaging to the eye and usually require surgery later on.

Asking the right questions

Puppies are too young to have had any conclusive tests for genetic complications, but their parents should have been tested *before* they were bred. The parents' good health strongly suggests that the puppy will follow suit.

The parents of the litter should have been x-rayed to show they are free of hip and elbow disorders. The x-rays are then examined by certified orthopedists at either the Orthopedic Foundation for Animals (OFA) or PennHip. A certificate is issued, stating that the parents are clear of these problems. The parents should also be certified as being free of eye abnormalities such as progressive retinal atrophy, an inherited disorder that causes blindness. The Canine Eye Registration Foundation (CERF) issues the certificates, and testing must be redone annually. Ask to see these certificates.

The only sure way of knowing whether a Rottweiler is free of the debilitating hip disorder known as *hip dysplasia* is through an OFA or PennHip screening. A preliminary x-ray can be done at 18 months, but a dog must be 24 months old before a final determination can be made.

Ask when the puppy had her last veterinary health check. You also need to know whether the sale of the puppy is contingent upon your own veterinarian giving the puppy a clean bill of health. Ask if the puppy will be replaced if she is found to have a hereditary fault. Discuss what kinds of faults are included in the breeder's guarantee and the age limitations for when they turn up.

Ask which inoculations have been given and how soon the next ones are due. Although it is not at all unusual for puppies to have roundworms, even from the best of breeders, you need to know when and if they have been wormed and what product was used.

My friend told me always to pick . . .

Friends, many of whom have never even owned a dog and who know absolutely nothing about Rotties, will usually offer all kinds of sage advice about how to pick a puppy. But when the big day comes, remember you are choosing this puppy for yourself and your family, not for anyone else.

Your pals down at the bowling alley may look at you with a bit more respect if you own the biggest, toughest Rottweiler on the block, but they don't have to live with the dog. The biggest, toughest puppy who comes streaking out of the whelping box to chew your shoes or swing on your pant leg may not necessarily be the right pup for you.

If you think this tiny tornado will grow up to provide you with that macho, tough-guy image, think again. Joining a gym and reinventing yourself as a latter-day Arnold Schwarzenegger could prove far less of a challenge than living with a Rottie you aren't able to handle.

Then there are all those romantic stories about the sickly runt of the litter who grows up to be the dog who wins the Westminster Kennel Club dog show. Were it only so! Taking home the forlorn little runt of any litter may well earn you a prize — for spending the most money on veterinary bills.

What you should be looking for is a healthy, happy Rottweiler pup who the breeder feels would be just right for the kind of guy or gal you happen to be. If your Rottie is going to be a welcome member of your family, the most easygoing, nicely adjusted pup in the litter is the only one you want to consider. If you use good sense in selecting your Rottweiler puppy, you'll have a friend whose intelligence and devotion will be everything the breed was intended to be.

Don't overlook the puppy's personality

An inscription in the temple of Apollo at Delphi says, "Know thyself." No one knows for sure just who wrote those memorable words, but I wouldn't be the least bit surprised if the guy who did was writing to someone who was about to buy a Rottweiler. The more you know about yourself, the more apt you are to get the right pup for you.

Will your personality meld with that of your Rottweiler? Will the way you handle life's little (and not so little) problems work for the Rottie puppy you will be bringing home?

If you are the type who handles problems by waiting until they disappear, forget about owning the little bruiser in the litter who is bound and determined to be king of the hill. Although he may be appealing, that little pink-tongued cutie you bring home is a lot smarter than you think. It won't take the little fellow long to figure out you are a *laissez faire* kind of a guy or gal, and the day he realizes he is no longer a weakling — watch out! Someone is going to be in charge, and it could well be the dog!

Bigger is not necessarily better when it comes to choosing your Rottweiler. Aside from the physical problems an oversized Rottweiler can develop, consider what your home and family are able to accommodate.

Some Rottweilers require a much firmer hand than others. The breed has a great capacity to learn, but each puppy learns at a different rate and one puppy may be a good deal slower to catch on than another. If you have patience that stretches from here to eternity, this won't bother you at all. But if you are equipped with a very short fuse, you may want to reconsider taking little Pokey home.

Breeder knows best

There's little doubt you know how you prefer to handle situations, but how much can you know about a puppy's personality when you only have a few minutes together? Probably not much. Aside from those pups who register at opposite ends of the temperament scale, it's pretty hard to tell a great deal about the rest of the litter.

An experienced breeder can give you a pretty good evaluation of the puppy you are considering. The breeder has been observing the litter since birth and has been through the growing-up process of Rottweiler pups time and time again. He or she knows a great deal about what to expect from each puppy in the litter. If you give the breeder even a general idea of your own personality, he or she can help tremendously in directing you to the right puppy.

Observe the puppy's behavior

The key characteristics in an adult Rottweiler's character are bravery, protectiveness, confidence, and devotion to family. By and large, you will find these characteristics in any well-bred adult Rottie. However, these characteristics are rooted in basic behaviors that can be seen even in youngsters.

Although definitive temperament testing can't be done on very young puppies, certain characteristic puppy behaviors can indicate how suitable a particular puppy will be for you and you for it. I am not trying to suggest that the following are characteristics are good or bad, because the same characteristic can be an asset in one situation and a liability in another. These are simply some of the factors you need to consider:

- **Dominance.** How the puppy interacts with her littermates is a strong indication of how dominant or submissive she will be as an adult.
- **Dependence.** One puppy will be the first out of the nest and rush out to meet every stranger who comes by. Another may only do so with the rest of the gang. The more dependent dog is usually more eager to please and easier to train. The more independent dog may prove to be stronger willed, but may not need as much attention and reassurance.
- **Energy.** Some puppies play until there is absolutely no littermate willing to go on, and then they will be the first awake to start over again. Other pups like to nap frequently and may be completely content to sit on some high perch for long stretches of time just observing the world.
- **Determination.** Some puppies seem to have only one thing in mind, and that is what they are trying to accomplish at the moment. Nothing can distract them. Other pups in the same litter can be redirected quite easily.
- **Aggressiveness.** Some puppies in a litter will not tolerate having their possessions tampered with and will respond angrily or by biting. This response can be directed toward littermates and/or toward humans. Uncontrolled aggressiveness can lead to serious problems, but harnessed it can serve a definite purpose.

Although a good part of how your Rottweiler behaves will be determined by how well the puppy is raised and trained, you can predict a lot by observing the way the puppy interacts with her littermates.

Knowing Which Important Papers You Need When You Walk out the Door

Before you leave with your young pup tucked under your arm, some very important transactions have to take place. First, the seller will want to get paid. Cash is always appreciated, as is a cashier's check or money order. If your payment is a personal check, the seller may want you to come back to pick up your puppy when the check has cleared the bank. Don't feel this is because you look untrustworthy or because the breeder is a suspicious old coot. What recourse does the breeder have after you are gone with the puppy if the check keeps bouncing right back no matter how many times it's deposited?

On the day the actual sale is completed, you are entitled to four very important documents:

- A health record, including an inoculation schedule
- A copy of the dog's pedigree
- The registration application
- A sales contract

But she picked me!

Some Enchanted Evening applies in plays, love songs, and movies. The two protagonists spot each other across a crowded room and somehow they know — it's happiness forever after. Good for songs and movies, but not so good when it comes to picking out your Rottweiler.

Undoubtedly, the aggressive little pup who knows no strangers will be the first one out of the chute and over to you. She will probably be happy to follow you to the ends of the earth, or if not there at least to the end of the hall. Does this mean you were meant for each other? In a good number of breeds I might unhesitatingly say yes, but in Rottweilers I would want to reserve judgment.

Make no mistake, I am not discounting friendliness and self-confidence — not by a long shot. But beware the absolutely reckless pup who plows straight ahead without thinking twice. Obviously you don't want a shrinking violet or you wouldn't be considering a Rottie. At the same time, you don't want a dog incapable of using a bit of Rottweiler discretion. Puppy bravery is all well and good, but it should be tempered with *some* good sense.

Ask the breeder for his opinion. If the person who knows the puppies best assures you that the puppy you want is a sensible one and has become totally smitten with you, the two of you (you and the puppy that is) can start singing love songs.

These papers, covered in more detail in the following sections, ensure your dog is a real Rottweiler. There should be no extra charge for these documents. Good breeders supply them with every puppy they sell.

If you want to be sure you are buying a purebred Rottweiler, do not be maneuvered into buying a "bargain pup" whose parents were "purebred, but we never got around to registering them" or who comes with excuses like "the mother was purebred and registered, but the people who owned the sire lost the dog's papers." The only way you can be sure you are getting a purebred Rottweiler is if the pup comes with an official registration application and at least a three-generation pedigree.

Health record

Most Rottweiler breeders have begun the necessary inoculations for their puppies by the time they are 7 or 8 weeks old. These inoculations protect the puppies against adenovirus, distemper, parainfluenza, and canine parvovirus (all deadly, communicable diseases covered at greater length in Chapter 12). These are diseases that can kill your puppy seemingly overnight.

A puppy should never be taken away from her original home before these initial inoculations have been at least started. There is a prescribed series of inoculations developed to combat these infectious diseases, and it is extremely important that you obtain a record of which shots have been given to your puppy and when. You must also have the type and make of serum used, so your veterinarian can continue with the appropriate inoculations as needed.

A rabies inoculation is also necessary, but in most cases it is not administered until a puppy is 4 to 6 months of age or older. Local ordinances may require that the rabies shot be given before that time. Check with your veterinarian, who will know what the law is in your area.

The chances that your dog will be infected with rabies by another pet dog are very remote. However, this doesn't preclude the possibility of your Rottweiler coming in contact with wild animals, who are always at risk of spreading rabies. Do not overlook the importance of inoculating against this possibility.

The health record should also say what kind of veterinary treatment the puppy has been given since birth. This will include records of exams, along with dates, and the type of medication used for each worming.

Pedigree

The pedigree is your dog's family tree. The breeder of every AKC-registered dog should supply the buyer with a copy of this document. The pedigree lists your puppy's ancestors back to at least the third generation by giving the registered names of each dog.

All purebred dogs have a pedigree. The pedigree does not imply that a dog is of show quality. It is just a chronological list of ancestors — nothing more, nothing less. Don't let anyone tell you otherwise.

A pedigree is read from left to right. The names are presented in pairs, and the first pair of names in the first column on the left are the puppy's *sire* (father) and *dam* (mother). The sire's ancestry, reading left to right, occupies the top half of the pedigree. The dam's ancestors appear on the bottom half. For each pair of names, the sire is on the top and the dam is on the bottom.

In most cases, pedigrees are hand-written or typed by the breeder. These unofficial documents tell you your puppy's ancestry, but like any document prepared by a human, they can contain spelling errors and other assorted mistakes. If you wish to obtain an Official Pedigree, you can obtain one by calling the AKC at 919-233-9767 or visiting the AKC online at `www.akc.org`. The information contained in an AKC document is taken from its computerized files. The registration application will contain a box you can check off if you want to order an Official Pedigree (which costs $17, in addition to the $10 registration fee).

A pedigree is just a list of ancestors. It is no guarantee of quality. If there is anything that indicates one pedigree is better than another, it is the titles the individual dogs in the pedigree have earned. Most of these titles will be indicated on the Official Pedigree. The titles can be earned for excellence of conformation and achievement in a host of sports and activities. Titles may also be awarded for producing many Champion puppies.

Even if you have not yet decided what the future holds in store for your puppy, you should understand that the titles on the pedigree tell you the dog's ancestors have excelled in certain respects — that they represent true Rottweiler character and intelligence. They also tell you the people who owned the title-holders were responsible individuals who felt an obligation to help their Rotties achieve their highest potential.

Registration application

The registration certificate is the canine world's birth certificate. When a breeder has a litter of puppies, the first thing he or she must do to get them registered is submit an application to register the entire litter with the AKC. The information about the litter's sire and dam is checked, and the AKC issues individual registration applications for each puppy in the litter. Breeders refer to these individual application as *blue slips,* just because they've always been printed on blue paper.

Breeders can either use the blue slip to transfer ownership of the puppy directly to you, or they can individually register all the puppies in the litter in their own name first. Most breeders will give you the blue slip when you buy the dog, and you will be responsible for sending it in. As with the Official Pedigree, the registration certificate is issued by the AKC. When the breeder sells you a Rottweiler, an official record of the transaction is entered on the registration application and mailed to the AKC, where it is permanently recorded in the AKC's computerized files.

Most breeders like to insert an official registered name for the puppy on the blue slip, or at least a prefix. A *kennel name* is the prefix or suffix used to identify the breeder or kennel that bred the dog. This kennel name is registered with the AKC and no other breeder may use it. Most breeders add this to a dog's individual name, so that the name ends up being something like Happy House Daisy or Hughie of High Acres. This permanently associates that puppy with that breeder. Actually, it is a compliment to the puppy that the breeder thinks highly enough of her to ensure the association. However, after a dog is individually registered with the AKC, the registered name can never be changed. You can, of course, call the puppy anything you choose.

When you buy a puppy, the registration application is transferred to you. This blue slip must be completed and returned to the AKC with the necessary fee ($10 as of this printing) no later than 12 months from the date of the puppy's birth. The puppy's birth date is printed on the blue slip.

Never, never, *never* accept a purebred puppy without either the blue slip or the actual registration certificate. Don't take anybody's word for it, don't accept any promises that the papers will be sent later, and don't listen to any excuses. Responsible breeders have all their papers in order at the time of sale.

Sales contract

A reputable breeder will supply a written agreement that lists everything that he or she is responsible for in connection with the sale of your Rottweiler. The contract will also list all the things you, as the buyer, are responsible for before the sale is actually final. The contract should be dated and signed by both the seller and the buyer. Sales contracts vary, but all assurances and anything that is a condition of the final sale should be itemized. Some of these conditions may be:

- **Whether the sale is contingent upon the dog passing a veterinarian's examination within 24 to 48 hours after she leaves the seller's premises.** There should be a clear statement of the refund policy if the dog does not pass the vet's exam.

- **Any conditions regarding the seller's requirement to spay or neuter the dog.**
- **Whether a Limited Registration accompanies the dog.** In a Limited Registration, the dog is ineligible to have offspring registered by the AKC.
- **Arrangements that must be followed if at any time in the dog's life, the buyer is unable to keep the dog.**
- **What conditions will apply if the dog develops genetic bone or eye diseases at maturity.**

Diet sheet

Your Rottweiler is the happy, healthy youngster she is because the breeder has properly fed and cared for her every step of the way. All established breeders have their own experienced way of doing so. Because they have been successful in breeding and raising their puppies, most breeders give the new owner a written record of the amount and kind of food a puppy has been eating. They will normally give you enough of the food the puppy has been eating to last until you are able to go out and buy some yourself. Follow these recommendations to the letter, at least for the first month or two after the puppy comes to live with you.

The diet sheet should indicate the number of times a day your puppy has been fed and the kind of vitamin supplementation or additions to the food she has been receiving. Following the prescribed procedure will reduce the chance of upset stomach and loose stools.

Some breeders add vitamin supplements to their dogs' and puppies' diets as a matter of course. Other breeders are adamantly opposed to supplements when well-balanced and nutritious food is given. Be sure you understand what your breeder's thoughts are on this issue and act accordingly.

Usually a breeder's diet sheet projects the increases and changes in food that will be necessary as your puppy grows from week to week. If the sheet does not include this information, ask the breeder for suggestions on increasing the size of meals and the eventual changeover to adult food.

In the unlikely event the breeder does not give you a diet sheet, your veterinarian will be able to advise you about what to feed your puppy. I also cover more about Rottweiler nutrition in Chapter 11.

Part III
Living with a Rottweiler

In this part . . .

In the chapters in this part, you'll get ready for your Rottweiler puppy by having on hand all the supplies and toys you'll need in the first few days. I also take you through the process of introducing your Rottweiler pup to the other members of his new community. And I give you some important and useful information on training your Rottie so that he's a valued and well-adjusted member of your family.

Chapter 5

Preparing for Your Puppy

In This Chapter

- Knowing what to include on your shopping list
- Finding the best leashes, collars, and crates for your Rottweiler
- Keeping your Rottie supplied with high-quality toys
- Getting the equipment you need to puppy-proof your home
- Using the right tools to keep your Rottweiler clean and healthy

Perhaps the next time you plan on bringing home a new dog, you should register for gifts at the local pet emporium and send out adoption announcements to friends and family. But for now you had better get down to making that list and checking it twice, because having everything in place *before* your Rottweiler arrives will save you some hectic days and sleepless nights.

You need equipment to keep that little tyke busy, other equipment to keep him in, and still other equipment to keep him out. He has to have a place to play and a place to sleep. You'll need some toys for training and some toys just for fun.

In this chapter, I give you a list of the basic equipment you need on hand, and then I go into more detail on the more critical items on the list so you know what to look for when you shop.

There are two dog-owner necessities that are as important as everything I discuss in this chapter, but they can't be purchased at any pet emporium or supermarket. They are patience and persistence. The other intangibles, like experience, respect, and a resounding sense of humor, come with time. Long-time dog owners know the importance of experience, respect, and a sense of humor, but they also know that without patience and persistence you can never achieve them.

Making Your Shopping List

If this is your first dog, you will probably need to start from scratch and buy everything on this list. If you've had a dog before, check to make sure that what you have will suit the size and needs of your Rottweiler puppy.

- Brushes, combs, and nail clippers
- Chewing deterrents
- Collars and leashes (see Figure 5-1)
- Doggy quick bath
- Feeding bowls and water dishes
- Fiberglass kennel crate or metal wire cage
- Food prescribed by the breeder
- Household odor neutralizer and cleaners
- Paneled fence partition or pen to cordon off a living area for the puppy
- Special dog shampoo
- Toys

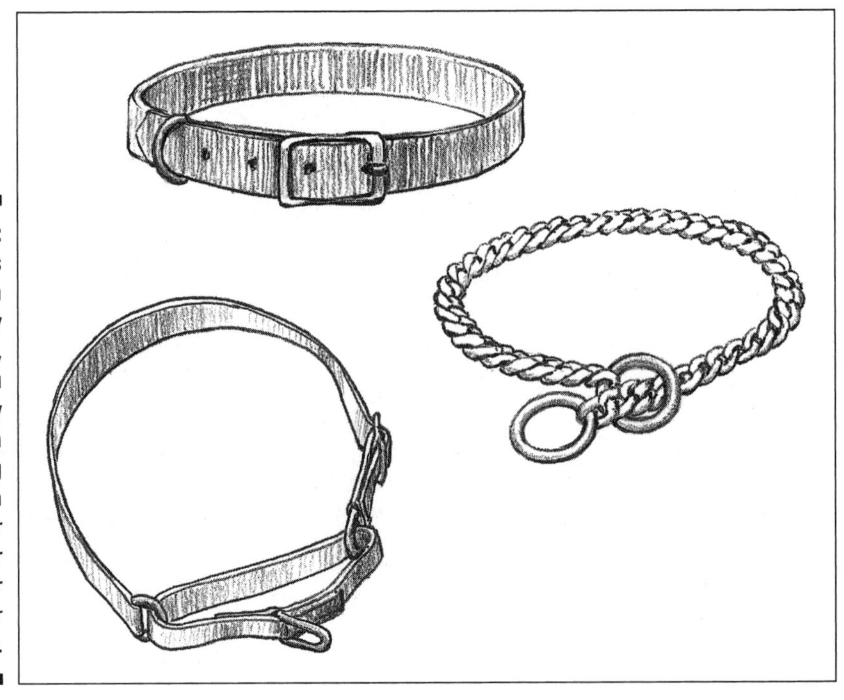

Figure 5-1: Collars come in many varieties, but you really only need a training collar and a soft leather collar for your Rottweiler pup.

All of this equipment can be purchased from local pet supply stores or the larger pet emporiums. Many supermarkets now carry a very extensive line of pet products as well, and if you have the opportunity to attend a dog show, you will find trade stands selling all the products you need.

When you go shopping, be sure to tell the shop owner or clerk that you are getting a Rottweiler. Toys and equipment suitable for a Chihuahua will not work for your Rottie. The shop owner or clerk may even have suggestions that will prevent you from having to replace all your equipment because your little Goliath has outgrown what you buy when he's a pup.

Finding the Right Leashes and Collars for Your Rottweiler

The collar that fits your little puppy today will probably just go around his wrist next week. Perhaps that's a bit of an exaggeration, but like shoes for kids, collars for young Rotties seem to be outgrown on the way home from the store.

Plan on buying the following different collars and leashes for your dog:

- **Baby collar.** This collar is just to get your puppy used to having something around his neck. Buckle collars made of *soft* leather or sturdy cloth work well. They are adjustable to about 14 inches, and even after the initial introduction period they can be used to carry the puppy's identification and rabies tags. This collar will be the first one to go around the puppy's neck, so the less noticeable it is, the better.
- **Training collar.** Also referred to as a *slip collar,* this link-chain collar is one you'll need by the time your Rottweiler pup is 3 to 4 months old, when basic training is about to begin. At that point, you can take the puppy with you to the store to be sure you get the proper size. The pet supply shop (or trade stand owner if you buy at a dog show) will be able to demonstrate how to measure and put on the link-chain training collar. (If they can't help, do your shopping elsewhere.)
- **Leashes.** The first leash you buy for your Rottweiler should be flexible and lightweight. (Actually, you can survive those first few days with a piece of light cotton clothesline.) When you first attach it to the puppy's collar, expect the little tyke to act as though he's being pursued by a king cobra. Fear not. Your little treasure will get over seeing the leash as a death threat fairly quickly. Obviously, avoiding a leash that's big and heavy will aid in the transition. Eventually you are going to need a 4-foot leather training leash, so my advice is to move right on up to that piece of equipment just as soon as your little pup graduates from the clothesline.

Getting the Right Equipment to Confine Your Dog When Necessary

Create a partitioned-off living area for your puppy. Wire paneled fence partitions, called *exercise pens,* are available at most pet supply shops. The panels are 3 or 4 feet high, and are well worth the cost. The kitchen is an ideal place to confine your puppy, because he will miss his mother and littermates very much and will almost immediately transfer this dependence to you and your family — and in most houses there is usually some member of the family in the kitchen to keep the puppy company. Plus, kitchen flooring is usually easiest to clean up in the event of an accident.

This fenced-off area provides a safe place for the puppy, as well. Not only does it keep the puppy out of mischief, but it also protects him from being bothered by (or bothering) other animals in the household (if there are any). It can also be a place where the children are told to leave the pup alone.

Kids and puppies were meant for each other, but make sure the initial introduction takes place slowly, especially if they have never met before. Rottweiler puppies are inclined to chase anything and anyone who runs. And when children are frightened, they run and scream, which only incites a puppy's chase instinct and even creates the urge to bite at the child's heels.

Puppies who have not been raised with small children may find these miniature humans very frightening. Most puppies love children, but it may take a bit of time for the puppy who is not used to children to feel comfortable around them. The fencing keeps the children at a safe distance and gives the puppy an opportunity to accept them gradually.

Crates and cages

Inside the fenced-off area I create for my pups, I always place a wire cage or a rigid fiberglass crate with the door open. The cage or crate quickly becomes the dog's sleeping den. These crates come in various sizes, and although the one that will accommodate the fully grown Rottweiler may seem terribly oversized for a very young puppy, you will be amazed at how big your puppy will grow in just a few weeks. So choose one that will accommodate your Rottweiler when he's fully grown.

A crate proves invaluable for both housebreaking and travel. When I have recommended crates to some first-time dog owners, you would think I had suggested locking their precious one in a trunk and throwing away the key.

At first, they consider the crate method of confinement (especially during housebreaking) to be cruel. But when they do as I suggest anyway, they invariably come back to thank me over and over, agreeing the crate is one of the most valuable training tools they have ever used.

Using a crate of the proper size reduces the average housebreaking time to a minimum and eliminates all the stress of constantly correcting a puppy for making mistakes in the home. Then too, there are those days when everything and everyone in the house seem to be working at odds. The children need time out, you need time out. At those times there is no better place for the family dog than his own little den with the door closed.

Crates provide a sense of safety and security. Most adult dogs use their crates voluntarily as a place to sleep. It becomes their cave or den, and in many cases a place to store their favorite toys or bones.

Dogs learn to look at their crates as safe and private quarters. Those of us who live on the earthquake-prone West Coast find our dogs make a bee-line for their crates at the first rumble. With some, it takes a good deal of coaxing to get them to come out of their shelter.

The fiberglass airline-type crates (like the one shown in Figure 5-2) are ideal for Rottweilers. They can be purchased from almost any pet supply shop. Check to see if the manufacturer's warranty states the crate is "airline approved" — just in case you and your dog decide to visit the relatives in Oshkosh. When traveling by air, an airline-approved crate is a requirement. Even when you decide to have your Rottweiler accompany you in the car, he is safest in his crate.

Buy an extra-large crate (approximately 40 inches long by 27 inches wide by 30 inches high). That size will accommodate the average full-grown male Rottweiler and allow him to stand up and turn around. Should your dog decide to grow beyond the norm, there is a giant-size crate available — but do remember, a crate is not a home gym, it's just for sleeping. Your dog should be able to comfortably stand up and turn around in the crate. He doesn't need to be able to walk around.

Naturally, an extra-large crate is much too roomy for a very young puppy, especially one you are trying to housebreak. Dogs do not like to relieve themselves where they sleep, but if the crate is large enough, they will eliminate at one end of the crate and sleep at the other. You can cut a plywood partition to reduce the inside space, as needed. If you don't want to bother with the cut-and-paste routine, you can purchase an inexpensive smaller crate and discard or sell it at your next garage sale as your dog outgrows it.

Figure 5-2: A fiberglass, airline-approved crate is ideal for Rottweilers.

In warm climates, some Rottie owners prefer wire crates, because they provide better air circulation. Wire crates come in all sizes, as well, and some have the additional advantage of being collapsible so that they can be folded flat if you need to transport them.

Outdoor runs

A securely fenced yard is the ideal place for your Rottweiler when he is outside. If you don't have a fenced yard, or if you do not want to see your rose bushes transplanted every few days, a dog run can be a godsend. Some of the larger pet emporiums carry very strong portable sections of chain-link fencing from which you can create any size run you choose.

Stocking up on Puppy-Proofing Supplies

Your Rottweiler will not spend his entire life inside his partitioned-off area, but trust me, sometimes you'll wish he did. Your puppy's safety and your sanity depend upon your ability to properly puppy-proof your home. As you do so, remember that what a Rottweiler puppy can't reach today, he will easily be able to dash off with tomorrow.

Mouth-size objects, electrical outlets, hanging lamp cords, and a host of other things you never looked upon as dangerous can be lethal to an inquisitive and mischievous puppy. Think of your Rottweiler puppy as one part private investigator and one part vacuum cleaner. That way, you will be much better equipped to protect your puppy and your belongings.

Puppies can get into places that defy the imagination. Be sure to get ties to keep the cupboard doors closed. Yours wouldn't be the first puppy to find a 10-pound sack of flour and decorate the kitchen with it.

More dangerous for the puppy is trying to digest a few sponges or the contents of any plastic bottle that can be chewed open. Many cleaning products, gardening supplies, and medicines can be poisonous and must be kept in securely latched or tied cupboards out of a puppy's reach.

Along with the fire department and police emergency numbers next to your telephone, keep the emergency number for your local veterinarian. Rottweiler puppies are constantly scooping up every item they find on the floor, and if your pup finds an object that fits into his mouth, he'll try his best to swallow it. Getting the pup to the vet quickly may save the little tyke's life.

Puppies are pros at chewing on things they shouldn't. But a product called Bitter Apple (it tastes just like it sounds!) is available at pet supply stores, hardware stores, and some pharmacies to help deter your pup from this common behavior. Bitter Apple is actually a furniture polish, but it is nonpoisonous and can be used to coat electrical wires and furniture legs. In most (but not all) cases, it will deter a puppy from damaging household items. I have also seen it applied to itchy spots to keep a dog from chewing himself.

If Bitter Apple does not deter your puppy, you can buy plastic tubing at hardware stores and place it around electrical cords and some furniture legs. The fencing panels I recommended will also help keep your puppy out of dangerous situations. And a daily puppy-proofing patrol will help you and your pet avoid damage and danger.

Supplying Your Pup with All the Toys His Heart Desires

Rottweilers love toys and games. There is seldom any problem in enticing them to play, and after a Rottie learns a game well, he becomes a master at coaxing you into playing it. The trick is in finding the right toys and teaching your dog games that are fun but that will not lead to complications or accidents.

Chew toys

Puppies have a strong need to chew. So if you don't want your puppy to chew on the furniture, you have to supply something for him to chew on instead. Chew toys help puppies through their teething periods and help them strengthen their jaws.

Providing your puppy with fun and interesting chew toys saves a great deal of wear and tear on your chair legs and encyclopedias. But you have to be careful about what kind of toys you select. What is safe and fun for your neighbor's Chihuahua could be swallowed or splintered (right along with the Chihuahua) by your Rottie before you can even yell, "Call the vet!"

Pet supply stores carry all kinds of toys. Some provide hours or days of chewing pleasure, whereas others are not much more than a quick snack. The dinosaur-size rawhide bones are good, as long as you keep your eye on the pup. Some puppies chew these rawhide bones for days. Other pups become masters at chewing off chunks and swallowing the pieces whole. The chunks can get caught in a dog's throat, so don't take the risk.

Rottweilers enjoy cured cattle and horse hooves as well, but the size of the hoof is important. If your big guy is the chew-and-swallow type, nothing smaller than an elephant hoof (if there is such a thing) is safe, but because harboring anything less than the entire elephant is illegal anyway, that pretty much eliminates hooves entirely.

Be careful of those toys sold in the pet section of your supermarket. Just because a toy is marketed for dogs does not mean that it is safe for your Rottie pup, who has jaws that seem capable of chewing through concrete!

A big fresh knuckle bone is a great chew toy for your Rottweiler — your pup will love the toy and will love *you* for getting it. Just make sure it is the bone of an animal that had very large knuckles.

For the vegetarians among you, you can buy things for your Rottweiler to chew on that have never lived. These are excellent manufactured substitutes that have different names, Nylabone and Gumabone among them. These hard nylon chew toys are next to indestructible, and puppies, even adult Rotties, can chew away to their hearts' content. Just make sure you buy the large sizes.

Play toys

Other things besides chew toys can keep your Rottweiler happy for hours. Kongs are super-tough rubber toys that are all but impossible to break. Available at your local pet emporium, Kongs are constructed with a hole in one end that can be stuffed with peanut butter or some other treat. Your Rottie will devote hours to attempting to get that wonderful stuff out of the toy.

Large Boomer Balls are made of nylon and can keep your Rottie entertained by the hour. They can be pushed and chased all over creation, so only allow your Rottie to play with Boomer Balls in a fenced area. (Some dogs are so focused on the balls they don't realize they have chased the thing a mile down the road or into the middle of rush-hour traffic!)

Rope toys take a tremendous amount of punishment before they give up the ghost. They are washable and come in all kinds of shapes and sizes. They're shakable and very throwable, so outdoors is probably the best place for playing with rope toys. You wouldn't want the rope toy to go flying into your objets d'art collection.

Toys to avoid

Don't think you are saving money by giving your pup an old sock or discarded slipper. Everything you and your family wear or have worn has your special smells, and dogs care not that you bought those socks or shoes last week if they are accustomed to playing with the older versions. A dog is unable to tell the difference between a discarded old loafer and your new dancing shoes. Don't confuse the issue.

Painted things are also no-nos. The toy may be as colorful as Disney World itself, but make sure the coloring agent is nontoxic.

Teddy bears and other stuffed toys are not a good idea either. Your Rottweiler can treasure and care for a favorite teddy bear for months on end, and then one day, for some transgression on the part of little Teddy that we know nothing about, the bear winds up inside your Rottweiler's tummy. When this happens, the three of you will be at the vet's office facing surgery.

Even before your Rottweiler swallows a stuffed animal, he will feel duty-bound to remove the eyes, nose, and squeaker from any stuffed toy immediately. That is part of being a dog. So is swallowing whatever is removed. Your Rottie is better off not eating little plastic parts, so don't offer them.

Finding the Right Grooming Tools

As a Rottie owner, you won't have long hair to deal with, but short hair still sheds. In fact, if you neglect to brush your Rottweiler, he will drop every unwanted hair exactly where you don't want it to be. Rottweilers shed a bit all through the year and go through major shedding periods in the spring and fall. Females tend to have a major shed when they come into heat, as well.

Even though your Rottie's hair is short, your house will still have some degree of doggie odor. All dogs have doggie odor — some more, some less. Still, having a dog in the house, even a dog the size of a Rottweiler, does not mean the place has to smell like a stable or even a doghouse. If you keep your Rottie's skin and coat clean, you will minimize the amount of odor that is present.

Realize of course, that if your Rottweiler has the run of the house and you aren't diligent about keeping him clean and shiny bright, his doggie odor is being transferred to every carpet, every chair, and every bedspread he rests on. Neglecting your Rottie's hygiene means extra work for whoever has the responsibility of keeping the house suitable for the human occupants.

A thorough 5-minute brushing every couple of days will suffice most of the year, but seasonal shedding and those special times of the year demand daily brushing to keep the hair from flying.

Certain tools can help you keep your Rottweiler — and your home — in great condition:

- **Slicker brush:** A *slicker brush,* which has bent wire bristles set in a flat rubber base, works well to remove all debris and loose hair. You can easily remove the loosened hair from the brush with a fine-tooth comb. Greyhound combs have fine teeth on one side and wider teeth on the other. This makes them useful for both removing hair from the brush and running through little tangles or mini-mats on the dog.For shedding periods, a shedding rake is very useful, because it removes more loose hairs.
- **Nail clipper and grinders:** Your Rottweiler's nails have to be attended to, and you'll find a variety of nail clippers and nail grinders to help you in this chore. Check out Chapter 12 for more information on using these supplies.
- **Dog shampoo:** When a brush and a promise are not quite enough, you can bathe your dog with a good shampoo made especially for dogs. Special dog shampoos are highly recommended, because their pH balance is set for a dog's needs — which are significantly different than a human's.
- **Dry bath products:** A wet bath is not the only approach to getting your Rottweiler's coat clean. Many dry bath products are extremely effective as well. You quickly rub in these products, and then wipe or brush them out, eliminating the mess and time involved in a wet bath.
- **Odor neutralizers:** Household odor neutralizers and cleaners should also end up in your shopping basket. As fastidious as you are, sometimes the doggie odors just get ahead of you. Supermarkets carry

sprays, candles, liquids, and plug-ins that help in these cases, but the pet emporiums often carry products that work better for pet odors. Also, many of the products you can buy at the grocery store may irritate an animal's skin, whereas the products you buy at the pet supply store are more likely to be dog-friendly.

Chapter 6

Welcome Home!

In This Chapter

- Getting ready for the reality of having a puppy in your home
- Knowing what to expect from a puppy, an adolescent, and a young adult dog
- Making it through the first week with your new Rottweiler
- House-training your pup with ease

Good parents, or people with good parenting potential, make good dog owners. Why? Because owning and caring for a dog is pretty similar to raising a child. The main difference is that with a child you eventually reach a point where you can wipe your hands and say, "Well, I've done a good job, and now you are on your own." That day never comes with a dog. And although Rottweiler lovers make extravagant claims for their dogs at times, they do realize that, in the end, the owner is completely and totally responsible for his or her dog.

The puppy doesn't learn until you teach her. A puppy, or grown dog for that matter, cannot eat until you feed her or turn on the faucet when she wants a drink of water. Dogs cannot let themselves out of the house to take care of bodily functions, and they don't have access to over-the-counter remedies when they are ill. You have to do all these things over and over — for the rest of the dog's life. And that is the case whether you feel you feel like doing them or not.

The first few weeks and months after your new Rottweiler puppy arrives, she needs the same kind of care and attention all babies need. When you finally get through that stage and adolescence sets in, you have to call upon all the patience in the world to work your way through that difficult time.

Being Prepared for Reality

A new puppy is capable of finding her way into situations you never thought possible for any dog to think up, much less one so young. And just in case you think you can eliminate all the problems of puppyhood by getting an adolescent or mature Rottie — forget it. Granted, you won't have the baby puppy problems; you'll only have the problems a more experienced adolescent or adult dog will present.

Give in and face facts: Bringing a new dog of any age into your home is going to present transition problems that have to be dealt with. It wouldn't be any different if you were bringing another human being into your home for the first time. If the new arrival were a baby, you would have infant problems. An adolescent would have all the challenges of that enigmatic stage, and certainly there's no need to tell you what having an adult move in with you would be like.

The two Ps come into play here: preparation and patience. Think, read, and ask for advice from your puppy's breeder. Breeders have lived through this transition many times, and if anyone can give you workable suggestions, it is the person who has gone through it all before.

Not only do breeders understand how Rottweilers react in most situations, they know how the dog you are taking home is inclined to behave. Believe me, having input on those two things alone can save you a good many headaches.

Keep in mind that everything in your home the new Rottie comes in contact with is entirely strange. To make matters worse, no one familiar is around to assure the newcomer that all is well. Beginning with the very first day your new Rottie enters your home, there are two very important rules to keep in mind:

- **Do not let your Rottie do anything on the first day or days that you will not want her to do for the rest of her life.** Think ahead — feeding your little pup buttered toast while she sits on your lap through breakfast may be fun when she's a tot. Where, however, will she sit and what will she eat when she weighs more than 100 pounds? For that matter, where will *you* sit?
- **Never be severe in correcting unwanted behavior.** Try to avoid nagging and correcting a new pup every time she turns around. New dogs, regardless of age, will make mistakes simply because they do not know the rules yet. Because this is the case, you're probably wondering how you can prevent your puppy from establishing bad habits yet still avoid constantly correcting your Rottie. The answer is actually quite simple: Avoid putting the new dog into situations where she will be breaking the rules.

If you allow your Rottie pup to sleep in bed with you the first few nights because she appears sad and lonely, don't expect her to be happy about banishment to her crate in the kitchen a week later. She will probably advise you in no uncertain terms that those arrangements are not acceptable.

Courage and aggressiveness are known and respected characteristics of the well bred Rottweiler. As a responsible owner, you must be certain that you are able to keep those breed traits under control at all times.

Photograph courtesy of Ron Kimball Photography

Although most of what is written about Rottweilers describes a formidable guardian of home and family, those who live with the breed know what a rollicking sense of humor lies behind that stoic reputation.

Photograph courtesy of Ron Kimball Photography

Your Rottweiler is always ready and willing to accompany you on a day-long hike or weekend adventure. When you're away from home, however, make sure you take along the supplies you may need in case of an emergency.

Photograph courtesy of Ron Kimball Photography

Photograph courtesy of Ron Kimball Photography

Your Rottweiler can enjoy a day at the beach as much as you do. When swimming ocean waters, be very familiar with currents and riptides, and never send your Rottie into waters that you wouldn't allow a child to enter.

Photograph courtesy of Ron Kimball Photography

Although the Rottweiler's muscular stature may indicate his forte is in strength rather than speed, do not underestimate his ability to shift into high gear when the occasion arises. More than one wrongdoer has learned this lesson, to the person's deep regret.

Photograph courtesy of Ron Kimball Photography

The official standard of the Rottweiler describes a robust and powerful dog with a substantial build that imparts an image of great strength, agility, and endurance.

Photograph courtesy of Ron Kimball Photography

The Rottweiler Standard describes the breed's expression as "noble, alert, and self-assured." This proud Rottie embraces every word of that description.

Photograph courtesy of Ron Kimball Photography

One of the most important lessons all dogs must learn as early as possible is to come when called, without hesitation. Never lose your temper or punish your dog if he doesn't respond immediately to your "come" command. If he associates the word "come" with negative consequences, he will delay returning even longer.

Photograph courtesy of Ron Kimball Photography

Even when you and your Rottweiler are in a dog park where having a dog off-leash is perfectly acceptable, make sure your Rottweiler has been properly socialized to accept other dogs. Some Rotties aren't able to handle being threatened or challenged without flying into a rage.

Dogs do not sweat through their pores in hot weather. Panting helps reduce their body temperatures. When your Rottie pants heavily, it's time to get him into an air-conditioned room or at least out of the sun and into a shaded area.

Photograph courtesy of Ron Kimball Photography

All dogs love to chew — especially when there isn't much going on to occupy their time. Rather than have your Rottie gnaw the time away on your best table or chair leg, be sure he has plenty of non-destructive toys instead. Some balls and rope toys are made especially for large dogs with strong jaws.

Photograph courtesy of Ron Kimball Photography

It is said that two dogs are just as easy to keep as one. In the case of Rottweilers, make sure your first dog is well trained before adding a second dog to the scene. Choose a new addition of the opposite sex; you'll avoid running into the confrontations and rivalry common between two same-sex dogs.

Frisbee is a game that most Rotties take to readily. It's also an excellent way to make sure that your dog is getting all the exercise he needs.

Most Rottweilers take great delight in retrieving a stick or ball from the surf and will do so beyond the point of exhaustion. Rest periods are important to avoid water accidents.

Photograph courtesy of Ron Kimball Photography

There is no better exercise for your Rottweiler than being able to stretch those muscles by running full speed in a totally unrestricted space, local ordinances permitting. However, make sure that the area is free of traffic hazards and that there is no danger of your Rottie harming another dog or running into a person who could be injured.

This handsome Rottie is anticipating a treat and seems to be totally oblivious of the chain-link collar he has around his neck. This type of collar is ideal for the many training sessions he will experience while growing up.

A Rottweiler who spends all his time with his owner soon begins to anticipate what you want him to do. There are times, though, when he has a look on his face that says, "I just don't understand you at all." And you won't be able to wipe the smile from your face.

Photograph courtesy of Ron Kimball Photography

A pup who is asleep in her crate when you can't be there to supervise or is confined in a nearby enclosure where she can see you but can't get underfoot is being protected, not mistreated. By gently confining the pup, you don't have to be a nag and the pup doesn't have to be confused about what is and isn't okay.

Bringing Your Pup Home Safely

The safest way to bring your puppy home is to get a pet carrier or cardboard box big enough for the puppy to stretch out comfortably with sides high enough so she can't climb out. Put a layer of newspapers at the bottom in case of accidents and a soft blanket or towel on top of that.

Ideally, another family member or friend should accompany you to do the driving or to hold the carrier that the puppy is in. All the better if you can hold the box on your lap. That way, your reassuring hand will be the first to stroke the puppy as she becomes accustomed to the strange and ever-changing new world.

Do your best to have your Rottie puppy come to live with you when you or another family member has a week or at least a few days off to be there most of the time. By the time a week has gone by, your puppy will have begun to forget all about her littermates and will begin to become a member of your family, even if the family is just the two of you.

If you can't manage a week off, try taking a Friday off and picking the puppy up early that day. It will give the two of you a full three days to get past that difficult transition.

Ideally, you should try to collect your puppy from the breeder in the morning so that the newcomer has at least one full day to acclimate to the overwhelming new world she is thrust in to. Then it won't be quite as bad when night falls.

Surviving the Difficult First Week

The first week is the tough one, especially for a very young puppy. When you take a puppy away from her littermates and put her into an entirely strange environment, the baby is going to be confused and lonely. No warm bodies to snuggle up to. No playmates for games. During the day it's bad enough, but the nights seem even worse.

Giving your dog a name — and using it

Decide on a name for your puppy before you bring the little tyke home, because it is one of the first things the pup should become familiar with. Name recognition is the puppy's first step in identifying with her new home. Notice that after just a couple of days of hearing that familiar word, the pup will respond by wagging what's left of her little tail and giving you that "you mean me?" look.

Use the name as often as you can. "Daisy, come!" "Daisy, outside?" Preface everything you say to your puppy with the puppy's name.

The subject of talking to your dog reminds me of an old English dog-training book I have in which the author is asked if a dog owner should talk to his dog — if it makes any sense to do so. The author's reply: "Bloody well do talk to your dog. Just make sure what you say makes sense!"

As brave as she was in the midst of her littermates, this is all very new and very bewildering for her. Expect some mournful complaints the first few nights. Usually, with a bit of help from you, the puppy will settle in and sleep the night through after that. However, some pups will keep up the lonely crying and howling night after night until you, your family, and the entire neighborhood are ready to move to another county. You may be amazed at how loud and how persistent a Rottie pup can be when it comes time to announce to the world that she is homesick and lonely.

The gang's all here

This is the time when your Rottie pup will meet everyone in the family and eventually everyone on the block and even everyone in town. Do not think for a minute that you should isolate your pup to ensure the Rottweiler's guarding or protective abilities. Meeting everyone in town with wagging tail will have no affect whatsoever on the territorial character of the adult Rottie. Believe me when I tell you the maturing Rottie will definitely know what is yours and will be as devoted as you are.

This is also the time your Rottie puppy will meet the family cat or other dogs in the household. ***Remember:*** Previous occupants deserve seniority treatment. Don't confine the pets who have already established residence. It is the puppy who is invading *their* territory. If you invested in the fence panels on your initial shopping list (covered in Chapter 5), this is the perfect time to set up the puppy enclosure in the kitchen. Let the previous residents check out the pup at their leisure and at the pace they choose.

Keep in mind that puppies don't use a great deal of sense in who they go rushing up to or who they will challenge to a puppy duel. A puppy's unsophisticated overtures of friendship may be entirely misread as aggression by an adult cat or dog and cause some very negative reactions.

For the first few nights after the new puppy arrives, put a box next to your bed and let the newcomer sleep there. If the puppy wakes up crying, a reassuring hand can be dropped down into the box without getting out of bed. The box-by-the-bed method teaches the puppy two important lessons:

- **The pup is really not alone in the world.**
- **You're there to protect her, and you'll be there no matter what.**

When you find the puppy has learned to sleep through the night without waking you up, you can change the puppy's sleeping quarters to the crate or cage you have purchased. Then, when the puppy is accustomed to that minor change, you can move the crate to the part of the house you prefer. You can do this more easily after the puppy has learned to be by herself for longer periods of time.

Dealing with Inevitable Baby Behavior

Everything is new for a puppy and every household rule has to be learned. Make everyone in your home understand that being consistent with the rules is a critical part of your Rottie's education. A puppy won't understand that lounging on the sofa is all right with the kids but not all right when Mom is looking.

No begging for food at the table means no begging at any table, any time, from any member of the family. Your first week with your Rottie, use a firm but gentle hand to consistently correct this behavior. Do you want a full-grown Rottweiler snatching your dinner from your plate?

Adorable/deplorable puppy antics

After the first day or so of unfamiliarity, your Rottie pup will begin to regain her confidence and start showing you a complete repertoire of antics that only puppies and kittens are capable of.

Unfortunately, as cute as some of these little behaviors are, many of them have to be curbed. Play biting, chewing, jumping up, dragging the sofa pillows off into the next room — all those things that are too cute for words now will *not* be things you'll appreciate in your adult Rottie. You'll have to harden your heart, be a killjoy, and nip bad habits in the bud. Teaching good behavior is *so* much easier to do than unlearn bad behavior.

Look at it this way — doing so will actually be teaching the pup those first two very important lifelong lessons: name recognition and the meaning of the word "no!"

Dealing with a lonely pup

Human babies cry. There are fretting cries, needy cries, and angry cries. Puppies are no different. They cry for all those same reasons, and they cry to express anxiety at being left alone. Teaching your Rottie that she will survive periods of being alone is important. Some puppies fret a bit and then settle down. Others are determined that you are going to give them the attention they want — or else. Do not let your Rottie get the idea that if she is persistent enough, salvation will come. After you teach your puppy this is so, life becomes a nightmare because the little monster will apply what she has learned to everything she wants or doesn't want.

Begin the training by confining your pup to her crate while you are in the same room. Some pups will be fine as long as they can see you. Others may decide they can only be happy under your feet. If the puppy begins to whine or bark, give a sharp "quiet!" command. Usually that does the trick. If not, you may have to rap the crate with the flat of your hand when you give the command. Almost invariably, the noise and simultaneous command will make the puppy pause, if not stop entirely.

You must have the last word, and if you are persistent you definitely will. Do not take the puppy out of the crate to comfort her. This is exactly what the complainer is after, and you will be teaching the puppy that the way to get what she wants is to be vocal about it.

Sometimes, with the more persistent little ones, sterner measures are necessary. Purchase a plastic spray bottle or water gun and fill it with water, adjusting the spray to a steady stream. The minute the barking or whining begins, command "quiet!" and give the pup a shot directly in her face. No harm is done, but puppies (even grown dogs) hate this. A few rounds with the water treatment usually get the message across.

Matching your dog's wits

Some dogs are determined not to be left outdoors alone at any time. Although I absolutely do not advocate banishing any dog at any age to the backyard, a little time alone outside in a securely fenced yard is not a bad thing. A friend of ours exhausted every known method to keep his young Rottie from standing at the fence and barking. Finally, in desperation, he rigged up a sound-activated water hose system so that the dog received a good blast of water every time he began barking. The Rottie learned very quickly that the consequences far exceeded the pleasure of vocalizing his unhappiness.

Another effective correction for puppies or barking adults is the shake can. A small aluminum soft drink can is ideal. First, empty the can. Then put a dozen pennies in the can and shake it — the noise is surprisingly loud, and if thrown at or near the puppy's crate it will surely startle the complainer. Be sure to give the "quiet!" command first, and immediately follow the command with the shake can if the dog does not comply.

When the puppy understands what the consequences are for whining or barking, you can stand in the next room. Just as soon as the racket starts, dash into the room and give your "quiet!" command. Follow up with the water or shake can, if necessary, but make sure you intervene each time and always use the same command. Don't make the mistake of saying "no" one time, "quiet" the next, and "stop" another time. This does nothing but confuse the dog.

Addressing house-training problems early

Some puppies get the housebreaking message right off the bat. Others may require all the patience reserves you have. You just never know how quickly (or slowly) your pup will get the message. But be patient, and eventually she will. Rotties are basically very clean, and when the breeder gets them off to a good start, housebreaking is a breeze. Still, accidents can and do happen. ***Remember:*** They're babies!

Avoiding the problem is the easiest way to approach this particular phase of your puppy's training. When it's time to go, a puppy will be inclined to return to the same area where she has previously relieved herself. If that's in the middle of your new white oriental rug, so be it. The puppy won't mind. But if the proper spot (with all the right smells) is outdoors, the puppy will begin to develop a yearning for that spot.

A puppy will let you know when she has to go. She will pace and circle and begin sniffing the ground. You'll see a mild sort of distressed expression and perhaps hear a little whine, seconds before "it" happens. As puppies begin to associate eliminating with that spot outdoors, they will become more and more insistent that they be given access to that spot.

If an accident occurs indoors, be sure to use an odor neutralizer to fully rid the spot of any smells that send the "return here" signal to the puppy.

Redirecting your puppy's chewing

Puppies chew. Grown dogs chew. The difference is that your adult Rottie has already learned what she can and cannot chew. The puppy hasn't learned this yet. Although Rotties are not as compulsive about chewing as some other breeds, when your Rottie does chew, you won't miss it. Never underestimate the power of those jaws.

A Chihuahua owner may return home to find their dog has left a tooth mark or two on the leg of the prized Chippendale table. A Rottie owner will wonder where the whole leg went. Bored Rotties are capable of reconstructing an entire household in a relatively short time. Be kind enough to your puppy to avoid leaving temptation in her path, especially during teething time.

Bitter Apple, Tabasco sauce, and other taste deterrents can help, but you can't cover your whole house with these products. When you can't keep an eye on your pup, confining her with a safe and enjoyable chew toy is the wisest approach (see Figure 6-1). In fact, you should always have something handy that the pup can chew on, even when you're there.

Surviving your pup's bursts of energy

I have always wondered what goes through puppies' minds when they suddenly decide to take off on a mad dash through the house as if the devil himself were right on their tails. You know, those headlong gallops 'round and 'round the dining room table or through the halls. If nothing else, it is a way for the pup to burn up some of that excess energy that all puppies seem to have.

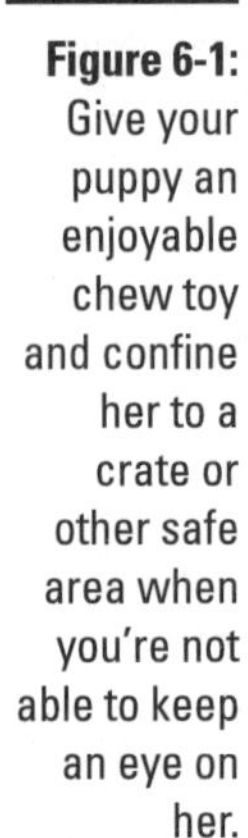

Figure 6-1: Give your puppy an enjoyable chew toy and confine her to a crate or other safe area when you're not able to keep an eye on her.

Photograph courtesy of John and Loraine Capurso

After they have one of those Indy 500 tears around the house, most pups immediately flop down and take a good long snooze. There is nothing wrong with your puppy if she does this. Just be careful that the pup doesn't crash into something and hurt herself — or that the older dog doesn't crash into the wall and hurt the wall. Also watch out for puppies who attempt to snap and grab at things as they go tearing around. This is definitely a no-no of the most serious kind!

Remember the Rottie's herding heritage — you do not want to awaken a Rottie's need to snatch at moving objects. This can lead to chasing and grabbing at joggers and cyclists. I can assure you none of them will appreciate being pulled down by your 100-pound cowgirl out on a roundup!

Managing play biting and growling

Although a little tough-guy growling and chewing on your hand may be cute in 2- to 3-month-old puppies, these are *extremely* dangerous habits to encourage. Rotties have an inherent desire to guard and protect. This trait has to be managed and directed by you.

Growling and attempting to snatch back things from your hand gives a Rottweiler puppy the idea that this behavior is just fine any time. This is not so, and it is your responsibility to make your Rottie understand this behavior is never permissible — not even "just for fun." Stop the behavior before it becomes a problem. A Rottweiler must learn to relinquish anything she may be holding in her mouth or standing watch over.

Begin this training very early by removing a play thing or food dish when the puppy is using them with the appropriate, "Daisy, leave it!" Do not tolerate any objections on the dog's part. You may even want to use your spray bottle here. I can not stress enough the importance of being fully in charge at all times.

No dog as large and as purposeful of character as a Rottweiler should ever be allowed to decide for herself what she can and cannot do!

Knowing What to Expect from Your Adolescent or Adult Rottweiler

Your Rottie puppy will pass through all the stages of maturity that all dogs go through. When you finally get through the dependency of infancy and the incessant curiosity of the Terrible Twos, you will plunge head on into adolescence. With some Rotties, particularly the boys, this period can be extremely challenging. It is a critical phase during which you must be especially wary of bad habits setting in and be persistent and consistent in training and maintaining the upper hand.

This doesn't mean every Rottie is going to start challenging you when she reaches adolescence. Some males have no great interest in becoming the leader of the pack. But a lot of them do. Females are less inclined to be rebellious but can easily become overprotective. It is up to you to make sure your Rottie doesn't get the ill-conceived idea that *she* is making the decisions.

If you've raised children, you'll recognize the signs of oncoming adolescence: grumbling, reluctance, inattention, a sullen attitude. If you haven't raised children, try thinking back on how you viewed the world at that same stage of your life.

Although dogs can't talk back, they can and do growl back. If you let puppy growls slip by uncorrected, you'll have a lot more difficulty trying to correct this behavior in adolescence. Even the Rottie who tried it in puppyhood and was corrected may take another shot at voicing disagreement in adolescence. The puppy who was permitted to get by with growling and puppy biting knows it's possible to rebel and escape unpunished. The big difference now, however, is that Baby Bruno weighs a hulking 100 pounds.

Recognizing the Instincts of the Breed

Your Rottweiler's bold attitude is as much a part of her genetic makeup as her black and tan color the breed sports. A brave heart is an inherent part of the breed's character — or at least, it should be. You can't change it, but you can direct and channel those instincts.

Guarding

The poor adolescent Rottie has a great deal to cope with just keeping those hormones from raging out of hand. On top of that, the young dog is constantly flipping back and forth between puppyhood and maturity. New and unaccustomed feelings are developing. At this stage, the guarding instinct also begins to develop, and no one is less confident about what to do with it than the Rottie herself. At this stage of their lives something deep within stirs and tells Rottweilers they should do something about the gardener coming around the side of the house, but they aren't sure of just what that "something" is.

Usually the budding guard dog will bark and then run off to hide. Another time your protector may beat a hasty retreat behind you and peek out between your legs, barking furiously to let you know the two of you are in danger. There's a problem, but the inexperienced Rottie just isn't sure what the problem is or what to do about it.

This is the time you have to step in and teach your protector that not all strangers intend harm, nor does the dog necessarily have to do anything about a stranger. If someone is to be a frequent visitor, introduce the person to your dog and get the two familiar with each other.

If you are the stranger (or even if you know a neighbor's dog), discretion is definitely the better part of valor. Never enter a friend's home or yard where a Rottweiler is on duty if the owner is not there, simply because the Rottie's first instinct is to protect and she may have a brief lapse of memory in regard to your friendship with her.

Advise friends and workers to come calling when you are home. Posting your yard or home with a "Guard Dog on Duty" warning of some kind would be entirely appropriate. Signs of this kind can be purchased at most hardware stores and pet supply shops. The merchants at dog shows often carry "Rottweiler on Duty" placards that are very effective for warding off unwelcome strangers. In many cases, these signs are posted even when there is no Rottweiler at home. Most would-be thieves are not particularly interested in testing the veracity of such a warning.

Dominance

Think again about the Rottweiler's origins and the characteristics insisted upon by those who shaped the breed: a positive attitude, boldness, courage, and determination. These are characteristics that do not come without willpower and an inborn sense of superiority. Neither are we able to pick and choose which of these qualities are a part of the breed's character. They come together, and together they can be molded into the fantastic animal the Rottweiler was meant to be. Without direction, they can result in a dog who is the absolute antithesis of what was intended.

The German breed standard points out that the Rottweiler has a strong instinct to retaliate when danger threatens. This characteristic was developed and encouraged in the breed. It is a good part of the reason Rotties are so well respected. Do note I said "a good part," and not "the whole story." This trait, combined with a unique level of trainability, makes the Rottie what she is — a discerning and highly controllable protector.

A well-informed owner and a well-devised training regimen are extremely important to the Rottweiler's stability and reliability. A Rottie who flies off the handle at any situation she deems threatening is not only useless as a companion but also a menace to society. Behavior of this kind should not be tolerated and would never be considered acceptable by knowledgeable and experienced breeders.

Throughout this book, I stress the importance of order in Rottie ownership. You and your human family are collectively your Rottie's pack leader. There must be *no* exceptions to this rule. If it is enforced, your Rottie will always look to you and your family for guidance in all things and you will not have a problem with dominance.

A Rottie who is pampered, whose every whim is catered to, begins to see herself as leader of the pack. Rotties who balk at giving up their playthings or who won't relinquish their spot on the sofa are trying to find their place in the order of things. It is up to you to let your dog know where her place is.

The pack leader does not arbitrate — the pack leader demands. There is no compromise. The members of the pack never have to wonder where their place is. Should any member forget her place or challenge the authority, the offender is quickly put back in line or ousted from the pack. There is no democracy in pack government, nor should there be in dog ownership.

Although kindness, respect, and tolerance must prevail in your relationship with your Rottie, there can never be a doubt as to who is in control. Anything less is a real disservice to your dog.

Dealing with Stress in Your Rottweiler

When a dog is unable to cope with the conditions she is experiencing, stress results. Sound familiar? In fact, all the things that stress *you* can also stress your dog. I don't mean going to work or driving in traffic, but being asked to do things you don't understand, or being separated from a loved one, or sudden, unexplained changes can stress us all — whether canine or human.

Being sure you don't pressure your dog too much

All Rotties, although somewhat similar, have individual personalities. They are no different than children in this respect. Some respond to a gentle reprimand, others don't seem to get the message unless three Marine drill sergeants are shouting out the order.

Each personality type requires an entirely different approach to training. The rough and ready, perhaps dominant, male needs to be handled differently than a quiet, compliant little female. (I am only using these as examples — not all males are bound to be bullies, nor are the females sure to be little angels!)

The more passive pup is a lot more anxious to comply and will not need or be able to handle the same kind of tough approach required for the extrovert. Bearing down too hard on the pup who was ready to comply in the first place can create a great deal of stress and confusion and interfere with learning. The passive puppy's first reaction to a command could then be fright rather than enthusiasm about being given an opportunity to perform for you.

Too much training before a pup is ready or being taught with too heavy a hand can upset some youngsters to the degree that they too can become neurotic and destructive. Pay attention to what your dog actually needs. Just because you once owned a dog who had to be run down by a bulldozer before the message got through doesn't mean you have to treat every dog that way. An observant owner very quickly learns which techniques work best with his or her dog.

Understanding separation anxiety

Separation anxiety is a far greater problem than most dog owners realize. This anxiety can be manifested in extremely destructive or neurotic behavior when the owner is absent. All too often this is dismissed as a temper tantrum, done out of spite or because the dog is just plain destructive. But in fact, your Rottweiler's destructive tendencies when you're away may be the result of a stress condition called *separation anxiety.*

Animal shelter managers say destructiveness caused by separation anxiety is the problem most likely to cause owners to abandon their dogs. This situation is especially sad because it is a problem that can be solved with a little training and patience.

In most cases, behavior of this kind is due to the dog's uncontrollable fear of being left alone. The behavior is almost to be expected from dogs who have been abandoned at some point in their lives. Some dogs who have been forced to undergo an extreme change in their living conditions will also exhibit this neurotic and destructive behavior.

Unwittingly, owners create or compound the problem by their own behavior. Do not add to your dog's insecurity by making your departure or return comparable to a soap opera cliff-hanger. Going to the store is not the Exodus, so don't make it that. Just go. When you return, don't carry on like a reenactment of the Return of the Prodigal Son. In fact, with a dog who is manifesting symptoms of separation anxiety, you're better off completely ignoring the dog for 10 or 15 minutes after you get back.

Confine all dogs to a safe area while you are gone, but especially do so with a dog experiencing separation anxiety. Instead of giving the dog yet another opportunity to reinforce her neurotic behavior — prevent it!

The drug Comicalm helps to relieve separation anxiety so that gradual retraining can take place. The drug is actually an antidepressant that works in much the same way as Prozac does in humans. If your Rottie is experiencing stress of this kind, discuss the problem with your veterinarian.

Housebreaking Your Rottweiler

Rottweilers generally are very easy to housebreak, because the breed is an exceptionally clean one. However, if you are inconsistent or lackadaisical in your approach, the Rottie gets a mixed message and as a consequence may well decide to do what has to be done wherever.

Young Rottie puppies have an amazing capacity to learn. But these young puppies also forget with great speed unless they are reminded of what they have learned by continual reinforcement.

The method of housebreaking I recommend is avoidance. I think the task of housebreaking gets progressively harder each time a puppy is allowed to have an accident indoors. Take your puppy outdoors to relieve herself after every meal, after every nap, and after every 15 or 20 minutes of playtime. Carry the puppy outdoors to avoid the opportunity of an accident occurring on the way out.

Housebreaking your Rottweiler becomes a much easier task when you use a crate. Begin by feeding your puppy in the crate. Keep the door closed and latched while the puppy is eating. When the meal is finished, open the crate and carry the puppy outdoors to the spot where you want the pup to learn to eliminate.

If you do not have outdoor access, or if you will be away from home for long periods of time, begin housebreaking by placing newspapers in some out-of-the-way corner that is easily accessible for the puppy. If you consistently take your puppy to the same spot, you will reinforce the habit of going there for that purpose.

Do not let the puppy loose after eating. Young puppies eliminate almost immediately after eating or drinking. They are also ready to relieve themselves when they first wake up and after playing. If you keep a watchful eye on your puppy, you will quickly learn when this is about to take place. A puppy usually circles and sniffs the floor just before she relieves herself.

If you are not able to watch your puppy every minute, she should be in her crate with the door securely latched. Each time you put your puppy in the crate, give her a small treat of some kind. Throw the treat to the back of the crate and encourage the puppy to walk in on her own. When she does, praise the puppy and perhaps hand her another piece of the treat through the wires of the crate.

A Rottweiler puppy of 8 to 12 weeks will not be able to contain herself for long periods of time. Puppies of that age must relieve themselves often. Your schedule must be adjusted accordingly. Also, make sure your puppy has relieved herself at night before the last member of the family goes to bed.

Your first priority in the morning is to get the puppy outdoors. Just how early this takes place will depend much more upon your puppy than upon you. If your Rottie is like most others, there will be no doubt in your mind when she needs to be let out. You will also very quickly learn to tell the difference between the puppy's emergency signals and just unhappy grumbling. Do not test the young puppy's ability to contain herself. Her vocal demand to be let out is confirmation that the housebreaking lesson is being learned.

If you find it necessary to be away from home all day, you will not be able to leave your puppy in a crate, because being confined for that long is just not fair to the pup. On the other hand, do not make the mistake of allowing her to roam the house or even a large room at will. Confine the puppy to a small room or partition off an area and cover the floor with newspaper. Make this area large enough so that the puppy will not have to relieve herself next to her bed, food bowl, or water bowl. You will soon find the puppy will be inclined to use one particular spot to perform her bowel and bladder functions. When you are home, you must take the puppy to this exact spot to eliminate at the appropriate time.

You're probably wondering whether your Rottie will eventually get to a level of maturity where she can let you know what she needs. The answer is yes — sort of. You will have to make allowances for those times when you don't fully understand what it is she's trying to tell you. There are days when your Rottie will give you the "I need to go outside" signal, and the minute you let her out she will turn around and demand to be let back in. Instead of accusing your Rottie of not telling the truth, you'll simply have to mark it down as just another thing you're failing to understand.

Chapter 7

Understanding How to Communicate with Your Rottweiler

In This Chapter

- Knowing the motivation behind your Rottweiler's behavior
- Seeing how both positive and negative behavior get reinforced
- Responding to your Rottweiler with kindness and patience under all circumstances
- Teaching your Rottie that people and other animals are fun to be around
- Reading your dog's behavior to understand what he's trying to tell you

Although a Rottweiler can be a brilliant dog, he isn't born knowing all the things you want him to know. Rottweilers have a tremendous capacity to learn, but if there is no one around to teach them or no one who can teach them properly, they will not be able to achieve that great potential. Every Rottie is born with a clean slate. It is you who will do the writing. Just make sure you write clearly and spell everything correctly!

Unfortunately, the things that work best for teaching humans cannot always be transferred to our dogs. What seems reasonable and logical to us may not apply to our dogs because (I know you're ahead of me here) they're dogs, not people! We all know this, of course, but when we accept our new pooch as a member of the family we tend to endow the dog with human qualities. Love your Rottie, be fair and kind to your Rottie, but do your Rottie a favor and remember that a dog is a dog and not a human. If you remember that, life will be easier for both you and your student.

Understanding Why Your Rottweiler Does What He Does

You and I obey the law because we know swift and unpleasant consequences could result if we break it. We don't have to actually experience the consequences to know this is the case. So how do we know? We know it because someone may have explained the consequences to us, or we may have read about what happens to lawbreakers, or perhaps we saw what may result in a movie or on television. We have the ability to conceptualize — to imagine, if you will.

Now, when it comes to our dogs' learning to obey the laws of the house, there are some things we know: Dogs understand things differently (sort of), and we cannot explain things to them the way we would to another human (most of the time).

If it sounds like I'm waffling, it's because I am. Some dog behaviorists tell us that all the canine world's behavior is purely instinctive and offer all kinds of proof for why this is so. Other behaviorists insist scientific studies prove dogs learn in a rational manner, much the same way young children do. We'll find out for sure, I guess, when we are able to teach our dogs to talk. I do believe, however, when and if that day arrives, how our dogs learn will be the least of what they'll have to tell us!

Words have no real meaning to a dog. It is what they associate the word with that counts in their minds. Actually, things are the same for us. We believe *sit* means "bend your knees and rest your rear end on a chair" because somebody taught us that's what it means. If you were taught that the word for this action was *martini,* you'd sit down every time someone offered you a cocktail! The point is, always use *exactly* the same word or phrase for what you want your dog to learn. If *sit* means "sit," and *get down* means "sit," and *take a seat* means "sit," and *sit, darn it* means "sit," your dog is going to get very confused.

What you'll find in this section about your role as teacher and your dog's role as student is based upon three things:

- What the instinctual behaviorists believe
- What the rational learning clan believes
- What living with dogs has taught me

Instinctual creatures

All dogs have some instinctive behaviors because they are, in fact, dogs. Great granddaddy wolf, from whom all the dogs of the world have descended, gave his descendants certain genes that have just hung in there through the ages. When humans recognized these hereditary inclinations, they manipulated the gene pools to either eradicate certain characteristics or to cultivate them.

A purebred dog will have some instinctive behaviors peculiar to all dogs and some that are specific to his own breed. We don't expect the Bulldog to have a burning desire to herd sheep, but we do know the Border Collie will. Border Collies herd because this is a trait passed down from wolf ancestors that has been selectively encouraged and refined for their breed. Granted, wolves had a much different purpose in mind when they herded together a group of animals, but humans took care of that by adding a pinch of reserve and a dash of trainability to suppress the desire to dine on the livestock.

Border Collies don't go to herding school to develop the desire to herd. They attend classes to learn how to do it to our liking. Guarding and protective breeds like our Rotties aren't sent off to school to give them the desire to protect — they already have that. They are given lessons in how to control and channel those protective instincts in a manner that will be both suitable and beneficial to their owners.

Eliminating a dog's breed-related behavior and responses is practically impossible. You can and should train your Rottweiler not to aggressively discourage strangers from entering your property, but it is against the breed's nature not to stand guard. Buying a breed that is naturally inclined to behave in a certain manner and then expecting it to react contrary to that natural instinct is not only pointless, it is unfair to the dog.

Thinking creatures

Despite all we know about how dogs behave instinctually, the only people I know who are willing to say dogs are unable to think things out are people who have never lived with a dog. When your Rottweiler starts hunting up his leash to let you know he's decided it's time for a stroll, or when he stands between your child and the street and refuses to budge, it's obvious dogs are rational, thinking creatures.

This is not to say a dog will always use the good sense he has. (Humans don't either, after all!) Dogs are inclined to be as wise as Methuselah at one time and absolutely witless at another. Don't expect your Rottie not to run off to romance the dog across the street just because it's rush hour. Left to his own devices, the instinct that takes your dog across the street will outweigh any sense he possesses and any love he may have for you. In other words, unless he has learned there are consequences to breaking the law (your law), your Rottweiler will follow his instincts.

Figuring Out How Behavior Gets Reinforced

Your Rottweiler learns to avoid breaking a specific law because every time he breaks that law he experiences something unpleasant: a snap of the leash, a harsh tone of voice from you, a correction. Breaking the law results in this unpleasant experience. To associate the unpleasant experience with the law-breaking act, the experience must occur immediately upon breaking the law.

This unpleasant experience must happen every time a certain behavior occurs — not some of the time but all of the time. Some of the time does not really mean much to the student dog. Negative experiences then become things that "just randomly happen," rather than being the consequences of a specific behavior.

You and I do the right thing because we have been lead to believe that "good" people do it this way and "bad" people do it the other way. We understand the concepts of *good* and *bad* — at least as they were taught to us. We do not need a piece of candy to encourage us as adults to eat our veggies. We eat them because they are good for us.

Our Rottweilers, on the other hand, are suckers for bribery. When your Rottie barks on command, he gets a doggie treat. He quickly learns barking equals treat. On the other hand, he also learns he cannot bark his head off any time he wants because that will lead to a rebuke or a squirt in the face rather than a treat or a pat on the head.

Why then, you will certainly get around to asking, does my dog insist upon doing things that will get him into trouble? He knows you will scold him when he empties the trash can and scatters its contents all over the kitchen, but he keeps doing it anyway. But it's not that simple. Evidently, he got some reward (a pork chop?) the first time he emptied the trash. He was able to topple the can again at another time and, lo and behold, he was rewarded with half a bag of potato chips.

Now, what is worse in your Rottie's mind — your being upset or his missing out on those gourmet treats? He hates the scolding, but his burning desire for those delectable morsels is satisfied when he raids the trash can. After several successful trash can raids, he knows for certain there is a pot of gold at the end of that rainbow. Forget the scolding! That comes later; the pork chop comes now.

Each time your Rottie repeats an undesirable act, it will be more difficult to remove that behavior from the dog's repertoire. That's why the best cure is prevention. Keep a tight lid on the trash can, and never allow behaviors to begin that you don't want to see repeated.

I'm using this common example to give you some idea about why a dog does or doesn't do what we think he should. Understanding how your dog gets from here to there will greatly increase your chances of success in teaching household rules or anything else you want your dog to learn.

Some young dogs are so wild and exuberant that it is almost impossible to get their attention long enough to get a point across to them. Food treats seem to work best with the enthusiastic types. The promise of some delicious tidbit will usually get the pup to concentrate.

Knowing How to Respond to Your Rottie When He Misbehaves

Knowing why dogs do what they do is one thing, but that understanding doesn't make his spreading the contents of the trash can all over the house any more acceptable. The trick is to handle the situation before it gets out of hand. And when it comes to Rottweilers, this can take more than a whispered, "no no, sweetheart."

Don't forget the breed's long, cultivated history of courage, determination, and fearlessness. That doesn't all go away because your Rottie senses you are unhappy about something. Punishment is entirely appropriate at certain times, but the punishment itself must be appropriate as well. Some things your Rottie does will be mildly upsetting; other things may make you furious. Don't make the mistake of interpreting your dog's actions in human terms. Vengeance and retaliation are human characteristics. What you may interpret as retaliation on the part of your dog is far more apt to be instinct or even anxiety and frustration. Although it may seem so, your Rottie did not diabolically plan to get back at you.

Separation anxiety, as I discuss in Chapter 6, can manifest itself in many ways. Dogs mildly affected will often seek out an object that is very personally "you." A shoe, an undergarment, or a glove are as close as your dog can get to you when you're gone, and your absence can best be endured through the dog's highly developed art of chewing. You come home and find your Bruno Maglies in shreds and assume your Rottweiler has done this to you because he is angry that you left him behind. But you have entirely misunderstood why he did what he did. He missed his lord and master, and got as close to him as he could in the best way he knew how. What you call retaliation, your Rottie calls devotion.

Assuming your Rottie has intentionally done something to spite you is a foolish error in judgment on your part. Flying off into a rage because of the behavior is both unfair and dangerous. Unfair because dogs are not vengeful creatures, and dangerous because a Rottweiler is not a breed whose history makes it willing to accept that kind of treatment. There is a vast difference between punishment for an infraction of rules and abuse.

If you respond with rage when your Rottie acts out of anxiety, you are only compounding the problem. When punishment is warranted, you must always remember three rules:

- **Be calm.**
- **Be fair.**
- **Be consistent.**

If you are unable to interact with a Rottweiler on that basis all the time and no matter what the circumstances, you should definitely not be a Rottie owner!

Socializing Your Rottweiler for His Own Happiness

Right on the heels of your Rottie's need for food and water comes a need for early and continual socialization. Our dogs no longer live in the wild, and if there is one lesson they all must learn, it is how to get along with humans. This does not necessarily mean your dog has to love every stranger that crosses his path. But it does mean the dog must understand that humans lay down the rules and regulations and the dog must learn to abide by them without hesitation.

Temperament is both hereditary and learned. Poor treatment and lack of socialization can ruin inherited good temperament. A Rottweiler puppy who has inherited bad temperament is dangerous as a companion or as a show dog and should certainly never be bred. But a well-bred dog who is not socialized can present just as many problems, and they are almost as difficult to overcome. So obtaining a happy puppy from a breeder who is determined to produce good temperaments and has taken all the necessary steps to provide the early socialization necessary is critical.

But just because the puppies in a litter are the result of such care does not mean socialization and temperament are a finished product. Not by a long shot! The responsible Rottweiler breeder begins the socialization process as the puppies enter the world. Constant handling, exposure to strange sights and sounds, weighing, and nail trimming are all experiences that help the growing Rottie understand that this is a human's world and that he is entirely safe and secure when he is with human beings. The puppy is learning that, after mom, the best care and comfort comes from people.

Everything puppies experience with people at this early age must be positive. Inoculations, a toenail nipped a bit too short, anything that causes discomfort for the puppy should be followed by reassurance and comfort to assure the youngster that all is well and that the discomfort was not intended.

Secluded, sheltered puppies who never see a stranger until they are ready to go off to their new homes are a poor risk in the temperament department. Their ability to take strangers and strange situations in stride has not been cultivated. That's why after the puppies have had their first inoculations, they should be given the benefit of as many strange sights, sounds, and people as possible.

Breeders also make it a point to introduce their puppies to strange environments. If the gang has been raised in the kitchen, a trip outdoors is arranged (weather permitting). One puppy at a time gets special attention in the family room.

Getting children to help in the socialization process

A household with dog-wise children, like the ones in Figure 7-1, is a fantastic environment for puppies to spend the first several weeks of their lives. Puppies and children have a natural affinity, and children who are well-trained in puppy care and sufficiently supervised have no equal in the socialization department. Children seem able to teach puppies things like eating from their own dish and behaving during cleanup with relative ease. They have a knack for breaking up puppy squabbles, and it seems to take children minutes to leash-train a puppy, whereas the same pup will balk and refuse when an adult tries the same thing.

We have friends who come to visit with their young daughter, and she brings a whole wardrobe of doll clothes to dress our puppies in. The puppies even have the opportunity to get rides in the doll carriage. The pups adore all the attention and go to their new homes thinking that children are the greatest playmates in the world.

Although children really are the best puppy socializers, be aware that children must be supervised, like the one in Figure 7-2, so that they understand how the puppy must be treated.

Be very careful about your children roughhousing with their playmates in your home. Rotties attach themselves to the children in the family and do not want them to be hurt. It is difficult for Rottweilers to tell when children are playing and when they are being harmed.

Figure 7-1: Dog-wise children make great companions for Rottweilers.

Photograph courtesy of Judith E. Strom

Continuing socialization in your pup's new home

At this early stage, puppies are becoming accustomed to different tones of voice and inflections. It is never too early for a puppy to learn the meaning of "no" — never followed by punishment of any kind, of course. Gently guiding a puppy away from danger with a firm "no!" prepares the pup to understand he cannot do just anything he may want to.

The socialization must continue when the puppy arrives at your home, as well. In fact, socialization must continue through the rest of the puppy's life with you. Granted, you will not want the entire neighborhood waiting with a drum and bugle corps when the pup first arrives, but increase the new sights, sounds, and people with each passing day.

It is also important to realize that a Rottweiler puppy may be as happy as a clam living at home with you and your family, but if you don't continue the socialization begun by the breeder, that sunny disposition will not extend outside your front door. From the day the young Rottweiler arrives at your home, you must be committed to helping the puppy meet and coexist with all human beings and animals. Do not worry about developing the Rottweiler's protective instinct. This instinct comes with maturity. *Never* encourage aggressive behavior on the part of your puppy, and don't encourage the pup to fear strangers.

Figure 7-2: Always be sure to supervise interactions between your Rottweiler and children.

Photograph courtesy of Judith E. Strom

Your puppy should go everywhere with you: the post office, along busy streets, to the shopping mall — wherever. Be prepared to create a stir wherever you go. The public seems to hold a special admiration for the Rottweiler, and although they may not want to approach a mature dog, most people will be quite taken with a Rottie baby and will undoubtedly want to pet your youngster. There is nothing in the world better for the puppy!

Carry treats with you when you go out. If your puppy backs off from a stranger, give the person one of the little snacks and have that person offer it to your puppy. Insist your young Rottweiler be amenable to the attention of any strangers you approve of, regardless of sex, age, or race. It is not up to your puppy to decide who he will or will not tolerate. You are in charge. You must call the shots. The leadership issue is determined very early.

All Rottweilers must learn to get along with other dogs as well as with humans. If you are fortunate enough to have a puppy preschool or dog training class nearby, attend regularly. A young Rottie who has been exposed to other dogs from puppyhood will learn to adapt to and accept other dogs and other breeds much more readily than one who seldom ever sees other dogs.

Listening When Your Rottie Speaks

You and I are accustomed to learning about each other by listening to what the other person has to say. The more attention we give the speaker and the more we dismiss our own preconceived notions and prejudices, the more apt we are to understand what the other person is really all about. Your relationship with your Rottweiler is based on exactly the same principle.

Dogs in the wild have communicated with each other through the use of growls, squeaks, and barks since the days when they were still wolves. Their major form of communication, though, is language. The canine world's body language is a much simpler and far less ambiguous one than our spoken language. A good part of it can be learned very quickly by understanding two of a dog's basic attitudes: active and passive.

Active versus passive behavior

Generally speaking, the active dog leans forward and up, while the passive dog moves backward and down. The challenging Rottie steps forward, stiff-legged, often with the hair on the back of his neck and shoulders standing up. The dog's head is up and he looks directly forward, staring at who or what is being challenged. A snarl emerges through clenched teeth. The tail is stiffened and carried in a semierect position. Everything about the dog's stance and attitude will indicate he plans to move ahead with whatever action must be taken.

Another dog would recognize the aggressive attitude this body language indicates and act accordingly — either actively or passively, depending on his status in the pack. The dog reacting passively does so with body language that is just the opposite of the active dog. The passive dog moves back and crouches down. The head is lowered and the ears are pinned back.

If you believe your brother when he says he talks to cats and there's no doubt in your mind the Horse Whisperer holds two-way conversations with his four-hoofed friends, you aren't entirely wrong. These people may simply have highly developed powers of observation and are able to interpret the nonverbal messages animals transmit.

The hidden meaning behind a dog's behavior

A Rottweiler's communication skills go far beyond exhibiting active or passive behavior, and your responsibility is to learn the language. The degree of success you will have in training and socializing your Rottie is in direct proportion to how much you understand of what your dog is trying to tell you. A Rottweiler seldom acts or reacts without giving some advance notice. Sometimes this is done in very subtle ways, but if you have made an effort to understand what these signals tell you, you will be fully prepared.

None of us may fully understand the reasons for every single thing our dogs do, but being attuned to the fact that they do have reasons will get us at least halfway there. For instance, even something as basic and apparently meaningless as your male dog wanting to lift his leg on every tree and fire hydrant you pass on the evening walk isn't meaningless. He does not do this simply because he wants to prolong the walk. Humans watch television or read newspapers to learn what's going on. We discuss what we've seen or heard with our friends and neighbors. When your Rottie sniffs the fire hydrant, he is reading the evening news by way of a scent-o-gram. He is finding out who passed by, when they passed by, and whether the passerby was a friend or not. When he lifts his leg, he is also leaving a note to say *he* stopped by.

What your body language says to your dog

Dogs are born with the ability to read body language — Rotties it seems, particularly so. They do it so well at times that some owners are willing to swear the breed is blessed with extrasensory perception. Your Rottie is reading you every step of the way — probably better than you read him.

Many owners new to training get very upset and angry if their dog doesn't perform in exactly the prescribed manner. Dogs read anger very easily. Your Rottweiler can learn to dislike a command very quickly because you fly off the handle if he doesn't perform as soon as you think he should. He associates the anger with the lesson and anticipates that immediately after you give the command, you will become angry with him.

The dog becomes confused because he is being given a command and then the commander gets hot under the collar, even though the dog is responding. The dog has no idea your anger is a reaction to the manner in which the command was obeyed.

Chapter 8

Training Your Rottweiler

In This Chapter

- Being your Rottweiler's leader
- Training your Rottie from the very first day
- Teaching your dog to sit, stay, come, lie down, and heel
- Taking advantage of training classes with your dog
- Dealing with emotional problems in your Rottweiler

A Rottweiler puppy's attention span is very short, and a youngster is not going to understand the more complex commands that an older dog will eventually learn to respond to. Still, this does not mean you should delay simple basic training. As soon as you bring your puppy home, household rules begin.

Assuming Your Role as Leader of the Pack

Puppy boot camp begins on the day the pup arrives, and guess who the drill sergeant is? Right — it's you! So you should keep in mind a few things that will help you accomplish all the goals you've set for your little trainee.

Using the proper approach, any dog can be taught to be a good canine citizen. Many dog owners do not understand how a dog learns, nor do they realize they can and should be breed-specific in their approach to training.

The Rottweiler is not only highly capable of learning, the breed thrives on training. Even young Rottie puppies have an amazing capacity to learn. This capacity is greater than most humans realize. Young puppies also forget with great speed unless they are reminded of what they have learned by continual reinforcement.

As a Rottie puppy leaves the nest, she begins to search for two things: a pack leader and the rules of the pack that the leader has set down. The mentally sound Rottweiler mother fulfills both of these needs unhesitatingly. However, a puppy's new owner often fails miserably in supplying these very basic needs. Instead, the owner immediately responds to the demands of the puppy, and Rottweiler puppies can quickly learn to be very demanding.

If your young puppy does not find her pack leader in you, she will assume those duties herself. If there are no rules imposed, the clever little Rottie puppy quickly learns to make the kind of rules she likes. The longer this goes on, the more difficult it will be to change.

If your Rottweiler finds a growl or a snap is the means to her end, rest assured that behavior will continue. In fact, the behavior will only increase. If that same challenge is met with a stern, uncompromising correction, your Rottie quickly learns bad behavior does not accomplish anything good.

When the pack leader talks, Rottweilers listen. Don't forget that. Through all your training you must remember to always be consistent and go about your business with an authoritative and commanding attitude. Your Rottie will respect this and learn much more quickly.

If you don't give your Rottie the leadership she wants and needs, your chances of winding up with a well-behaved dog are very slim at best. This doesn't mean you can't praise and pet your dog when she responds correctly. You can be as enthusiastic and jolly as you want to be when you get what you want, but be direct and forceful at all times when you are giving your commands.

Knowing What to Expect of Your Rottie

If you own a Rottweiler, you should aim for certain basic behavior minimums right from the first day your puppy enters your home. The rewards of owning this great breed are practically limitless, but to gain access to what has earned Rotties their great reputation, you must provide the framework within which your dog will reliably operate.

Here is a checklist that all Rottweiler owners should consider a basic part of their dog's education.

- **Walk on a leash quietly at your side, even on a crowded street.**
- **Allow any stranger to pet her when you give the okay.**
- **Come immediately when called.**

- **Sit and lie down on command and remain in position until you say otherwise.**
- **Be tolerant of other dogs and pets.**
- **Show no unprovoked aggressiveness toward any person.**

These are behaviors that every companion Rottweiler must be taught and consider an ordinary, everyday way of behaving. Your Rottie is more than capable of mastering all the items on this checklist, and it is up to you to make sure the dog is given the opportunity to do so.

Starting with the Basics

When you first bring your puppy into your home, you can start with some very basic training. This training will lay the foundation for your future training efforts and let your Rottweiler know from the very first day that you're the one in charge.

Name recognition and "no"

The two most important early lessons your Rottweiler puppy will learn are the meaning of "no" and her name. Use your pup's name in conjunction with every command you give. "No" is the command the puppy can begin learning the minute she first arrives in your home. Frightening the puppy into learning the meaning of "no" isn't necessary, but you should never give this or any other command you are not prepared and able to enforce. The only way a puppy learns to obey commands is to realize that once they are issued, commands must be followed.

The power of positive reinforcement

The Rottweiler is easily trained to almost any task. As you train, however, remember that the breed does not comprehend violent treatment, nor does a Rottweiler need it. Positive reinforcement is the key to successfully training a Rottie, and it produces a happy, confident companion. Your Rottweiler puppy should always be a winner.

Make sure you are in the right frame of mind for training sessions. Training should never take place when you are irritated, distressed, or preoccupied. A quiet place away from the maddening crowds is where you should begin.

Say "Daisy, no!" just as soon as she grabs the end of the tablecloth or eyeballs the electric plug on the wall. Screaming "no" *after* the damage is done does nothing to further her education. Dogs do not associate a reprimand with something they've done in the past. In fact, reprimands after the fact will probably confuse your dog rather than teach her that you do not approve. As a dog owners, you need to fine-tune your timing for praise as well as for corrections.

In addition to including your puppy's name in every command you give, use it every time you speak to the dog: "Want to go outside, Daisy?", "Come Daisy, come!" Repetition counts, and soon just saying the pup's name will make that little stub of a tail wag.

Using a collar and leash

It is never too early to accustom your Rottweiler puppy to her leash and collar. The leash and collar are your fail-safe way of keeping your dog under control. No dog should ever be outdoors or in an unsecured area without a collar around her neck and the leash held securely in your hand.

Begin getting your puppy accustomed to the new experience of wearing a collar by leaving a soft collar around her neck for a few minutes at a time. Gradually extend the time you leave the collar on. Most Rottweiler puppies become accustomed to their collars very quickly, and after a few scratches to remove it, they forget they are even wearing one.

While you are playing with the puppy, attach a lightweight leash to the collar. Do not try to guide the puppy anywhere at first. The point here is to accustom the puppy to the feeling of having something hanging from the collar.

At first, follow the puppy while you hold the leash. After a bit, try to encourage the puppy to follow you as you move away. If she is reluctant to cooperate, coax her along with a treat of some kind. Hold the treat in front of the puppy's nose to encourage her to follow you. Just as soon as she takes a few steps toward you, praise her enthusiastically, give her a tiny bit of the treat, and continue to do so as you move slowly along.

Make the initial sessions short and fun. Continue the lessons in your home or yard until the puppy is completely unconcerned with the fact that she is on a leash. With a treat in one hand and the leash in the other, you can begin to use both to guide the puppy in the direction you want to go. Begin your first walks in front of the house and eventually extend them down the street and around the block. Try to encourage the pup to walk on your left side — this will come in handy in your later training work.

Teaching Your Rottweiler the Most Important Commands

Although there is virtually no limit to the levels of obedience training to which you and your dog can go, every pet Rottweiler should know several basic commands that will make their lives easier. In the following sections, I cover these behaviors that should be a part of your Rottie's repertoire — "come," "sit," "stay," "down," and "heel."

"Come"

One of the most important lessons for a Rottie puppy to learn is to come when called. Learning to come on command could save your Rottweiler's life when the two of you venture out into the world. "Come" is the command a dog must obey without hesitation, but the dog should not associate that command with fear. Your dog's response to her name and the word "come" should always be associated with a pleasant experience, such as great praise and petting or a food treat.

All too often, novice trainers get very angry at their dog for not responding immediately to the "come" command. When the dog finally does come, or after a chase, the owner scolds the dog for not obeying. The dog begins to associate "come" with an unpleasant result.

Never allow your puppy to associate the "come" command — or any command — with anger or punishment. If you call your pup to come for a scolding or a trip to the vet or to be dragged inside after a play session, why should the dog come when you call? Remember, Rottweilers are *smart*.

Avoiding bad habits is much easier than correcting them. Avoid at all costs giving the "come" command unless you are able to make sure your puppy comes to you. Begin teaching the "come" command when the puppy is already on her way to you or while walking or running away from the youngster. Clap your hands and sound very happy and excited about having the puppy join in on this game. Be reasonable though — don't expect the just-learning young puppy to come dashing over to you when she is engrossed in some wonderful adventure.

If you save "Daisy, come" for when she's already headed toward you, and use lots of praise when her majesty arrives, soon the royal rascal will learn the word is associated with her being absolutely wonderful and that coming to you brings many pats and hugs.

Later, as a puppy grows more self-confident and independent, you may want to attach a long leash or rope to the puppy's collar to ensure the correct response. Again, do not chase or punish your puppy for not obeying the "come" command. Doing so in the initial stages of training makes the youngster associate the command with something to fear, and this will result in avoidance rather than the immediate response you desire. Praising your puppy and giving her a treat when she does come to you, even if the pup takes her time in getting to you, are critical.

When your very young Rottie puppy learns you are the pack leader, she will be very dependent upon you. Your pup will want to stay as close to you as possible, especially in strange surroundings. When your puppy sees you moving away, her natural inclination will be to go right along with you. This is a perfect time to teach the "come" command.

"Sit"

Most Rottie puppies learn to sit easily, often in just a few minutes — especially if it seems to be a game and a food treat is involved.

Your puppy should always be on collar and leash for her lessons. Young puppies are not beyond getting up and walking away when they have decided you and your lessons are boring.

Give the command "Daisy, sit" immediately before pushing down on her hindquarters or scooping her hind legs under her, gently molding her into a sit position. Praise your puppy lavishly when she does sit, even though you're the one who made it happen. Again, a food treat always seems to get the lesson across to the learning youngster.

Let your hand rest on the dog's rump to reinforce the idea that the dog must sit until you say otherwise. If your dog makes an attempt to get up, repeat the command while exerting pressure on her rear end until the correct position is assumed. Make your Rottie stay in this position for a few seconds, then *slowly* increase the time as the lessons progress over the next few weeks.

Do not test a very young puppy's patience to the limits. As brilliant as the Rottweiler is, remember that you're dealing with a baby. The attention span of any youngster, whether canine or human, is relatively short.

When you do decide your puppy can get up, call her name, say "Daisy, okay," and make a big fuss. Praise and a food treat are in order every time your puppy responds correctly. Continue to help your puppy assume proper positions or respond to commands until she performs on her own. This way your puppy always gets it right every time. You are training with *positive reinforcement.*

"Stay"

When your Rottweiler has mastered "sit," you can start working on the "stay" command. With your dog on her leash and at your left side, give the "Daisy, sit" command. Put the palm of your right hand in front of her eyes and say "Daisy, stay." Take a small step forward.

Any attempt on your Rottweiler's part to get up must be corrected at once, returning her to the sit position, holding your palm up, and repeating "Daisy, stay!" When your Rottie begins to understand what you want, you can gradually increase the distance you step away. With a long leash attached to your dog's collar (here again, lightweight rope is fine), start with a few steps and extend that to several yards. Your Rottweiler must eventually learn that the "stay" command must be obeyed no matter how far away you are. Later on, with advanced training, your dog will obey the "stay" command even when you move entirely out of sight.

As your Rottie masters this lesson and is able to remain sitting for as long as you dictate, avoid calling your dog to you. This makes the dog overly anxious to get up and run to you. Instead, walk back to your dog and say "okay," which is a signal that the command is over. Later, when your Rottweiler becomes more reliable, you can call her to you.

Keep the "stay" part of the lesson to a minimum until the puppy is at least 5 or 6 months old. Everything in a very young Rottie's makeup urges her to stay close to you wherever you go. The puppy has bonded to you, and forcing her to operate against her natural instincts can be bewildering. The important thing here is to teach the puppy that your command is to be obeyed until and unless you give a different command.

"Down"

When your Rottie has mastered the "sit" and "stay" commands, you can begin work on "down." The down position is especially useful if you want your Rottie to remain in a particular place for an extended period of time. A dog is usually far more inclined to stay put when she is lying down than when she is sitting.

Use the "down" command only when you want the dog to lie down. If you want your dog to get off your sofa or to stop jumping up on people, use the "off" command. Don't interchange the two commands. Doing so only serves to confuse the dog and will delay the response you want.

Teaching the "down" command to some Rottweilers may take a little more time and patience than the other commands, because the down position is a submissive one for dogs. Therefore, the more forceful breeds (and the individual dogs within those breeds who are inclined to be more dominant) may take more time to develop any enthusiasm for this exercise.

With your Rottweiler sitting in front of and facing you, hold a treat in your right hand and gather up the slack in the leash in your left hand. Hold the treat under the dog's nose and slowly bring your hand down to the ground. Your dog will follow the treat with her head and neck. As she does, give the command "Daisy, down!" and exert light pressure on her shoulders with your left hand. If your pup resists the pressure, do not continue pushing down — doing so will only create more resistance.

An alternative method of getting your Rottie headed into the down position is to move around to the dog's right side and draw her attention downward with your right hand. Then slide your left arm under the dog's front legs and gently slide them forward. In the case of a puppy, you will undoubtedly have to be on your knees next to the dog to do this.

As your Rottweiler's forelegs begin to slide out in front of her, keep moving the treat along the ground until her whole body is lying on the ground. When she has assumed the position, give her the treat and a lot of praise. Continue assisting her into the down position until she does so on her own. Be firm and be patient.

You can teach your Rottie to stay in the down position by following the same basic procedure you use in getting her to stay while sitting. With your dog on leash and at your left side, give the "Daisy, down" command. Put the palm of your right hand in front of her eyes and say, "Daisy, stay!" Take a small step forward. If she attempts to get up, firmly say, "Daisy, down," and then "Daisy, stay!" While you are saying this, raise your hand, palm toward the dog, and again command, "Daisy, stay!"

When your Rottie begins to understand what you want, you can gradually increase the distance you step back. Use the same long leash you use for the sit and stay exercise, starting with a few steps back and gradually increasing the distance to several yards.

"Heel"

Walking a Rottie puppy who is attempting to pull your arm out of its socket is difficult enough, but when your Rottweiler reaches 110-plus pounds you are going to find yourself in a horizontal position hanging onto the leash as she races down the street with you screaming behind. So training your Rottweiler to walk on a loose leash and obey the "heel" command is very important.

Many people become frightened when they see a Rottweiler coming down the street. A Rottweiler lunging at the end of the leash, even if it is done out of friendliness and to greet the passerby, can be extremely intimidating.

A link-chain training collar is very useful for leash lessons. It provides both quick pressure around the neck and a zipping sound, both of which get the dog's attention. Some people refer to this as a *choke collar,* but don't worry — the link-chain collar used properly does not choke a dog. The pet store from which you purchase the collar will be able to show you the proper way to put it on your dog.

Do not leave the link-chain collar on your puppy when training sessions are finished. Because the collar fits loosely, it can get hooked on protruding objects and cause injury or even death. Also, when the link-chain collar is used, your Rottie knows it's get-down-to-business time and not just a casual saunter.

As you train your puppy to walk along on the leash, you should insist the youngster walk on your left side (see Figure 8-1). The leash should cross your body from the dog's collar to your right hand. The excess portion of the leash should be folded into your right hand and your left hand is then free on the leash to make corrections. Keep the leash slack and only tighten it to give a quick jerk to get your dog back in position.

Figure 8-1: Train your Rottweiler to walk on your left side.

A quick, short jerk on the leash with your left hand will keep your dog from lunging to the side, pulling ahead, or lagging behind. As you make a correction, say, "Daisy, heel." Keep the leash slack as long as your dog maintains the proper position at your side. Insisting that your Rottie walk quietly along with no pressure or strain on the leash will avoid giving the dog the urge to pull you along.

If your dog begins to drift away, give the leash a sharp jerk and guide the dog back to your left side. Do not pull on the lead with steady pressure. What is needed is a sharp jerking motion to get your dog's attention.

I've heard obedience trainers tell students that success in training will be in direct proportion to the jerk at the end of the lead. Everyone in the class usually doubles up with laughter at this point, but it is a point well made. Eventually, your pup will automatically go to your left side as you walk along.

In learning to heel, your Rottweiler will walk on your left side with her shoulder next to your leg no matter which direction you may go or how quickly you turn. Your fingers should be able to touch your dog's shoulder with your left arm hanging directly down at your left side. If you have to swing your arm out or bend your fingers, the dog is not in the right place.

The dog should not lag behind, move on ahead of you, or drift away from your side. Insisting on heeling in a precise way is very important when the two of you are out walking in public places. A Rottie who obeys this command properly will make a far more tractable companion when the two of you are in crowded or confusing situations.

If you plan to progress on to formal obedience training, "heel" is one of the lessons that all trainers will demand your dog follows to a T. Well, it's not really a T at all. In fact, in obedience competition your dog will have to be able to maintain the precise position even if you walk in an X, Y, or Z!

To teach your dog to heel, begin with your Rottweiler sitting at your left side with her shoulder next to your leg. Step forward on your right foot, and as you take your first step give the command "Daisy, heel!" The leash should be slack. When you start off, your dog will probably move out with you. If she attempts to pull away in any direction, give the sharp jerk and command "Daisy, heel." Do not keep the leash taut and attempt to pull the dog back into position. The well-trained Rottie will maintain the correct position no matter how fast or slow you go and no matter which direction you turn, including your doing an abrupt about-face.

There is one exception to the sharp jerk correction. Occasionally, dogs are frightened or intimidated by the heel exercise. In this case, coax the dog into position and try to make obeying a fun game and worthy of a treat when done well.

Attending Training Classes with Your Rottweiler

There are few limits to what a patient, consistent owner can teach his Rottweiler. For the advanced basic obedience course, which all Rottweilers should have, and for work beyond that, consider getting local professional assistance.

Qualified professional trainers have had a lot of experience in avoiding the pitfalls of basic training and can help you to avoid these mistakes as well. Even Rottweiler owners who have never trained a dog before have found that with professional assistance, their dogs have become superstars.

Training classes are particularly important for your Rottie's socialization. All dogs, not just Rottweilers, need to have class experiences, once they have an attention span. This is another form of socialization. The dog will learn that she must obey even when there are other dogs and people around. These classes also keep the Rottweiler ever-mindful of the fact that she must get along with other people and other dogs. Many parks and recreation facilities offer free classes. Or you can sign up for group lessons at training schools or very formal (and sometimes very expensive) individual lessons with private trainers. However, private lessons defeat the distraction and socialization aspects of training.

Some obedience schools will take your Rottweiler and train her for you. A Rottweiler can and will learn with any good professional. However, unless your schedule gives you no time at all to train your own dog, having someone else train the dog for you is last on my list of recommendations. The rapport that develops between an owner who has trained his Rottie to be a pleasant companion and a good canine citizen is very special — well worth the time and patience it requires. Most Rottie breeders agree that if you don't have time to work with your dog, you should not own a Rottweiler.

Finding a Good Dog Trainer

When you decide to seek the help of a dog trainer, you will probably be overwhelmed by the number of them available. All will claim to have years of experience and use a training method known only to them but guaranteed to make your dog a canine *Jeopardy!* winner and a shoo-in for a costarring role in the next *Lassie* film.

Take promises of overnight success with a grain of salt. Smart as our Rotties are, good trainers take as much time with each dog as is necessary, and no two dogs learn at the same rate. Good dog training is about training your dog well, not how fast the dog completes the course.

Don't misunderstand what a dog trainer's real purpose is. The ideal trainer is one who is experienced at teaching you to train your dog. The fact that an outsider is able to have your Rottweiler behave like a perfect lady will have no effect upon her behavior at home if you are not equipped to enforce the rules.

Here are some tips for finding a trainer who will be able to teach you and your Rottie what you both need to know and in a manner that is suitable for the breed:

- **Always check to see how long the trainer has been in business and whether she has references you can contact.**
- **Choose a trainer with a working knowledge of many breeds and with a good understanding of their origin, purpose, and differences.** It is extremely important that the trainer have an awareness of the different instinctual behaviors found in the different breeds of dogs.
- **Find a trainer who has had considerable prior experience in training Rottweilers and who likes the breed.**
- **Be wary of a trainer who promises overnight perfection or makes claims that sound too good to be true.**
- **Don't sign up with a professional trainer unless he puts what he intends to teach your dog in writing and will always offer post-training assistance if you experience problems.**
- **If there are specific things you don't want your dog to learn or if there are training methods you object to, make your wishes clear to the trainer.** The trainer's methods or goals may be in conflict with yours.
- **Ask the trainer what is required in the various levels of obedience training.** If she can't explain this to you in terms you understand, find another trainer.
- **Get the trainer's standard rate list.** Professional trainers provide this so that you will know beforehand just how much your dog's education will cost.

Experienced professionals have no difficulty discussing any of the items in this list. They have the knowledge to back up their answers and do not feel threatened by your questions. Be very wary of any trainer who is unable or reluctant to answer the questions you pose.

Although many trainers have proven to be extremely capable of training Rottweilers, there is no substitute for trainers who have bred and raised the breed themselves.

Dealing with Emotional Conflicts

It's virtually impossible for two animals (human or otherwise) to have a relationship without an occasional conflict. That's life. However, when emotions constantly run at a high pitch, that's a problem, both for us and our dogs.

Animal behaviorists who have been called in to deal with incorrigible dogs often report that the problems are environmental. When the dog is moved out of a hostile environment and into one that is serene and accommodating, what appeared to be hopeless behavior resolves itself.

Particularly sensitive breeds are highly susceptible to environmental conditions. When I say *sensitive,* I do not necessarily mean shy or fragile dogs. I believe that the more intelligent breeds are especially attuned to their owner's feelings and are at the greatest risk in this area. I include the Rottweiler among these breeds.

It may well be the human members of the family who are at the root of a dog's behavior problems, but unfortunately, it is more apt to be the dog who will suffer the consequences.

Those of us who admire the Rottweiler are fully aware that if left unchecked, the breed's determined character can be a distinct liability rather than the asset it was intended to be. Fearlessness, determination, and a high energy level are the components that help create the free-spirited character that is another admirable Rottweiler trait. However, when your Rottie is consistently allowed to do what she wants to do, when she wants to do it, she may have great difficulty following the rules when you find it is necessary to impose them.

Rotties who have convinced themselves their way is the only way can respond to having their reins tightened with some highly unacceptable behavior. An inability to focus, aggressiveness, and often outright rebellion are not uncommon reactions. Behavior of this kind is undesirable in any dog, but it's inexcusable and dangerous in a Rottweiler.

Although we cannot be permissive in dealing with a Rottie, neither can we be overbearing. A dog with the strength of character a well-bred Rottie normally possesses must be given direction, but you cannot constantly browbeat and harass a Rottweiler without ill effects. Hitting your Rottie or frenzied yelling at every minor infraction create a dog who lives in constant confusion and fear.

If your Rottie is acting and reacting in any of these socially unacceptable ways, the cause may or may not be the manner in which you have been approaching the dog's training and discipline. Regardless of whether the mistake is yours, you must seek professional help to assist you and your dog to get back on track right away. Even initial indications of rebellion or retaliation out of fear are cause for immediate concern.

Where should you go for help? A professional trainer can help you. So can a responsible breeder (yet another reason to stay in touch with the dog's breeder). If you haven't remained in touch with your pup's breeder, this is the time to correct that situation. An experienced breeder will undoubtedly be able to suggest who would be most able to help you through your problem.

The proper solution may be a trainer experienced in dealing with problem Rotties, or your dog's behavior may warrant finding an animal behaviorist. You and you alone are responsible for the behavior of your Rottie, and it is up to you to find the most suitable solution to any behavior problems that develop.

Chapter 9

Having Fun with Your Rottweiler

In This Chapter

- Playing casual games with your Rottweiler
- Taking advantage of dog-friendly parks, beaches, and hiking trails
- Working with your Rottweiler in more serious, breed-related activities
- Competing in sporting events with your Rottweiler
- Bringing a smile to someone else's face by doing therapy work with your Rottie

When you are sharing your life with a Rottweiler, you should spend a lot of time out and about, because your well-trained pal can accompany you to pretty much anywhere dogs are allowed. Many Rotties go to work with their owners and have learned all the office rules, becoming a welcomed member of the staff. Small-business owners feel just that much safer when their Rottweiler is on the premises. After all, would-be thieves would prefer plying their trade somewhere that doesn't involve dealing with a 100-pound canine deterrent.

But the kind of Rottweiler who is welcomed out in public is the one who has been properly trained and is accustomed to regularly interacting with people. If your dog lives with you at home and only gets out into the real world once in a blue moon (whenever that is), it's only natural that the dog will be extremely curious, distracted, and perhaps even leery of his surroundings. Strangers, strange voices, and strange hands could be very intimidating and set your Rottie on edge. The dog who never gets out is an accident waiting to happen. Think about people who have been confined indoors for many, many years. Their excursions out into the big wide world are not going to be as much fun as they would be for someone who has interacted with strangers and strange situations every day.

One thing a lot of dog owners don't seem to understand is that training has to take place both at home and "out there" — wherever you are and whatever you do when you aren't home. For some this means the shopping mall, for others it could be the park or a beach. Many Rotties perform like clockwork at home, but the picture changes rapidly when they're out on the town. When they get out to the dog park and see the gang, or if they're off leash on a hike and a bunny bounces by, perfectly trained dogs suddenly become stone deaf. However, if you train your dog in all sorts of situations, your dog will behave like the well-trained dog he is, wherever the two of you happen to go.

Many of the activities you enjoy are ones that your Rottie can share and will enjoy simply because it means spending time with you. The two of you can do lots of activities that are great fun for the dog — and the exercise certainly won't hurt you either. In this chapter, I cover all kinds of activities that you and your Rottweiler can do together. If you're looking for ways to have fun, you've come to the right place!

Playing Games with Your Rottie

Just because your Rottweiler has the stoic countenance of his German ancestry, don't think for a moment he doesn't enjoy having fun. Although Rottweilers can thoroughly enjoy the more formal pursuits of obedience trials and tracking, what the two of you can enjoy certainly doesn't stop with activities that have rules. Rotties are great at soccer, whizzes at fetching, and masters at hide-and-seek.

If you have kids in your family, all the better. Kids and dogs create games they seem able to play for hours on end, day after day, without ever seeming the least bit bored. However, supervision by an adult is the key. If an accident occurs, the dog is always at fault, and no one is in charge without the adult present. Rotties make compatible playmates, however, depending upon three things:

- **How well socialized your Rottie is.**
- **How effective those early lessons were on what is permissible and what is not when playing with children.** Don't forget, in many cases your Rottie will far outweigh the child he is playing with, so the dog must understand that roughhousing is taboo.
- **The age of the children.** Kids have to be old enough to understand what can injure a puppy or even a grown dog. What may seem great fun to the child could be harmful to the dog or cause a defense reaction on the dog's part.

Dogs have ways of communicating with us that take some time and patience to learn and understand. Although dogs and very young children have no language with which to communicate, they still seem to do quite well by using gestures and facial expressions. We can only wonder who taught our Rotties to respond to a child's giggles or outright laughter with a wagging tail. Who informed our dogs they should show outward signs of agitation or sound the alarm when the baby starts to cry?

The patience of a Rottie who has grown up with children is astounding at times. A dog, even a very young puppy, can spend an entire morning or afternoon with a child and never get bored or run out of things to do. I have seen huge males sit poker-faced while their young mistresses dress them up as everything from Arabian sheiks to Paris streetwalkers.

Small children always seem fascinated by what is in a dog's food dish. And, like all dogs, Rottweilers have a natural instinct to protect their food and will often react with a snap or a real bite before they even realize what they have done. When there are toddlers present, always feed your Rottie in his crate. At the same time, teach children they should never put their hands in your dog's food dish.

Although kids seem to come by the games in the following sections naturally, there is certainly no reason in the world you can't play, too. After a long week in the office or studying for exams, a few let's-forget-everything-and-go-for-it hours can do everyone some good.

Following the bouncing ball

Balls and Rottweilers go together. Old, beat-up footballs, basketballs, and soccer balls can usually be picked up at garage sales and flea markets for next to nothing. The balls can provide more fun for your Rottie, your kids, and yourself than the most expensive dog toy the pet emporiums could possibly offer.

When selecting balls for puppies, make sure the balls are big enough that they can't be swallowed. If the ball fits inside the puppy's mouth, it could easily get lodged in his throat and cause the puppy to choke.

Kicking that soccer ball around with your Rottie playing guard can go on for hours. A good many Rotties become so expert at guarding the ball that their human opponents have to be right on their toes to even think of getting past them.

Basketballs are too big for Rotties to grasp, so they very quickly learn to manipulate the ball with their noses. A Rottweiler can become so engrossed in nudging the ball back and forth that he can forget about time or possible danger.

Make sure you only allow your Rottie to play ball on his own in a safe area. Your own fenced yard is fine (if the posies don't mind being trampled on!). Never allow your Rottie to play ball in an area where there is traffic. Chasing the ball will be far more important to your dog than watching for careless drivers.

Playing a rousing game of fetch

Most Rottweiler puppies will chase after just about anything that rolls along the ground or flies through the air. Getting the pup to bring it back to you may prove to be a different story. The easiest way is to start off with two balls or toss toys. Throw one a few feet away. When the puppy picks it up, he will probably do a lot of proud prancing and dancing around. Encourage the pup to come back by praising and by waving the second toy. Getting the pup interested in the second toy will bring the youngster back to you, and if you indicate you are going to throw the second item, the first toy or ball will probably be dropped in front of you. When the pup does drop the toy, give lots of praise.

The pup will soon get the idea that you will not be throwing something again until the object is brought back to you. When the puppy returns with the object but does not want to relinquish his hold, you can gently remove the toy from the dog's mouth and say "drop" as you place the toy on the ground.

Although most Rottweilers love to bring back things you've thrown, there is an occasional dog that looks at what you've tossed, then back at you with an expression of, "Well, she mustn't want it if she threw it away." This is very unusual for a Rottie, but it does happen. Even the disinterested dog can eventually be taught to fetch, but this becomes another lesson to be learned and will never fall under the dog's heading of "favorite games."

Getting a game of hide-and-seek going

Hide-and-seek is a game that can be played two different ways. In the first version, you're the one who hides. This can best be accomplished by having someone hold your Rottie on a leash while you find a nearby place to hide. Call the dog's name and have the other person unsnap the leash and say, "find!" Keep calling until the dog finds you, and then give lots of praise. Eventually, you will be able to stop calling out and the person holding the dog will only have to say "find."

Another variation of hide-and-seek is done with one of your dog's favorite toys. Rub the toy briskly between the palms of your hands. Let your dog see the toy but then have the holder distract the dog while you go off and conceal the object in a place that is, at first, close by. Have the holder release the dog and give the "find" command. You can stand near but not right next to the hidden object and also repeat the "find" command. If the toy is one the dog knows by name, use a command like "find the squeaky" or "find the ball." You may have to lead the dog to the toy a time or two, but most Rotties get the idea very quickly. When your Rottie understands the game, you won't have to stand near the object at all.

If you don't have anyone to help you with these hide-and-seek games, you can give your Rottie the "sit and stay" command while you hide the toy or yourself out of the dog's sight. When you've hidden the toy, give the "okay" command to let your dog know the sit and stay is done, and then follow with "find."

Taking Advantage of Dog-Friendly Parks

Unfortunately, because of neglectful dog owners, it is becoming increasingly difficult to find parks and recreational areas that allow dogs, and even fewer that permit dogs ever to be off-leash. This is understandable, because not all people love dogs as much as you and I do. Even those who like dogs don't appreciate being harassed or threatened by someone else's dog or stepping in a pile of dog poop.

Although your well-trained Rottie would never think of threatening anyone, many people are thoroughly convinced that all Rottweilers are dangerous and become terrified at the sight of one, particularly if he is off-leash. My best advice is to keep your Rottie on a leash at all times when you are in a public recreation area. The popular Flexi-leads can extend themselves up to 25 feet if there is no one around to bother you, but the retractable leads give you constant control over your dog at all times.

If you want to use a nearby park, check with the local Department of Parks and Recreation to see what the rules are that apply to dogs. Some parks allow dogs only during certain low-use hours, and some even allow dogs to be off-leash during specified time periods.

Many communities are creating special dog parks or are fencing in certain portions of public parks in which dogs are allowed to be off leash. The value of these dedicated areas is that they give a dog plenty of opportunity for some serious exercise and help improve socialization by letting the dog run with other canine pals.

Even when you are in a dog park where having your dog off-leash is perfectly acceptable, make sure your Rottie has been properly socialized to accept other dogs. Is your Rottie of a nature to withstand being threatened or challenged by another dog without flying into a rage?

Even though your dog, and nine out of ten of the other dogs at the park, may be well socialized, the tenth dog may be the culprit. You know, like the kid who can't seem to get through a single school recess without antagonizing someone? The additional problem with dogs in groups is that even though a troublemaker may pick on just a single dog to fight with, fighting ignites a pack reaction, and soon every dog with a single aggressive bone in his body has to dive into the fray.

When trying out an off-leash dog park, remember that you and your dog are the new kids on the block. Proceed with care and make sure no bullies are present. If a dog seems determined to rule the pack through aggression, take your Rottie home and try the park another time. Most Rotties will not tolerate being pushed around for no good reason, and even though they may not start a fight, the average Rottweiler is more than capable of finishing one.

Enjoying the Water with Your Dog

Although there is nothing in the breed's history to indicate the Rottweiler has ever served as a water dog, they *love* the water. Retrieving from a pond, a lake, or even the ocean is the Rottweiler's idea of good clean fun. Some even like to relax on rafts like their human friends (see Figure 9-1).

Even though Rotties like water, don't make the mistake of throwing your puppy, or even your grown dog, into the water on your first visit to the beach. If you allow the dog to become accustomed to the water gradually, you'll wind up with an excellent swimmer on your hands.

I usually take puppies who haven't been introduced to the ocean down to the beach on a calm day when the surf is relatively gentle. The sound and ominous look of huge crashing waves can be very frightening to a pup. On puppy days, we also take along the older dogs who like the ocean. This gives the pup or new dog confidence that he will not be eaten alive by this huge wet beast.

Figure 9-1: Rottweilers are huge fans of the water. Just be sure the water your Rottweiler swims in is safe.

Photograph courtesy of John and Loraine Capurso

If you don't have a seasoned dog for your dog to follow, attach a long leash to your dog's collar and walk through the shallows at a leisurely pace, allowing your dog to trail along and very gradually get his feet wet. If you walk too rapidly, the pup will begin to splash himself, and cold water on the tummy can be a little intimidating for the first-timer.

After your Rottie decides water sports are the next best thing to a steak dinner, be sure the dog doesn't become totally exhausted. Some dogs will retrieve sticks or balls out of the water for as long as there is someone around to throw for them. Dogs are like children in that regard, so it is up to you to set some sensible limits.

Ocean and river swimming can be dangerous. Consider currents, rip tides, and the size of the surf before you let your Rottweiler enter the water. If you wouldn't let your child swim there, don't allow your Rottie to. Talk to lifeguards or people familiar with the beaches and tides in your area so that you don't make the fatal mistake of sending your Rottie off into a hazardous situation.

Swimming pools have no tides or surf to contend with, but make sure your Rottie is completely familiar with how and where to get out. Begin by taking your dog down to the far end of the pool, and then allow the dog to follow you to the exit that will be easiest for the dog to use. Do this several times and your Rottie will quickly learn how to get out on his own. Never leave a dog in or near a pool on his own unless you are *absolutely certain* that the dog is able to get out of the pool.

Responsible beach-going

Ocean and lake ecology is at an extremely fragile state at present, and quite frankly, most conservationists would like to keep dogs off our beaches entirely. They are not being unfair if you stop to look at the consequences. There are many additives contained in today's commercial dog foods that are not environmentally friendly. When dogs eliminate along beaches, the harmful materials eventually wash down into the water and are capable of killing marine life.

You may think your dog's feces once a day or once a week could not possibly do any great harm to vast bodies of water, but multiply what your dog is responsible for by the hundreds of dogs who live in your area and the number of days and weeks in a year and you can see where the difficulty lies. If you take your Rottie to the beach, plan to pick up any droppings. Commercial concerns do enough damage to our waters. We who profess to be nature lovers and lovers of all animals need not contribute to the problem.

When you are on the beach, keep your dog on a leash unless you are in a really remote area where it is practical and legal for the dog to run free. Do consider the fact that many people go to the beach to relax and read, and they don't enjoy having someone's massive Rottie leaping over them or kicking up sand.

Hitting the Trails with Your Rottie

Being able to hike through the beautiful trails cut through some of our state and national parks is wonderful, and who better to share the beauty of it all than your Rottweiler pal? Your dog may not relate to the aesthetics of it on the same level as you do, but rest assured he is able to enjoy it in his own way. The camaraderie and the opportunities for your dog to enjoy all the wondrous sights and smells of nature make for a perfect day.

Most national parks allow dogs but have very strict leash laws to protect the wildlife. It is very difficult for any dog to resist taking off after a rabbit or deer, and most urban dogs can chase an animal for miles before they realize they are lost.

Equip yourself properly on your hikes. Stash any emergency and first aid materials that may be appropriate to the time of the year and the terrain in your backpack. Park rangers and the Department of Parks and Recreation can advise you on what may be worthwhile to carry along with you in case of emergency.

Hiking supplies for both dogs and dog owners are available at specialty shops and through pet supply catalogs. In fact, hiking with dogs has become so popular that there is a wide range of equipment geared to the canine set alone: collapsible food and drink containers, booties to protect your dog's feet from sharp rocks or freezing terrain, rainwear, and even doggie sun shades and sunglasses. And just so all of your Rottie's camping and hiking equipment doesn't become an additional burden for you, there are doggie backpacks designed to help your dog carry whatever he may need along the trail.

Helping Your Rottie Do What He Was Bred to Do

A Rottweiler's genetics give this clever and talented breed the ability to perform well on so many levels that most owners are never able to really exhaust their dogs' full capacity to perform.

The chapters in Part I highlight the many duties that have been assigned to the Rottweiler through the ages. Even though science has developed a myriad of ways to replace the need for our Rottie's services, that doesn't eliminate the breed's ability to perform them. In the following sections, I give you a look at just a few of the many ways in which this ingenious breed can serve his owners.

Make sure each step is a clean step

The well-trained Rottie can go pretty much anywhere you can go, unless dogs are specifically prohibited. (Always check on that ahead of time.) But no matter where you go with your Rottweiler, make sure you clean up after him. It doesn't take more than a minute to place your hand inside a plastic bag, pick up the droppings, and turn the bag inside out. Or you may prefer to carry a poop scooper and plastic zip-close bag. Whatever works best for you is what you should use, but use something. If you and your neighbors are diligent about picking up after your pooches, you will be allowed to continue using the parks and outdoor recreation areas. If you're not, you'll spoil it for everyone.

Herding tests and trials

Herding trials are sponsored by many organizations — the American Kennel Club is just one of them. The American Kennel Club's trials are limited to all dogs over 9 months of age who are registered with the organization as a herding breed (and Rotties are!). There are two levels of tests and three levels of trials.

Even though Rottweilers have been flexing their herding muscles since the days of ancient Rome, it wasn't until 1994 that the American Kennel Club admitted the breed to the list of those eligible for compete for herding titles. Since that time, the Rottie has proven capable of herding just about anything herdable: sheep, cattle (see Figure 9-2), horses, and even ducks and geese.

Herding tested

The herding test is a very simple test that is designed to see whether the dog is willing to respond to the handler. The test also shows whether the dog is able to control the movement of the livestock — which can be sheep, goats, cattle, or ducks.

To pass the test a dog has to be able to:

- **Stay on command.**
- **Obey two commands to change the direction of the livestock.**
- **Halt the livestock on command.**
- **Come on recall.**

Ten minutes are allowed for the exercises. The Rottie must pass two of these basic tests with two different judges presiding. There is no score — the dog simply passes or fails. If the dog is successful on both attempts, the official Herding Tested degree (HT) is awarded.

Figure 9-2: Rottweilers are extremely adept at herding competitions.

Photograph courtesy of Judith E. Strom

Pre-trial testing

With an HT degree under his belt, a Rottie becomes eligible for the pre-trial test. The challenges here are:

- **Guide the livestock through obstacles.**
- **Stop the livestock.**
- **Turn the livestock in a different direction.**
- **Reverse the direction in which the livestock is moving.**
- **Pen the livestock within ten minutes.**

This is simply a pass or fail event with no scores. Two successful tests under two different judges are required to earn the Pre-Trial Tested (PT) title.

Herding trials

In herding trials, the Rottweiler is given the option of competing in three different designated courses. Each course demonstrates different areas of working ability, and each of these options has three levels of accomplishment: Herding Started (HS), Herding Intermediate (HI), and Advanced. Success in the Advanced level earns the dog a Herding Excellent (HX) title, the loftiest degree attainable by a herding dog.

In herding trials, a dog must score a minimum of 60 out of a possible 100 points. The points are divided into six categories of proficiency, and the competing dog must earn at least half of the points allotted to each category in order to qualify. The courses are complex.

The requirements for all of the AKC's herding program can be obtained directly from the AKC at 5580 Centerview Drive, Raleigh, NC 27606 or by calling 919-233-9767.

Schutzhund

Note: Unfortunately, Schutzhund training carries a negative connotation in the U.S. Irrespective of the ultimately positive goals of the training, the fully-controlled, assertive behavior required of the dogs is perceived by the general public and legislators as encouraging dangerous behavior. In order to avoid this perception, the AKC has made a hard-and-fast rule that no AKC-affiliated club can be involved in this or any sport that includes aggression toward man. Because Schutzhund training is so intricately involved in the development of the Rottweiler, the general details are presented here for the interest and consideration of the reader.

Schutzhund (German for "protection dog") is a way to give your Rottweiler work to do in order to reach his true potential. This program isn't just busywork for a Rottie; it is a program that, in the end, will provide you with a dog who is not only your friend and companion, but who can protect you if the need arises.

The Schutzhund sport began in Germany about 100 years ago as a means of testing and maintaining the character and usefulness of working dogs. It sprang from the peasant farmers' need to train their herding dogs to also protect the livestock from predators and poachers. Though born of the aristocracy, Captain Max von Stephanitz admired the impressive capabilities of the peasants' herding dogs. Having always been an animal lover, he decided to try his hand at dog breeding — but not just random dog breeding or breeding of dogs purely for entertainment or exhibition. He had a definite plan in mind. His goal was to breed the ultimate shepherd dog. The dogs he observed in the shepherds' fields were, in his mind, the finest and most intelligent working dogs of his day.

Von Stephanitz became actively involved in the *Verein fur Deutsche Schaferhunde* (SV), the national German Shepherd Dog club, and helped shift the direction of the organization toward carefully recording and registering the dogs that would be produced to develop the breed he had in mind. Captain von Stephanitz installed himself as president of the organization and dictated the rules, regulations, and criteria by which dogs would be deemed worthy to be included in the stud book of the SV. The captain's goals were the goals of the organization, and fortunately, for his breed and the many other German breeds that would eventually follow suit, von Stephanitz's unswerving dedication was to the preservation of intelligence and trainability. Beauty he cared nothing about.

The SV also organized training contests for dogs, configured to include tests measuring excellence in obedience, tracking, and protection. Those tests were the foundation for the Schutzhund trials of today.

Schutzhund trials test on three distinct areas. The first two, obedience and tracking, are very similar to the obedience and tracking trials offered by the AKC. The third area is ability and courage in protection work. Schutzhund devotees value all three areas equally and believe they are interdependent in creating a top-quality, all-around working dog. There are three levels of proficiency — Schutzhund I, II, and III — with increasingly difficult skills and demands for each. Before any dog can even begin to compete for one of these titles, he must successfully pass a preliminary test for steadiness.

Schutzhund tracking

The tracking phase tests a dog's trainability as well as his tracking ability and endurance. As in the other two phases of Schutzhund work, temperament plays an important role in the tracking test. It begins with a temperament test given by the presiding judge. The dog must be neither shy nor independently aggressive. To be successful in this aspect of the trial, a dog must be completely reliable, and neither shyness nor uncontrollable aggressiveness lend themselves to the prerequisite stability.

In the test, a track is laid on a natural surface of either grass or dirt. The track includes some turns. The person making the trail drops objects along the way directly on the track. While on leash, the dog is expected to follow the track and locate and indicate the objects.

Tracking isn't just part of Schutzhund. A successful Rottie can earn tracking titles at AKC events. The Tracking Dog (TD) is the first rung up the ladder, followed by Tracking Dog Excellent (TDX), which is a bit more difficult. The top title is the challenging Variable Surface Tracker (VST), which is a test over changing urban terrain. Some Rotties are absolute whizzes at sniffing their way to stardom, and others, well, they simply turn their noses up at the whole affair.

Schutzhund obedience

In the obedience phase, the dog's temperament is tested along with his physical soundness and willingness to work for humans. The dog is given a sequence of heeling exercises, during the course of which groups of strangers must be negotiated and a gun is fired. All this is to observe emotional stability. The standard "sit," "stay," and "down" commands are given while the handler continues to move along, and the dog is required to remain in position until the handler indicates the dog should catch up or change positions.

Other exercises test a dog's ability to continue to follow through on the handler's instruction whether or not the handler is in sight. And finally, the dog is required to retrieve objects over both flat and elevated surfaces.

Schutzhund protection work

The protection work phase tests the dog's courage and puts his agility and strength to the test, as well. The protecting phase includes finding and apprehending a person under the direction of the handler. The dog is expected to perform these exercises with sufficient aggression, but only under the strict command and control of his handler. Although all this does, in fact, test the dog's courage, it also measures the dog's ability to refrain from becoming aggressive without the handler's instruction to do so.

Don't make the common mistake of thinking that a Schutzhund-trained dog is a fighting machine. Schutzhund relies heavily upon the complete cooperation of both dog and handler, and no properly trained Schutzhund dog would ever act aggressively toward a human or other animal without the explicit instruction of his handler. Schutzhund training is by and for the dog and handler team.

Guard work

Although many different names are given to dogs who do guard work — *attack dogs, guard dogs, protection dogs,* and *patrol dogs* among them — all dogs trained for this purpose are highly specialized dogs who should remain in the hands of skilled, professional trainers. They are *not* household pets. These dogs are trained specifically to be spontaneously aggressive in performing their duties, even without commands from a handler. Their job is normally to protect property or individuals.

A Rottweiler owner should *never* attempt to train his dog for guard work without the supervision of a highly qualified and experienced trainer. Guard work taught by an amateur can unleash aggressive tendencies in a Rottweiler that may be difficult, if not impossible, to redirect.

Generally speaking, guard dogs have been trained to protect a given area or person with any and all force necessary. If what they have been trained to protect is invaded, they will attack and, if necessary, bite intruders without waiting for a command to do so. It should be obvious what a lethal weapon this would be in a residential neighborhood or any area into which an unsuspecting person could inadvertently trespass.

Whenever there is a need for this kind of dog, it is best obtained from trained professionals who are experienced in providing services of this kind. Posted signs, fencing, and a myriad of other requirements are usually required by law when you keep a trained guard dog.

Carting

All carting requires is one Rottie, something that needs to be hauled, and a cart. The cart can either be professionally manufactured or homemade. Rottweilers just love carting, and if there are children around to be carted, most Rotties are in seventh heaven.

We have friends whose young son was born with a handicap that makes it extremely difficult for the boy to walk any great distance. The family has a Rottweiler who absolutely adores the boy, and the dog somehow seems to understand that he brings great joy into his young master's life as he transports the youngster around the neighborhood and on outings the family takes together into the desert or on hiking trails.

A good many Rotties are still used to haul goods in the more remote and less affluent villages throughout Europe. On a recent winter trip to Russia, we found it not the least bit unusual to find several children on a sled attached to the family Rottweiler's harness as they trucked down the icy streets of both downtown St. Petersburg and Moscow.

The South African Kennel Union provides highly regimented competitions for excellence in carting, with specific degrees and qualifications that apply to both individual and team competitors. It is an extremely popular event and has been attracting more and more interest in the United States as well.

Search and rescue work

Search and rescue teams have proven their worth beyond a shadow of a doubt in assisting local law enforcement in countless ways. Searching for and finding lost children and adults are just a few of the many ways these canines have proven themselves heroes and lifesavers. Search and rescue teams are also invaluable at disaster sites, where they can find trapped victims faster than any manmade equipment can.

Search and rescue work requires a dog who has a good sense of smell, a great sense of urgency, and the physical strength and stamina required to perform long, sometimes exhausting searches. Water, land, and snow specialists have been able to perform incredible rescues. In fact, many say search-and-rescue dogs are more useful in some rescue operations than a human ever could be.

Search and rescue is a team effort. That means *you* must be in as good shape as your dog. It also means you have to train just as often and just as hard.

Many volunteer organizations assist in training both dog and handler for search and rescue work. The handler is given instructions in first aid, map reading, and even water rescue. The dogs are highly trained in tracking, hauling, and alerting their handlers when a person is located.

Keeping in Mind Some Other Fun Things to Do with Your Rottweiler

There's not a whole lot you've read about the Rottweiler so far that somehow doesn't work its way back to the same basic truth: This is a breed whose entire history revolves around serving humanity: guarding, fighting, herding, hauling, and tracking — the list goes on and on. It all sounds terribly serious, doesn't it? But if you've been living with a Rottie, even if it's been just a few weeks, keep in mind that there is another side to this breed — an energetic, fun-loving, enthusiastic side.

When all that energy and enthusiasm is harnessed and channeled constructively, there are few heights a Rottie cannot reach in the canine world. Rotties are natural athletes and they can run, jump, sniff, or strut with the best of them. Some of their abilities provide unquestionable service to people, and others, well, just prove that Bruno is not all work and no play. There are some fun pursuits that both your Rottie and you will enjoy so much that you just may get addicted.

There's no business like show business

Have you ever considered going into show business? Dog show business, that is. The Rottweiler is a very popular show dog. Many owners who had thought of their Rottweiler only as a friend and companion have entered the dog show world and found it to be an exciting and fascinating hobby. The dog show fraternity extends around the entire world and affords competitors an opportunity to create new friendships from all walks of life. It is an activity in which one person or an entire family can participate.

In the United States, the American Kennel Club sponsors many kinds of competitive events in which all registered purebred dogs may compete. They run the gamut from very formal events like the Westminster Kennel Club Show to local match shows.

Dog shows are called *conformation events,* because dogs are judged by how well they conform to the breed standard.

Conformation shows are currently the most popular and well-attended dog events. The original purpose of conformation shows was to give breeders a means of comparing their stock to that of other fanciers and thereby improve their breeding programs.

Today, not all people who participate in conformation shows intend to become breeders. Many simply find enjoyment in the competitive aspect of these events. Conformation dog shows take place nearly every weekend of the year in one part of the country or another and are open to all unneutered, AKC-registered dogs.

Choosing which kind of show to participate in

Generally speaking, conformation shows fall into two major categories: match shows and championship events.

Match shows

Match shows are primarily staged for young or inexperienced dogs who are not ready to compete for championship points. In most cases, classes are offered for dogs from about 3 months of age and older.

Matches are great places for beginners to learn how to show their own dogs. These matches are far more informal than championship events. Because they are more laid-back, there is plenty of time for the novice handler to make mistakes along with everyone else and to ask questions and seek assistance from more experienced exhibitors or from the show judges.

Match shows can be held for all breeds of dogs recognized by the AKC, or they can be specialty matches — matches for just one particular breed of dog. When there is a club devoted to a specific breed in an area, that club will often hold these match shows so that the newer club members and the young puppies will have an opportunity to gain some experience. Rottweiler breeders are usually aware of local Rottweilers-only specialty matches, and if you have any interest at all, you can check with the breeder where you got your pal. Information regarding these matches can usually also be found in the classified sections of Sunday newspapers under "Dogs for Sale."

Matches can be entered on the day of the show. Most clubs accept entries on the grounds of the show site on the morning of the event. The person taking your entry will be able to help you fill out the form and give you the preliminary instructions you will need. All the information required is on your Rottie's registration certificate, so you may want to make a photocopy of that and bring it along with you.

Championship shows

Championship shows are a lot more formal than match shows, so I recommend entering them only after you've gained some experience by showing in a few match shows first. The championship shows are sponsored by various all-breed kennel clubs or, in some instances, by a club specializing in one particular breed of dog. The AKC can provide you with information about an all-breed kennel club in your area, and the American Rottweiler Club can let you know if there is a local Rottweiler club in your area.

For a dog to become an AKC champion, he must be awarded a total of 15 championship points. Points at a show are awarded to the best male and best female non-champions in each breed. Only one male and one female in each breed win points at a dog show. The number of championship points that can be won at a particular show is based on the number of entries in the dog's breed and sex, but it's never 15. That means the dog must win the points at several shows to become a champion. Of the 15 points required, two of the wins must be what are called *majors* (that is, a show at which three or more points are offered). These two majors have to be won under two different judges.

How do you enter a championship show? All clubs sponsoring an AKC championship show must issue what is called a *premium list.* A premium list contains all the information you will need to enter that club's show. These premium lists are sent out by a professional show superintendent several weeks before the date you must enter the show. (Unlike match shows, which can be entered the same day, championship shows must be entered in advance.)

If you want to get on the mailing list for these premium lists, you must advise the show superintendent in your area. A list of show superintendents can be obtained from the AKC. When your name is on a show superintendent's list, you will continue to receive premium lists for all shows staged by that organization as long as you continue to show your dog.

The premium list gives you the date, location, and closing date for entries for a particular show. It also lists the entry fee, the judges for each of the breeds eligible to compete at the show, and the prizes that will be awarded in each breed. Generally, dog shows in the United States do not offer cash prizes. The prizes are trophies, ribbons, and similar mementos.

Also included in the premium list is the entry form, which you must complete to enter the show. All of the information you need to complete the entry form appears on your dog's AKC registration certificate. The information that you enter on this form will appear in the catalog on the day of the show.

Picking a class

When you enter your dog in a show, you can choose from several classes. Read the information contained in the premium list carefully. Often there are lower rates for puppy classes, as well as other exceptions that you should be aware of.

Listed In Table 9-1 are the classes in which you can enter your Rottweiler at AKC shows. As you read the requirements for the different classes, it will become apparent that the classes are organized according to a dog's age and prior accomplishments. If you are a beginner, I strongly advise entering your Rottweiler in the Puppy class if he is young enough. If your Rottweiler is over

12 months old, enter him in the 12- to 18-Month class. Those Rottweilers who have passed the 18-month cutoff can be entered in the Novice class. Judges are far more forgiving of immaturity and lack of experience in these classes than they would be in some of the other classes that normally accommodate more seasoned dogs and handlers.

Each of the classes in Table 9-1 is divided by sex, and all dogs must be at least 6 months old on the day of the show to be eligible.

Table 9-1 Dog Show Classes

Class	Description
Puppy class	Pups under 12 months of age on the day of show, who are not champions.
12- to 18-Month class	Dogs at least 12 months old but under 18 months on the day of the show, who are not champions.
Novice class	Dogs born in the United States, Canada, Mexico, or Bermuda, who have not earned three first-place ribbons in the Novice class or one first-place ribbon in the Bred-by-Exhibitor, American-Bred, or Open class. Dogs in this class may not have won any points toward their championships.
Bred-by-Exhibitor class	Dogs being shown by any one of the breeders of record who is also an owner or co-owner. The dog may also be shown by a member of the immediate family of any one of the breeders of record. No champions of record are eligible for this class.
American-Bred class	For any dog whelped in the United States as the result of a mating that took place in the United States, who is not yet a champion.
Open class	Any dog 6 months or older.
Best of Breed	This class is for champions only, so you probably won't have to worry about this one for a while.

You must include the dog's sex on the entry blank so that your Rottweiler is not put into the wrong class.

In dog show terminology, males are referred to as *dogs* and females as *bitches.* While at the show, only the males are dogs, and your beloved and adored Daisy will have to suffer being referred to as a bitch.

Showing your own dog

Getting ready for a dog show begins long before you actually walk into the ring at a championship show. Beginners have a great deal to learn. At first it may seem totally overwhelming, but keep in mind that everyone was a novice at one time. No matter how the pros may whirl and twirl around you, remember that they didn't know how to do all that when they entered their first show.

Much of what you need to know you can find in books and magazine articles. Read everything you can. Attend dog shows and observe the people in the ring who are winning with their Rottweilers. You will quickly see how much skilled handling enhances a dog's looks and his chances of winning.

The next step is to begin to master the art of handling your own Rottweiler. This can start just as soon as you bring your puppy home. Teaching your puppy to stand still while he is being brushed is the first phase of learning the proper stance in the show ring.

Rottweilers are examined by the judge while the dog is *stacked* (standing evenly on his four legs). It is bottom-line important that your Rottweiler not be apprehensive when the judge attempts to examine him. You can practice this at home whenever strangers stop by. If your Rottie is going to be a show dog, the more strangers who are allowed to put their hands on your dog, the better. The dog must be completely at ease when the judge does his or her examination. Any attempt to snap at the judge will result in your being dismissed from the ring immediately.

Many all-breed clubs sponsor handling classes for people who want to show their own dog. These classes are usually taught by professional dog handlers, who will be able to offer you worthwhile tips both on handling in general and showing your Rottweiler specifically. In these classes, you will discover a great deal about general ring procedures. At the same time, your Rottweiler will become accustomed to being handled by strangers. As you attend more classes you will observe your Rottweiler growing confident and less distracted, which makes good presentation easier for both you and your dog.

Although showing dogs is an enjoyable hobby, it takes hard work and a lot of study to master the art of handling your dog well. Patience and practice will help make you proficient. You will not become an expert overnight.

Professional handlers offer their services to those who do not want to handle their own dog at a show or who are unable to do so. These professionals can be contacted at most dog shows. When they have completed their work for the day, they are happy to discuss the possibility and the practicality of having your Rottweiler professionally handled.

Participating in obedience trials

Obedience trials are held at both championship shows and at matches, along with the conformation events. The same informal entry procedures that applies to conformation matches apply to obedience trials, as well. And the same formal rules apply when you are entering an obedience competition held in conjunction with a championship show.

Obedience classes are definitely a prerequisite. Obedience competition work is based entirely on how well your dog performs a set series of exercises, and the requirements are very precise. The exercises range from the basics like heel, sit, and down in the Novice class, on through to scent discrimination and directed jumping in the Utility class.

Rottweilers, like the one shown in Figure 9-3, have proven to be excellent candidates for obedience work. Many have earned advanced titles through the years, and the breed is proud to claim title-holders in even the most demanding of the categories.

Don't let the rules, regulations, and titles intimidate you. Actually, obedience competition follows in a very logical order that makes it easy to learn and easy to follow. Instructional classes must come first, and even if you decide you don't want to enter shows, what you and your dog learn in obedience training is priceless. From there on, it is step by step up the ladder, and by the time you complete a step you will already know how to go on to the next level.

Figure 9-3: This Rottweiler shows off his proud accomplishment of a second place at an obedience show.

Photograph courtesy of John and Loraine Capurso

Competitive sports for Rottweilers

If you and your Rottweiler are getting bored with playing fetch in your backyard and you'd like to test yourself and your dog, check out one of these competitive sports together.

Flyball

Flyball is certainly one of the most exciting activities you and your Rottie can choose from the breed's never-ending list of fun things to do. The degree to which your Rottweiler is obsessed with his tennis ball will determine, in good part, how successful he may be at flyball.

In flyball, the dogs are organized into two teams, with four dogs on each team. The teams race relay-style. At the signal, each dog must clear four hurdles, release a ball from the flyball box, catch it in the air, and return with the ball to the starting point so that the next team member can start off. The team that races the fastest wins, and the speed and excitement make for a very enthusiastic ringside audience.

If you want information on rules, training, and where flyball events are held, contact the North American Flyball Association, 1002 East Samuel Avenue, Peoria Heights, IL 61614.

Freestyle

Canine freestyle is a relatively new canine sport with one paw in obedience and the other in dance. Many of the basic obedience exercises are called upon, but in freestyle, dog and handler set a complicated routine to music.

There are two main approaches to freestyle in the United States. The Canine Freestyle Federation puts the spotlight primarily on the dogs and their movements, with the handlers being as inconspicuous as possible. Musical Canine Sports International is a bit more flamboyant, with more emphasis on the handler's costuming and movement. Both approaches seem to attract staunch followers, and both are growing rapidly in popularity.

Teamwork and coordination are prime factors in freestyle. Scoring is based on the performance of both dog and handler. Execution of some of the standard obedience movements is required, but nonstandard movements that the dogs are called upon to perform also weigh heavily. Enthusiasm, degree of difficulty of the movements, and appropriateness of the music and its interpretation are additional scoring factors.

For more information on freestyle, contact Musical Canine Sports International, c/o Val Culpin, 3466 Creston Drive, Abbotsford, British Columbia, Canada V2T 5B9, or the Canine Freestyle Federation, c/o Alison Jaskiewicz, 576 Jackson Road, Mason, NH 03048.

Frisbee

Not all dogs are mad about playing Frisbee. However, if your Rottie decides catching that plastic disc while he flies through the air is a jolly good time, it could well become an obsession for both of you. Some Rotties will take to catching and retrieving a Frisbee at their first try and get better and better with each catch. Other Rotties need to develop a liking for the object first, and one of the easiest ways to do this is to use the Frisbee initially as a food dish.

Whether your Rottie's interest is mild or extreme, Frisbee is excellent exercise and can help keep your pal in great shape. If you find your Rottie is a Frisbee fanatic, there's no limit to the heights to which the two of you can soar. There are local, regional, national, and international Frisbee competitions, and prizes range anywhere from a couple of hundred dollars into the thousands. There are even international Frisbee teams that meet annually for the World Cup!

If this seems like something you and your canine athlete may be interested in, there are countless books, Web sites, and videos that can help launch you on your way to stardom. For more information about Frisbee contests, call Alpo Frisbee Contest at 888-444-ALPO, or Friskies Canine Frisbee Championships at 800-423-3268.

Agility

Agility competition is simply an obstacle course for dogs. Everyone involved (and everyone who watches) appears to be having the time of their lives, and the sport has become outrageously popular at dog shows and fairs throughout the world. There are tunnels, catwalks, seesaws, and numerous other obstacles that the canine contestants have to master off leash while they are being timed.

The idea for agility competition began in England and caught the public's attention when it was first presented at the world famed Crufts Dog Show in London in 1978. By 1986 it was already a major event in Great Britain and had caught on so well in the U.S. that the United States Dog Agility Association (USDAA) was organized.

The enthusiasm of the dogs and the supportive roar of the crowd at ringside as their favorite dog jumps over, under, around, and through the obstacles gives an electric feeling to the event, and the canine participants seem to thrive on it all. Agility competition does require teamwork, because the handler has to act as navigator for the dog. Although the dogs do all the maneuvering, the handler is the one who directs the dog, because the sequence of the individual obstacles is different at every event. Both the AKC and the USDAA can provide additional information, as well as names and addresses of the organizations sponsoring events nearest to your home. Contact the USDAA at P.O. Box 850955, Richardson, TX 75085-0955.

Canine Good Citizen

The purpose of the Canine Good Citizen program (CGC) is to demonstrate that a dog is a well-mannered asset to the canine community. CGC really isn't a competition of any kind, because a dog is scored completely on his ability to master the basic requirements for a well-behaved dog. There are ten parts to the CGC test, and the dog must pass all ten in order to be awarded the CGC certificate. They are:

- **Having a good appearance and grooming.** The dog must be clean and appear to be free of parasites.
- **Accepting a friendly stranger.** The dog is required to allow a friendly stranger to approach and speak to the handler.
- **Walking on a loose leash.** The dog has to walk along attentively next to the handler.
- **Walking through a crowd.** The dog is required to walk along, paying attention to the handler, without interfering with other people or dogs.
- **Sitting and lying down on command and staying in place.** The dog has to respond to each of the handler's commands.
- **Coming when called.** After being put in a sit or down position 10 feet away, the dog must return to the handler when called.
- **Sitting while being touched by a stranger.** A friendly stranger must be able to pet the dog.
- **Having a positive reaction to another dog.** The dog has to keep his attention on the handler even in the presence of another dog.
- **Having a calm reaction to distracting sights or noises.** These distractions can be an unusual or loud noise, a bicycle going by, or an unusual object.
- **Dealing well with supervised separation.** The dog must wait calmly while held on a lead by a stranger (supervisor), while the owner is out of sight for 3 minutes.

Anyone interested in this program can obtain information regarding the rules, and when and where testing is held, directly from the AKC.

Helping Your Dog Help Others

You and your dog can be a great form of therapy for people in need. I can just hear you now: "You think working with the sick, the handicapped, and the aged is fun?" Actually, yes. You and your Rottweiler may not be rolling in the aisles after a therapy visit, but you'll be amazed at the warm and cozy feeling you'll come away with when you've spent the day bringing a little sunshine into some lives that otherwise can be quite dreary. Children and elderly people especially seem to light up when they are visited by dogs (see Figure 9-4), and they are amazed at how sweet and attentive these big dogs can be.

Figure 9-4: You and your Rottweiler can bring a smile to the face of someone who otherwise may not get many visitors. Nothing is more rewarding for you or your dog.

Photograph courtesy of John and Loraine Capurso

There is great therapeutic value to the patients who come in contact with dogs. Medical journals have substantiated stress reduction and lowered blood pressure as a result of these human-to-animal associations. And what *you'll* get out of it is beyond measure; trust me.

Two organizations — the Delta Society and Therapy Dogs International — test and register Rottweilers and other breeds that are temperamentally suitable to visit hospitals and homes for the aged. Rottweilers can also be trained in a wide range of assistance roles. Their keen awareness makes them ideal companions for the hard of hearing and the sight-impaired. For more information on therapy work, contact Therapy Dogs International at 88 Bartley Road, Flanders, NJ 07836, or the Delta Society at 289 Perimeter Road East, Renton, VA 98055-1329.

Part IV

Keeping Your Rottweiler Healthy

In this part . . .

The chapters in this part cover everything from feeding and exercising your Rottweiler to taking care of him when he gets sick. In this part, you'll figure out how to prevent health problems from starting, and you'll get useful information on recognizing and dealing with them if they affect your Rottweiler. You'll also find great tips for avoiding emergencies and dealing with them if and when they come up. If you're looking for information on any facet of your Rottie's health, you've come to the right part.

Chapter 10

Getting to Know Your Rottweiler . . . Inside and Out

In This Chapter

- Knowing the anatomy of your Rottweiler
- Being aware of some inherited health problems that may affect your dog
- Considering the possibility of breeding your dog
- Spaying or neutering your Rottweiler
- Finding a vet and establishing a good relationship

You know what a good Rottweiler is and what it looks like. You shopped 'til you dropped and managed to find the perfect breeder, and you were lucky enough to be able to get the first perfect (well, at least *near* perfect) pup. Now that you and your little gangbuster have begun life together, you no doubt want to make sure all that time invested in finding the little tyke was not for naught, and your new best friend will remain happy and healthy.

You start by discovering what the different parts of your dog's anatomy are called. Yes, this is your course in Rottweiler anatomy. After this quick introductory course, you'll be able to call up your vet and say your Rottie injured her hock, rather than saying she has a boo-boo on that bump that's just above her foot.

In this chapter, you also get the scoop on inherited problems and diseases that may affect your Rottweiler. And you gain information to help you decide whether to breed your dog or whether to spay or neuter. Finally, I give you some tips for finding a good vet and establishing a solid working relationship with him.

Through experience, your breeder was able to supply you with a healthy, well-socialized puppy. Keeping the pup that way is more about preventive maintenance than it is about anything else.

Exploring the Anatomy of the Rottweiler

As we explore the Rottweiler's external features, refer to Figure 10-1 and follow along.

Because we all know which end of the dog the nose is on, I start there. What the nose is set into is called the *muzzle.* The muzzle fits right into the *skull,* which is what holds the eyes and ears in place. Right at the top back of the skull you'll feel a fairly prominent ridge of bone, which corresponds to the little ridge of bone that is at the top back of your own skull. In dogs it is called the *occiput.*

Right behind the occiput is the *crest* of the neck, which is where the neck begins. The part that follows the crest is the *neck* (of course!), and that runs down into the *shoulders.*

If you run your hand from the crest and down the neck, your hand will come to a stop at the *withers.* Lots of people call that point the top of the shoulders, but you'll sound very hip if you say, "Oh, you mean here, right at my dog's withers?"

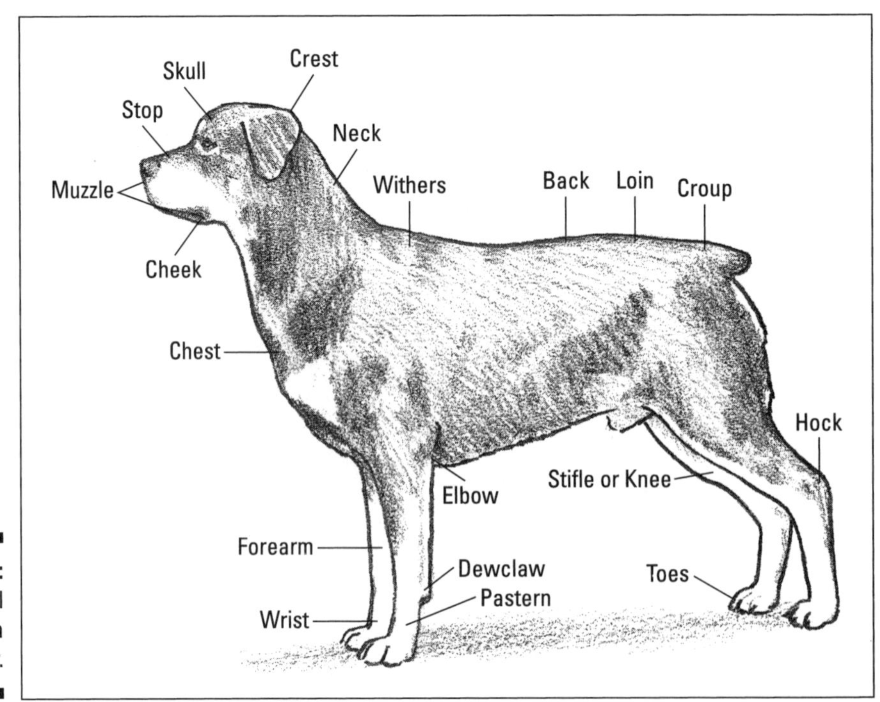

Figure 10-1: The external features of a Rottweiler.

After that, much like you and I, your Rottie has a *back*. The line of the back, all the way to the end of the dog, is called the *topline*. The back extends clear on to the *hips*. Anatomy experts say only part of that is really the back on a dog, but we're not anatomy experts, so calling it the back is perfectly fine.

The area on the dog's side, between where the rib cage ends and the pelvis begins, is called the *loin*. The *croup* (it has nothing to do with the cough human babies get) is the part of the body above the hind legs, and it extends from the loin to the base of the tail at the *buttocks*. (Buttocks are buttocks — no matter who they're on.)

Moving down, you come to the *upper thigh*, which is the place that corresponds to your own thighs. The next area down is called the *lower thigh*, and below it is the *hock* joint. Next down from the hock is the rear *pastern*, the area between the foot and the wrist.

That little claw-like thing near the bottom inside edge of the Rottie's leg is called a *dewclaw*. (What it has to do with dew is beyond me.) Actually, the dewclaw is an undeveloped toe that harks back to before the time your Rottweiler's ancestors had even become wolves. And that, my friends, is far back! Dewclaws grow on the front legs as well, but don't panic if your dog doesn't have any dewclaws. Most breeders remove them just a few days after the puppies are born.

Heading back up the rear leg, on its bottom side and between the upper and lower thigh, you'll find the *stifle* joint. The stifle corresponds to a human's knee.

Now you're up in front of the Rottie again. You know what *feet* are, and just above the Rottie's front feet is the area between the foot and the wrist, called the *pastern*.

The *forearm* is the area between the wrist and the elbow. It hooks up to the *upper arm*, which connects to the bottom edge of the *shoulder blade*. And lo and behold, you've come full circle and you've passed your Rottweiler Anatomy 101 course with flying colors!

When all the parts hang together correctly so the dog moves like one collective unit, the doggy set refers to this as being *sound*. When you watch your Rottweiler move around with strength and ease, with her legs moving directly forward with purpose, you can then say, "My, my, isn't she a sound looking Rottweiler!"

Identifying Inherited Health Problems and Diseases

Like all breeds of domesticated dogs, including the mixed breeds, the Rottweiler has its share of hereditary problems. Fortunately, the problems are relatively few. And any genetic problems I describe here are far less apt to be present in the Rottweiler you buy from a reputable breeder, because a reputable breeder's stock is tested and rigidly selected to avoid these problems. These are complications that exist in the breed, however, and you should discuss them with the breeder before you purchase your dog. If you ever suspect symptoms of any of these problems in your Rottweiler, make an appointment to see your veterinarian without delay.

The reputable Rottweiler breeder is aware of genetic breed problems. Even though breeders constantly test and do their utmost to breed around inheritable problems, they're not God, and occasionally one of the following problems can arise in even the best-planned litter.

There is a misconception that wild dogs and *feral* dogs (domesticated dogs who have returned to a wild state), have no hereditary diseases or infirmities. But this is entirely untrue. There are documented cases of both canines and felines captured in the wild who have shown evidence of developing eye and bone abnormalities. Untreated, the afflicted animals would perish. This only goes to prove that domesticated animals are not alone in developing genetic dysfunctions. The difference is that affected wild animals often don't survive long enough to breed.

We who control the breeding of our domesticated dogs are intent upon saving all the puppies in a litter. In preserving life, we also perpetuate health problems. Our humanitarian proclivities thus have a downside as well. This has made genetic testing and screening an important part of all modern breeding programs.

Hip dysplasia

Hip dysplasia is an orthopedic problem that affects most large and many smaller breeds of dogs. A malformation of the hip joints, it usually occurs unilaterally, meaning in both hips. Hip dysplasia can vary in degree, from the mildest form that is undetectable other than by x-ray, on through to extremely serious and painful cases that require surgery.

The normal hip can best be described as a ball and socket arrangement (see Figure 10-2). The upper bone of the rear leg (the femur) has a head that should fit neatly and firmly into the socket of the pelvis. A well-knit ball and socket allows the femur to rotate freely within the socket, but it is held firmly in place. In a dog with hip dysplasia, the socket is shallow, allowing the femur head to slip and slide. The shallower the socket, the more sliding and the more it impairs movement and causes pain.

Hip dysplasia is considered to be *polygenetic,* which means it is caused by the interaction of several genes, making it extremely hard to predict. Although it can be detected in the individual adult dog, only the law of averages reduces the occurrence when breeding individual dogs x-rayed clear of the problem.

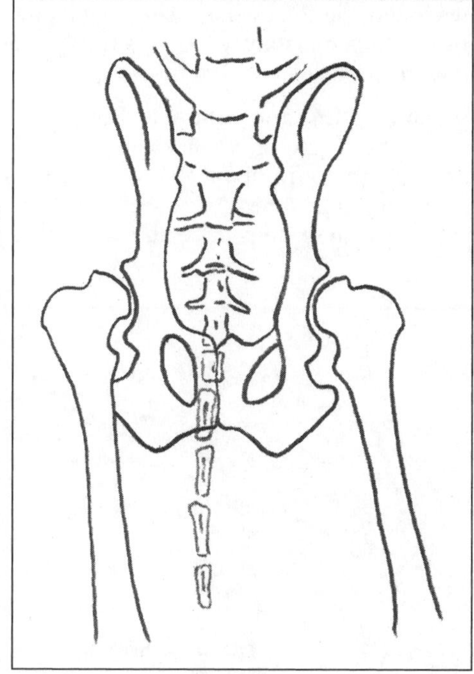

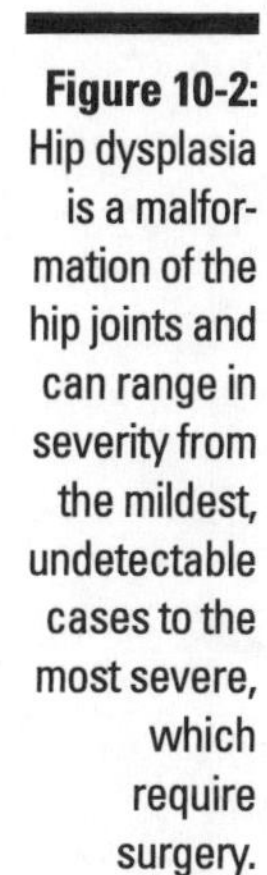

Figure 10-2: Hip dysplasia is a malformation of the hip joints and can range in severity from the mildest, undetectable cases to the most severe, which require surgery.

Osteochondritis dissecans

Osteochondritis dissecans (OCD) is a condition in which the cartilage lining the bone surfaces in the shoulder joint, elbow joint, or stifle and hock joints thickens until it enlarges and cracks. When that happens, the bone beneath it becomes inflamed and deteriorates. The resultant lameness varies from an occasional limp to a chronic condition, depending on how much cartilage is affected. In Rottweilers, OCD can occur more frequently in males. The area most commonly affected is the elbow, and this is referred to as *elbow dysplasia.*

Eye problems

Rottweilers can be affected by any of several eye conditions:

- **Entropion:** In a dog with *entropion,* the eyelids are turned inward so that the eyelashes constantly rub against and irritate the eyeball (see Figure 10-3). Untreated, entropion can severely damage vision. A simple veterinary procedure can fully correct the condition.
- **Ectropian:** *Ectropion* is a condition of the eyelid that causes the lid to roll out and hang down, exposing the eyeball. The sagging eyelid forms a pocket that traps debris, which constantly irritates the eye. This condition can be corrected with surgery.
- **Progressive retinal atrophy (PRA) and cataracts:** Both progressive retinal atrophy and cataracts are degenerative diseases of the eye that can lead to total blindness. Though not rampant in Rottweilers, cases have been reported. Tests conducted by a registered ophthalmologist can assure Rottweiler owners that their dogs have no concerns in this area.

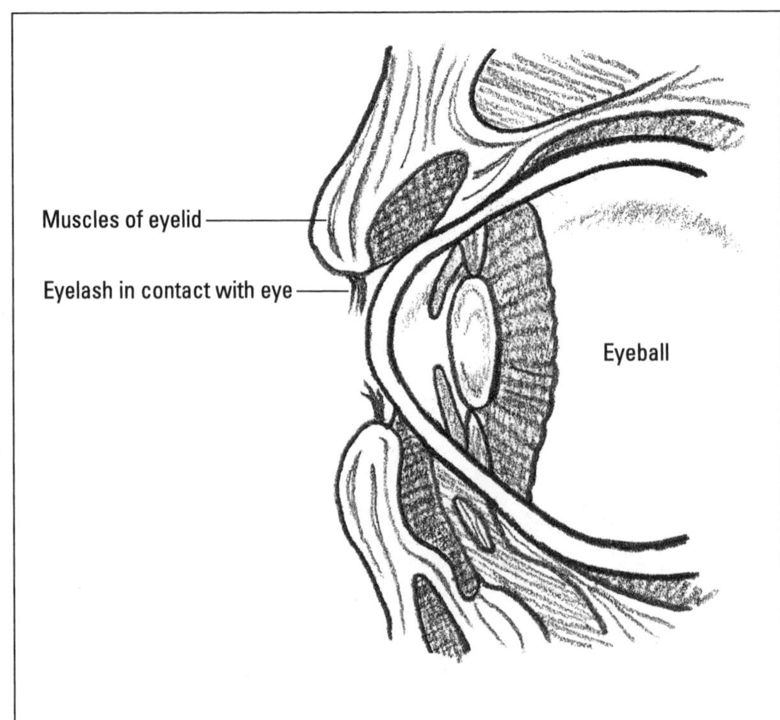

Figure 10-3: Entropion is a condition in which the dog's eyelid turns inward, causing the eyelashes to rub against and irritate the eyeball.

Demodectic mange

Demodectic mange is a form of skin infection caused by a parasite that lives in the hair follicles. Susceptibility is believed to be hereditary in some lines of the breed. Damage to the coat and skin varies to the degree in which it affects an individual dog. It can be extremely severe in dogs whose immune systems are weakened at puberty or by some diseases.

Checking Your Dog's Health Regularly

We humans have medical insurance because we know how staggering those hospital bills can be without it. Your Rottweiler's medical bills may not be quite as high as your own, but they won't be cheap. A good many of the causes for expensive treatment could be prevented by regular checkups. The old adage "An ounce of prevention is worth a pound of cure" certainly applies here.

You can easily forget to look at and into certain parts of your Rottie's anatomy as you go through your busy life. Create a checklist containing all the things you should be looking for as you groom your dog. Post that where you groom your dog so that you can glance at it while you are brushing her. Here are some key things to look for as you groom:

- **Skin should be free of eruptions.**
- **Coat should be thick, lustrous, and clean.**
- **Ears should be clean, without an offensive odor.**
- **Teeth should be white without accumulated tartar.**
- **Eyes should be clear and bright with no discharge or irritation.**
- **Nails should be short, with no cracks or ragged edges.**
- **Check the rectal temperature whenever your dog appears out of sorts.** Normal is between 101.5 and 102 degrees Fahrenheit.

Make it a habit to check all the points on this list regularly. You can do it as part of your grooming session or when you're just hanging around with your dog and cuddling. (See Chapter 12 for more information on each of the items on the list.)

Healthy, wealthy, and wise

A well-bred and well-socialized Rottie will not only make you the envy of most dog owners, but she will also keep you from going to the poorhouse. Sick dogs are not only an unhappy situation, but they also cost money. If you don't believe me, just ask your veterinarian.

You and your well-bred Rottie will share a relatively carefree life together if you give your pal reasonable care and lots of training and affection. With that all-important preventive maintenance you won't have to worry about renting space at the vet's office.

Deciding Whether to Breed Your Rottweiler

If you want my quick and easy answer to the question of whether you should breed your dog, here it is: Don't! Believe me, there is a great deal more to consider than the fun you may have with a half dozen or more chubby little Rottweilers wagging their stubby little tails at you.

The first thing you should do before you think further about the possibility of adding to the world's Rottweiler population is pay a visit to your local Humane Society or animal shelter. Thousands of purebred dogs are in need of rescue all over the country. Unfortunately, a good percentage of them are Rottweilers. The American Humane Society reports approximately 15 million healthy and friendly dogs and cats were euthanized in 1998 alone. Many of them were born into good homes but obviously fell into the hands of irresponsible buyers.

Something else you have to give serious thought to is the suitability of your Rottweiler for breeding. Not all Rotties, even though well bred, are suitable as breeding stock. If you discussed your breeding plans with the person from whom you purchased your dog, a responsible breeder will undoubtedly have selected a pup for you that was worthy of being bred. The operative word here, of course, is *worthy.* Your Rottie may be the smartest gal who has hit the boards since Lassie came home, she could be the most courageous and protective Rottie in town, and the dog may love you beyond all reason, but none of these are sound reasons for producing offspring.

If the dog's breeder sold the dog to you specifically as a pet, the breeder obviously had no desire to have the dog bred. You should respect that experienced person's wishes. If you are unable to get in touch with the breeder, or if you doubt the credentials of the person from whom you purchased your dog, do some research and find a local breeder who has a reputation for producing show-quality Rotties. This is the best person to advise you on whether your male or female should be bred.

Bet You Didn't Know

All too often I hear people who have purchased purebred pets say, "Brandy needs to have a litter to complete her development" or "Jack needs a girlfriend to relieve his frustration." Believe me when I say neither Brandy nor Jack needs a sexual liaison to make their lives complete. Actually, especially in the case of Jack or any other male, breeding will only serve to *increase* his frustration rather than relieve it.

Even if your Rottie is of the quality that warrants breeding, you must consider the consequences. Having a litter of puppies can easily bring your dog population to eight or ten overnight. This can be great fun for the entire family for the first couple of weeks, when the puppies spend their lives nursing and sleeping. But do note, I said *for the first couple of weeks.* The day will come very quickly when your Rottweiler will look at you as if to say, "Well, you wanted puppies. Now take care of them!"

It won't be long before the puppies will not only outgrow the whelping box, they'll outgrow the whole room! Then, too, they will have transferred their dependence from their mother to you — and they will want to be with you *all the time!* Think back on the patience and work involved in housebreaking and training your single Rottweiler puppy. Now multiply that by eight or ten.

Realize the commitment you will have to make to be on hand when weaning time comes. Newly weaned puppies need four meals a day. Will you or a responsible member of the family be on hand to feed the pups morning, noon, evening, and night?

Not only will the puppies object to being shunted off into the garage or the backyard, but treating them this way will do nothing for their temperaments. Rottie puppies must have *continuous* human contact from birth if they are to achieve their potential as companions. Ask yourself if you are willing to give them all the time they need and deserve until you have found a responsible home for each puppy in the litter. This may take weeks, sometimes months. And that's after you have already decided it is time for the puppies to be off to their new homes.

When those cute little puppies start growing by leaps and bounds (none of them old enough to housebreak!), getting them off to their new homes is going to be your top priority. But that priority *cannot* interfere with your making absolutely positive that the person relieving you of your burden is the right person to own a Rottweiler.

There is constant lobbying throughout America to restrict the rights of all dog owners and dog breeders because of the pet overpopulation problem and the unending need to destroy unwanted animals. Thoughtful dog owners leave the breeding process to experienced individuals who have the facilities to keep all resulting offspring on their premises until suitable and responsible homes can be found.

All too often, people are willing to commit to all the hard work and time involved in raising a litter of Rottweilers in anticipation of financial gain. Think again! Consider the cost of a stud fee and prenatal veterinary expenses. Then add the cost of possible whelping problems, health checks, and the necessary inoculation series and food for the puppies. These will all put a very large dent in any anticipated profits.

Many parents want to have their young children experience "the miracle of birth" by letting them watch their dog give birth to puppies. But remember that you can rent videos of all kinds of animals giving birth. Handling the experience this way saves adding to pet overpopulation. In addition, all too often the miracle of birth is accompanied by the miracle of death. You cannot control what your children will see.

Spaying or Neutering Your Dog

Female dogs are *spayed,* which means their uterus and ovaries are removed. Male dogs are *neutered,* which means their testicles are removed. Spaying or neutering will not change the personality of your Rottweiler and will help your dog avoid many health and behavior problems.

Males who have not been altered have the natural instinct to lift their legs and urinate on objects to mark the territory in which they live. Teaching an unaltered male not to lift his leg in your home can be extremely difficult. Then, too, the unaltered male Rottweiler has that ongoing need to prove he's the toughest guy on the block, and he also has a greater tendency to roam if there is a female in heat in the area. Males also can suffer from enlarged or infected prostates if left intact.

Females who have not been spayed have two estrus cycles each year, and those cycles are accompanied by a bloody discharge. Not only will there be extensive soiling of the area in which the dog is allowed, but, much more disastrous, she could become pregnant. Unspayed females also have a much higher risk of developing *pyometra* (a potentially deadly uterine infection) or mammary cancer later in life.

Spaying and neutering are not reversible procedures. If you are considering the possibility of showing your Rottweiler, keep in mind that altered animals are not allowed to compete in American Kennel Club or United Kennel Club conformation dog shows. Altered dogs may, however, compete in all performance events except Beagle trials. (And you wouldn't enter your Rottie in a Beagle trial anyway.)

Looking for the Best Veterinarian on Your Dog's Behalf

No one knows more about the best veterinarian for your Rottweiler puppy than the breeder from whom you purchased the pup. If you are fortunate enough to live in the same area, your problems are solved. You can continue right on with the vet who has known your puppy since birth.

Unfortunately, that may not be possible because of distance. And I do recommend that you have a veterinarian that you can get to in a hurry. As good as a veterinarian may be, if he or she lives hours away and you have an emergency situation on your hands, that extra time needed to get to your vet may end up costing your dog her life.

Still, your breeder may be able to help by asking friends or fellow dog breeders in your area to provide recommendations. Your neighbors may be able to help you in this respect as well. Do check ahead though. Pay the recommended veterinary hospital a visit before you bring your puppy home. Inspect the premises and discuss Rottweiler care with the vet. Some veterinarians have had little or no experience with Rotties and may even be intimidated by the prospect of working with one.

If the facility and the person you speak to meet your approval, make an appointment to take your puppy there for her first checkup and insist that you see the same veterinarian each time your dog pays a visit. Some clinics have several veterinarians in attendance and it becomes the luck of the draw as to who will see your Rottie. Don't let that happen. Veterinary visits can be traumatic enough for some dogs, and being treated by a complete stranger each time can only add to a dog's anxiety. On the other hand, if your dog seems to take a disliking to a particular vet, ask if there may be value in having someone else look at your dog. Some Rotties will instantly like or dislike someone, and they're not about to change their minds.

If your Rottie doesn't approve of anyone at the hospital, it may well be that your *dog* is the one who needs a personality adjustment. That's up to you. No veterinarian should have to face being eaten alive while trying to be helpful.

Chapter 11

Feeding and Exercising Your Rottweiler

In This Chapter

- Figuring out what and how much to feed your Rottweiler
- Considering your dog's special needs as he ages or gets sick
- Giving your Rottweiler the exercise he needs to stay fit and healthy

Nutrition and exercise are two crucial elements in your dog's overall health. And in this chapter, I explore both of these, letting you know the important issues to keep in mind.

Answering Your Questions about Your Rottie's Nutrition

Responsible Rottweiler owners are often overwhelmed by all the dog food options available. They commonly have questions about which food to feed and how much of it, not to mention what the right balance of fat and protein is for their dog. In this section, I answer these questions and more.

Which food should I feed?

There is no one answer to the question of what the best food is for your Rottweiler. I have spoken to successful Rottweiler breeders in many parts of the world, and each person seems to have his own "tried and true, absolutely the best, under no circumstances would I ever change" method. Probably the best answer to the question is, feed your dog what works best — not necessarily what the dog *likes* best, but what is most apt to keep the dog looking and acting the way a Rottweiler should.

All about potatoes (the couch variety)

Maybe having your wardrobe reduced to a patch quilt or watching your furniture being redesigned by a bored Rottie doesn't bother you. Perhaps the fact that neither you nor your Rottie can bend over to touch your toes doesn't make you depressed. Then the two of you will not have to be concerned about becoming couch potatoes. Just remember that neither one of you will live as long or as well as you may have if you'd eaten right and gotten enough exercise.

Eating properly and maintaining a sensible exercise program will keep you both happier and healthier for a lot longer, but it is *you* who will have to design the menus and implement the exercise program. Your Rottweiler will be happy to help, but he won't be able to get you into your jogging shorts, nor can he cook. If you aren't up to thinking about your own health, at least remember your dog's welfare and give him the best nutrition and exercise possible.

Who can tell you which food that is? I sincerely recommend you consult with the breeder from whom you purchased your dog. I can only assume you decided upon that breeder because the adult dogs at his kennel were in fine fettle and the puppies in the litter you selected yours from were equally healthy. That means whatever your breeder has been doing works for the dogs he is breeding.

How much is enough?

The correct amount of food to maintain a Rottweiler's optimum condition varies as much from dog to dog as it does from human to human. It is impossible to state any specific amount of food your dog should be given — and be wary of anyone who says otherwise. Much depends upon the amount of exercise your dog is getting (which uses up the calories consumed). A Rottie who spends the entire day pounding the pavement doing police work needs considerably more food than the house dog whose exercise is limited to a leisurely walk around the block once a day. As a general guideline, I would say the correct amount of food for a normally active Rottweiler is the amount he will eat readily in about 15 minutes. What your dog does not eat in that length of time should be taken up and discarded. Leaving food out for extended periods of time can lead to erratic and finicky eating habits.

When it comes to feeding, use your common sense. Remember that the Rottie was originally bred to be a working dog — herding cattle, pulling carts, or putting in a hard day at the Colosseum. Meals were of questionable nutritional value back then, but the quantities were undoubtedly large and probably were not served until after a long, grueling day's work.

Today's Rottweiler has inherited the constitution of a combat hero, and an appetite to go with it, but many Rotties only burn enough calories to accommodate an office clerk. Rotties can gain weight very easily if their food intake is not controlled and they are not given sufficient exercise.

A way to determine whether your Rottie is receiving the right amount of food is to closely monitor the dog's condition. You should be able to feel (but not see) his ribs and backbone through a slight layer of muscle and fat.

Fresh water and a properly prepared balanced diet, containing all the essential nutrients in correct proportions, are all a healthy dog needs to be offered. If your Rottie will not eat the food offered, it is because he is either not hungry or does not feel well. If the former is the case, your dog will eat when he *is* hungry. If you suspect your Rottie is not well, an appointment with your veterinarian is definitely in order.

How much protein and fat does my dog need?

Dogs, whether Rottweilers or Chihuahuas, are *carnivorous* (meat-eating) animals, and although the vegetable content of your dog's diet should not be overlooked, a dog's physiology and anatomy are based upon eating animal protein. Protein and fat are absolutely essential in a dog's diet. The animal protein and fat your dog needs can be replaced by some vegetable proteins, but the amounts and the kind required necessitate a diet with some meat in it. Don't try to force your dog to go against his nature. If you prefer a pet that eats no meat, consider a rabbit instead.

A great deal of research is conducted by manufacturers of the leading brands of dog food to determine the exact ratio of vitamins and minerals necessary to maintain your dog's well-being. Research teams have determined the ideal balance of minerals, protein, carbohydrates, and trace elements a dog needs. So many excellent commercial dog foods are available today that it seems a waste of time, effort, and money to try to duplicate the nutritional content of these carefully thought-out products by cooking food from scratch. Reading dog food labels carefully or consulting with your veterinarian is important. Your vet can assist you in selecting the best moist or dry food for your Rottweiler.

Will that inexpensive grocery-store brand be good enough?

Dog food manufacturing has become so sophisticated that it is now possible to buy food for dogs living almost any lifestyle from sedentary to highly active. This applies to both canned and dry foods. But, like most other things in life, you get what you pay for. It costs the manufacturer more to produce a nutritionally balanced, high-quality food that is easily digested by a dog than it does to produce a brand that provides only marginal nutrition.

Whether canned or dry, look for a food in which the main ingredient is derived from meat, poultry, or fish. You cannot purchase a top-quality dog food for the same price as one that lacks the nutritional value you are looking for. In many cases, you will find your Rottie not only needs less of the better food, but there will be fewer feces to clean up as well.

By law, all dog food labels, like the one shown in Figure 11-1, must list all the ingredients in descending order by weight. As in food for human consumption, the food's main ingredient is listed first, the next most prominent follows, and so on down the line. A food in which meat or poultry appears first on the ingredients list provides more canine nutrition per pound of food than one that lists a grain product as the leading ingredient. The diet based on meat or poultry also costs more than a food whose primary content is inexpensive fillers, but you will need to feed your dog less of the meat-based product. In the end, the cheaper grain-based product is not really much of a savings, and the meat-based product is a lot better for your dog.

Ingredients: Chicken, Corn Meal, Chicken By-Product Meal, Ground Grain Sorghum, Ground Whole Grain Barley, Chicken Meal, Chicken Fat (preserved with mixed Tocopherols, a source of Vitamin E, and Citric Acid), Dried Beet Pulp (sugar removed), Natural Chicken Flavor, Dried Egg Product, Brewers Dried Yeast, Potassium Chloride, Salt, Choline Chloride, Calcium Carbonate, DL-Methionine, Ferrous Sulfate, Vitamin E Supplement, Zinc Oxide, Ascorbic Acid (source of Vitamin C), Dicalcium Phosphate, Manganese Sulfate, Copper Sulfate, Manganese Oxide, Vitamin B_{12} Supplement, Vitamin A Acetate, Calcium Pantothenate, Biotin, Lecithin, Rosemary Extract, Thiamine Mononitrate (source of Vitamin B_1), Niacin, Riboflavin Supplement (source of Vitamin B_2), Pyridoxine Hydrochloride (source of Vitamin B_6), Inositol, Vitamin D_3 Supplement, Potassium Iodide, Folic Acid, Cobalt Carbonate.

Guaranteed Analysis:

Crude Protein not less than	26.0%
Crude Fat not less than	14.0%
Crude Fiber not more than	4.0%
Moisture not more than	10.0%

Animal feeding tests using Association of American Feed Control Official's procedures substantiate that this product provides complete and balanced nutrition for adult dogs.

DOG'S LIFE DOG FOOD

Figure 11-1: Dog food labels list all the ingredients in descending order by weight. Look for a food with meat or poultry listed as the first ingredient.

Adapting Your Dog's Diet as His Needs Change

Most manufacturers of premium dog food now produce special diets for weaning puppies, as well as growing, overweight, underweight, and older dogs. The calorie and nutritional content in these foods is adjusted to suit the particular needs a dog has at each period in his life.

Appearance isn't everything

Dog foods advertised and packaged to look like a steak or a block of cheese are done up that way to appeal to the dog *owner,* not the dog. Chances are the manufacturer used a lot of chemicals to make the food look that way. The better dog foods are not manufactured to resemble products that appeal to humans. Your dog could care less that a food looks like a juicy steak or a wedge of Wisconsin cheddar. All your Rottweiler cares about is how his food smells and tastes. The "looks like" dog foods are manufactured that way to tempt *you.* So unless you do, in fact, plan to join your dog for dinner, don't waste your money.

Be careful of those canned or moist products that are advertised as having the look of "rich red beef," or the dry foods that are red in color. In most cases, the color is put there to appeal to *you.* It looks that way through the use of red dye. Dyes and chemical preservatives are no better for your dog than they are for you.

A good red dye test is to place a small amount of canned food or moistened dry food on a piece of white paper towel. Check the food in half an hour or so to see if there is any red staining on the towel. If there is, you can rest assured the color is there to appeal to your eye and not your dog's.

Using the correctly formulated food for each stage of your dog's life is very important. A food that is too rich can cause your dog just as many problems as one that is not rich enough. Read the labels on the can or box, study the promotional literature that is published by the manufacturer of the dog food you are considering, and seek the advice of those who are experienced in raising Rottweilers.

Feeding puppies

A good puppy diet consists of at least 20 percent protein, but protein is not the only nutrient essential for growth. Puppies also need fat. Fat has the calories that a puppy's little energy-burning furnace needs to keep it stoked. Fat also produces healthy skin and helps build resistance to disease. Animal fats should make up approximately 10 percent of a puppy's diet.

Carbohydrates also supply energy and provide the bulk that is a necessity in the Rottweiler puppy's diet. Potatoes, rice, and even pasta are good sources of carbohydrates. If you feed these foods to your puppy, just be sure they are well cooked, because a young puppy won't be able to process these foods if they are not.

Puppy foods must also be easily digestible and contain all the important vitamins and minerals, including calcium and phosphorous. Calcium and phosphorous are extremely important for bone growth. They work in tandem to do their job, but they must be present in the right proportions to be effective.

Be careful here though: Too little calcium can subject a young dog to bone deformities such as rickets; too much calcium is suspected of causing many of the bone diseases dog breeders are dealing with today.

A great deal of controversy surrounds the use of vitamin supplements for dogs. Many breeders believe that hereditary conditions are not entirely to blame for the high incidence of orthopedic problems modern dogs face. They suspect these problems are exacerbated by overuse of vitamin supplements. Their suspicions are not without merit, because most high-quality commercial dog foods are well balanced and highly fortified. Supplementation could easily throw that balance off and lead to growth problems. Before adding any supplement to the food you give your dog, discuss the product with both your dog's breeder and your veterinarian. If you do decide to use a supplement, never exceed the prescribed dosage.

All this should make it quite clear that cooking your own properly balanced dog food from scratch is something that requires a good deal of knowledge about nutrition. I sincerely advise talking to your breeder or veterinarian if you are thinking about adopting a feeding plan that is not based on a prepared top-quality and scientifically balanced commercial dog food.

Maintaining your dog's current weight

As dogs mature, their energy requirements decrease — I said "decrease," not "stop"! If the dog is extremely active, whether the activity is fun or work, the dog will burn more calories than the same dog napping around the house all day long. A well-balanced maintenance diet eliminates any complicated guesswork as to supplying all nutritional needs.

Feeding an aging Rottweiler

As your Rottie ages, getting out of bed in the morning is no less difficult for him than it is for his aging owner. There is less activity and a slower metabolism, but like his aging owner, the elderly Rottie will probably still feel entitled to the same size food portions. A senior food will enable you to reduce your dog's caloric intake without reducing his rations.

Unfortunately, you're going to have to steel yourself and start cutting back on the amount of food the old-timer is being given. Fatty foods and gas-producing vegetables are no-nos at this point in your dog's life. Solid food, especially meat, should be chopped or ground so it is not swallowed in large chunks.

Activity should be reduced in its intensity but should not be stopped. The old folks need exercise, albeit for shorter periods, but a nice long walk every day will keep them healthier and you'll see just how much they look forward to it.

Meeting Your Rottweiler's Special Nutritional Needs

The diets described in the preceding sections are those fed under normal circumstances as your little pup progresses from puppyhood to adulthood and eventually to old age. There are exceptions to the everyday rules, however, and at those times, diets must be adjusted accordingly. I cover these adjustments in the following sections.

Chicken soup for the ailing pooch

When your Rottweiler is under the weather, diet becomes a very important part of the recuperative process. Sick dogs need a diet that is low in carbohydrates but high in vitamins, minerals, and fat. Rather than attempting to mix food on your own to accomplish this end, you are much better off speaking to your vet about a prescription diet that is specially formulated for this purpose.

Other dogs may have chronic gastrointestinal problems of various kinds that require an entirely different approach to nutrition. Normally speaking, dogs with conditions of this nature need food that is easily digestible but low in fat. Prescription diets are advised. As a general rule, it is best to speak to your veterinarian about foods if your Rottweiler is experiencing anything but optimum health.

What to do for the tubby Rottweiler

Watch your Rottie's midsection. Dogs, young or old, don't become obese overnight. The excess weight comes on gradually, and your eye may accustom itself to the gradual gains so that nothing seems out of the ordinary. Periodic hops onto the scale will be very helpful in monitoring your dog's weight.

Your Rottweiler may seem fit as a fiddle, but I still strongly suggest twice-a-year visits to the vet's office for weight control and preventive maintenance. Most vets have scales made especially for weighing animals and will automatically have your Rottie hop on as part of their normal office procedure. If your dog tips the scales way over, your vet can advise you on how much he needs to lose and how you should go about seeing to the loss.

Commercial reducing diets are available through your veterinarian that will keep your dog satisfied but are low in calories. Using these special foods will enable your dog to lose weight without feeling like you're running him through boot camp.

If your Rottie is not overeating and is getting sufficient exercise, there may be some other cause for his weight gain. Have your vet look into this.

Getting Your Rottweiler the Exercise He Needs

So far you've done nothing but read about what *you* must do for your Rottie. Now here's something your Rottie can do for *you.* It may not be something that tops your holiday wish list, but like elementary school math and cod liver oil, you will be a better person because of it. What could that possibly be? It's exercise!

Exercise is something your Rottie needs, and it is also something that will improve your own health and state of mind. Fortunately, you do not have to become a marathon runner to give your Rottie the exercise he needs. Walking at a pace that lets your body know you are doing something more than just slogging along is a good pace for both you and your dog.

If improving your health isn't incentive enough to get you out and moving, think about exercise this way: It's a nonprescription mood relaxer for your dog. Although Rotties aren't classed among the high-strung breeds, remember their heritage: herding, carting, taking on all comers in the arena — all pursuits that required a higher than average energy level. That energy doesn't just go away because you'd like it to. It will be used in some way, and if you would prefer that your dog does so by eating the sofa or taking down the wallpaper, so be it. Most Rottweiler owners, however, would prefer to have their dogs use up their energy taking a good brisk walk, playing catch, or bringing back a Frisbee.

Don't expect your Rottie to get exercise on his own unless there's another dog around, and even then he probably won't be all that active after he emerges from puppyhood. As maturity and then old age set in, you'll find Rotties become less and less inclined to be self-starters in the exercise department. However, if their lord and master (that's you, in case you forgot!) is involved, a Rottie of any age is ready, willing, and able to enjoy outdoor activities. Supervising your Rottie's exercise is always best; that way you'll be sure the dog is getting enough of the right kind of it.

Rottweilers are susceptible to bloat (see Chapter 13 for more on this life-threatening condition). Both veterinarians and Rottweiler breeders caution against feeding immediately before or after strenuous exercise, because they believe it can bring on bloat.

Puppy exercise

If you watch puppies at play with their littermates, you will see frequent but brief bouts of high-level activity. This rush of activity is nearly always followed by a good long nap. Puppies need exercise, but only as much as they themselves want to get, and then they should be given ample time to rest.

Just as soon as you and your puppy master the collar and leash, the two of you can be off to explore the neighborhood and perhaps the nearby park (that is, of course, after all inoculations are up to date). Visiting a park gives you both the exercise you need, and when you're out and about you'll be working on your tyke's socialization process as well.

Don't expect a baby pup to take a 10-mile hike. The smart pup will plunk his little rear down and refuse to budge, and you will have to tote him all the way back home. However, your pup may try to please you by struggling to keep up and exerting himself beyond what is reasonable. So be sure to shoot for brief periods of exercise with lots of rest in between.

Adolescents and healthy adults

After he's out of puppyhood, your Rottweiler will probably be able to outwalk you any day of the week and still be up for some aerobics afterward. He'll also be ready for every conceivable game you can think up and will probably want to continue far longer than is good for either one of you.

Just as you should do for yourself, whenever you start a new form of exercise for your Rottie, do so gradually and increase the duration very slowly. Jogging with a young Rottie — at least one under 18 months of age — isn't a good idea. When a dog has reached 18 months of age, his bones and muscles have formed and strengthened to the point where the jarring involved in running will not do permanent damage.

If you live near a lake, most Rotties love to swim and there couldn't be any better exercise. Any place that is safe for you to swim will be safe for your Rottie as well. Don't let your Rottie swim in a place you think is too dirty or too dangerous for you. If you're planning on swimming in the ocean, make sure you understand the dangers involved and are aware of the areas in which riptides and undercurrents prevail. Rotties who love the water can be too adventurous for their own good. Make sure you don't send your pal into a dangerous situation. (For more information on getting your Rottie in the water, check out Chapter 9.)

Be extremely careful when exercising your Rottweiler in hot weather. Confine exercise periods to the early morning hours before temperatures rise or to the evening after temperatures drop.

Regardless of the dog's age, be sensitive to bone or joint injuries sustained while exercising or playing games. Always inspect sore or tender areas, and if they seem particularly painful for the dog, see your vet immediately. Concrete walkways and stony paths can be hard on a Rottweiler's feet. Inspect your dog's foot pads for cuts and abrasions often if exercise takes place on cement.

65 and counting: Exercise for seniors

Just because the old-timers have reached the twilight of their years doesn't mean they have to stop living! The older Rottweiler will still enjoy taking those walks with you every day. Maybe he won't be thrilled about heading outdoors on cold or blustery days, but when the weather is fair there is absolutely no reason why the two of you can't take a nice leisurely walk around the block or down to the park.

Don't push it, and don't be too hasty about throwing balls and Frisbees even though the old codger may think he's still capable of doing the 100-yard dash. Be kind and careful with the old folks (human and canine), and they'll be with you for a long, long time.

Chapter 12

Preventing Health Problems

In This Chapter

- Vaccinating your dog to prevent potentially serious health problems
- Preventing parasites from making your dog their home
- Getting tips on grooming your dog
- Knowing what to look for when you groom your Rottweiler

In this day of high medical costs, for both humans and animals, an ounce of prevention is most certainly worth a pound of cure. Pay attention to your Rottweiler and deal with problems as soon as they arise — before they become serious.

Rottweilers are, by and large, a healthy breed. Compared to a good number of other breeds, they are what can be referred to *as low-maintenance.* But *low* maintenance doesn't mean *no* maintenance. Rottweilers are living, breathing creatures subject to various accidents and ailments as they progress from puppyhood into adulthood.

In this chapter, I give you some valuable information that can help your Rottweiler lead a long, happy, and healthy life — everything from vaccinations to grooming (which is a great way for you to keep track of your Rottweiler's physical well-being as well).

Vaccinating Your Dog Against Deadly Diseases

Diseases that once were fatal to many dogs are now very effectively dealt with through the use of vaccines. The danger of your Rottweiler being infected with distemper, hepatitis, hardpad, leptospirosis, or the extremely virulent parvovirus is unlikely, just as long as the dog is properly inoculated and the recommended series of booster shots is given.

Cases of rabies among well-cared-for dogs are practically unheard of in the United States. Still, dogs who come in contact with wild animals of any kind can be at risk if they are not properly immunized. Even city dogs can come across rats, squirrels, rabbits, and many other small rodents — all of which have been known to carry rabies — so it is important to have your dog immunized no matter where you live.

Vaccines work by introducing a minute amount of a specific disease into your dog's system so that the dog can build up an immune response to the disease. Then, if the dog is exposed to the disease in the future, she will be able to ward off the disease. (This is the same way vaccines work in humans, by the way.) The appropriate age of your dog and the timing of the vaccines vary from region to region. So be sure to discuss this schedule with your own veterinarian on your dog's first visit.

On rare occasions, some dogs do not, for one reason or another, develop full immunity against infectious diseases. So be familiar with the signs of these illnesses, in case your Rottweiler is one of the few who is not completely immune and actually does develop the disease.

All responsible breeders give their puppies at least one if not two temporary shots against infectious diseases before the puppies leave for their new homes. But complete immunity can only be expected after all booster inoculations have been given at the prescribed intervals.

Canine parvovirus

Canine parvovirus (commonly called *parvo*) is a particularly infectious gastrointestinal disease. It can be contracted by direct contact or by being exposed to areas where infected dogs have been housed. Although dogs of all ages can be and are infected by parvo, this disease is particularly fatal to puppies.

Symptoms include acute diarrhea, often bloody, with yellow- or gray-colored stools. Soaring temperatures, sometimes as high as 106 degrees, are not uncommon — particularly in puppies.

Death can follow as quickly as one to three days after the first symptoms appear, so early treatment is critical. If you suspect that your dog may have this disease, contact your veterinarian immediately!

Canine virus distemper

An extremely high fever can be the first sign of distemper, which is a very serious and often fatal disease. Mortality among puppies and adult dogs who have not been immunized is extremely high. Other signs may be loss of appetite, diarrhea, and blood in the stools, followed by dehydration.

Respiratory infections of all kinds are apt to accompany these conditions. Symptoms can appear as quickly as a week after exposure.

Hardpad

Considered to be a secondary infection, hardpad often accompanies distemper. A symptom is hardening of the pads of the dog's feet, but the virus eventually attacks the central nervous system, causing convulsions and encephalitis.

Infectious canine hepatitis

Infectious canine hepatitis is a liver infection of particularly extreme virulence. It is a different virus than the one that affects people, but it attacks some of the same organs. Canine hepatitis eventually affects many other parts of the body with varying degrees of intensity, so that the infected dog can run the entire range of signs, from watery eyes, listlessness, and loss of appetite to violent trembling, labored breathing, vomiting, and extreme thirst. Infection normally occurs through exposure to the urine of animals affected with the disease. Symptoms can appear within a week of exposure.

Leptospirosis

Leptospirosis is a bacterial disease contracted by direct exposure to the urine of an affected animal. Both wild and domestic animals can get leptospirosis, and it can be contracted by one animal simply sniffing a tree or bush on which an affected animal has urinated.

Lepto (as it is known) can be contagious to humans as well as animals and can be fatal to both. Rapidly fluctuating temperatures, total loss of maneuverability, bleeding gums, and bloody diarrhea are all signs. The mortality rate is extremely high.

Leptospirosis is not prevalent in all sections of the country, so discuss this vaccination with your veterinarian — particularly if you intend to travel with your dog.

Rabies

Rabies infection normally occurs through a bite from an infected animal. All mammals are subject to infection. The rabies virus affects dog through inflammation of the spinal cord and central nervous system. Rabies symptoms may not be as detectable as those of other diseases because they often resemble the symptoms of other, less virulent diseases. Withdrawal and personality changes are common symptoms, as well as the myriad of symptoms associated with the other diseases described in the previous sections.

Humans who are bitten by any animal suspected of being rabid should seek the advice of their personal physician immediately. If your dog is bitten by an animal who could be rabid, call your veterinarian without delay.

Bordatella

Although bordatella (commonly referred to as *kennel cough*) is highly infectious, it is actually not a serious disease. Kennel cough can be compared to a mild case of the flu in human beings. Infected dogs act and eat normally. The symptoms of the disease are far worse than the disease itself. Symptoms are particularly nerve-wracking because there is a persistent hacking cough that sounds as though the dog will surely bring up everything she has ever eaten.

The name of the disease is misleading, because it suggests that a dog must be exposed to a kennel environment in order to be infected. In reality, kennel cough can be easily passed on from one dog to another with even casual contact. In severe cases of kennel cough, antibiotics are sometimes prescribed in order to avoid secondary infections, such as pneumonia.

An intranasal vaccine is available that provides immunity. This type of vaccination is advised for any dog who visits dog parks or is taken to a boarding kennel. In fact, most boarding kennels now insist upon proof of protection against kennel cough before they will accept a dog for boarding.

The Great Vaccination Debate

All over the world, debates rage over whether a dog should or should not continue to receive annual inoculations against infectious diseases after the important first year. Some people believe that annual revaccinations are vital to a dog's health, and others believe just as strongly that we are overvaccinating our dogs and doing them more harm than good. Somewhere in the middle are those who think revaccination is a good idea, but it should be done less often — perhaps once every 3 years instead of annually.

Strong evidence can be found to substantiate all sides of the debate. Those opposed cite occurrences of chronic health problems, sterility, and aborted litters as a result of over-administration of the vaccines. Those who oppose abolishing the annual shots argue that the number of negative reactions to annual vaccines is such a small percentage of the vaccinated population that the benefits far outweigh any small risks.

The problem is that nobody knows exactly how long immunity from a vaccine lasts in dogs. What we do know is that many of the infectious diseases (the distemper virus leading them all) ran rampant before these vaccines were developed. In many cases, contracting the diseases meant certain death.

There does seem to be growing agreement that vaccines have a longer period of effectiveness than previously believed. A 2- or 3-year interval between the first set of shots and revaccination is probably appropriate. Some cities and counties have changed their rabies vaccination requirements to reflect this trend.

Most breeders recommend that the puppy owner wait as long as possible to give a rabies shot — up to 1 year of age if at all possible. Thereafter, give rabies inoculations as required, but never any less than 2 weeks before or after any other vaccine.

There is also some debate about how many shots to give at once. Veterinarians have traditionally combined as many inoculations as possible into one shot. But this can be a big viral load for a dog to cope with all at once. Many puppies are extremely sensitive to the five-, six- and seven-in-one vaccines using modified live virus. (This vaccine is known as *DHLPP.*) Some pups get very ill within 2 or 3 days of receiving the vaccines, or within a couple of weeks. In other cases, seizures and/or symptoms of hypothyroidism, liver and kidney problems, and heart complications show up several years later. Many breeders now recommend giving separate shots over a longer period of time. Discuss this with the breeder who sells you your puppy, and insist your veterinarian follow the breeder's recommendations to the letter.

If you know your dog is sensitive to the multi-vaccine shots, insist on seeing the vial containing the vaccine your veterinarian uses before the inoculation is given. Many owners' hearts have been broken and pocketbooks emptied because the veterinarian has cavalierly dismissed any concerns the owners may have.

There is no doubt that some risk exists in administering any vaccine. How that risk stands against the possible loss of a dog through omitting the inoculations is a question that can only be answered by the individual dog owner.

Paying Attention to Parasites

Potential parasitic invasions can take place both inside and outside your Rottweiler — and at least one form of parasite is *both* internal and external. Cleanliness, regular grooming, and biannual stool examinations by your veterinarian can keep parasite infestations to a minimum, but do not be upset or surprised to find that even with your best efforts some of these nasty creatures will find their way into your home or inside your Rottie's skin or tummy.

The most common external parasites are fleas and ticks. The most common internal parasites are roundworms, tapeworms, and heartworms, all of which are best diagnosed and treated by your veterinarian. Great advances are constantly being made in dealing with all these parasites, and what used to be complicated, messy, and time-consuming treatments have been replaced and/or simplified over the years.

Fleas

No matter how careful and fastidious you may be in the care of your Rottweiler, fleas can still be a problem. By just playing in the yard or even going on daily walks, your dog can bring fleas into your home. Once there, the little creatures multiply with amazing speed. Cats with outdoor access compound this already difficult problem by attracting fleas on their neighborhood patrols and bringing them back home on their fur.

If you live in a northern climate where there are heavy frosts and freezing temperatures, you have a winter respite from the flea problem, because fleas cannot survive these conditions. People who live in the warmer climates face the flea problem year-round.

Unfortunately, flea baths will not get rid of all the fleas. If you find even one flea on your dog, there are undoubtedly hundreds and perhaps thousands of them lurking in the carpeting and furniture throughout your home. The minute your Rottweiler completes her flea bath, the fleas are ready and able to return to their host.

Aside from the discomfort flea bites cause your dog, the severe scratching they induce can cause what are known as *hot spots.* Hot spots are created when a dog chews and scratches so hard that the skin is broken. If not attended to promptly, these sores can form moist, painful abscesses and all the hair surrounding the area falls out.

Fleas also act as hosts for tapeworm eggs, carrying them wherever they go. When a dog swallows a flea (which happens often as the dog tries to get at the itching bite), the tapeworm eggs grow in the dog's intestines. Unfortunately, if your dog has fleas, she will almost invariably have tapeworms.

After your home and dog have been infested, there is only one surefire way of eliminating a flea problem and keeping it in check. It takes a bit of planning, but is well worth the time:

1. **Make an appointment for your Rottweiler to be given a flea bath by your veterinarian or a professional groomer.**

   Most groomers use products that will completely rid your Rottie of fleas. Leave this bath to the professionals, who will make sure every part of your dog is washed safely and thoroughly.

2. **While the dog is out being bathed, have a commercial pest-control service come to your home to get rid of all the fleas that are sitting around waiting for her to return.**

   If you bring your dog home before your home is treated, the fleas will be back on the dog within hours. The service will spray both the interior of your home and the surrounding property. Most of these companies guarantee the effectiveness of their work for several months.

3. **The day *after* your Rottie comes home from her bath, give an insect growth regulator to your dog.**

   These new flea-control products can be used monthly or year-round, and they control fleas by stopping their reproduction cycle. The nice thing is that these products are deadly *only* to fleas. They have no effect on mammals at all. There are pills you can give your dog or liquids that are placed on the dog's skin between the shoulder blades. Administered regularly, these preventives are proving to be highly effective in keeping both fleas and ticks off of household pets.

Although home spraying is effective, there is a downside. Your home must be vacated and kept closed for at least a few hours after the spraying, and toxic chemicals are used for this operation. Some services are now using nontoxic sprays, so, if possible, seek them out.

Lice

Well-cared-for Rottweilers seldom have a problem with lice, because the parasites are spread by direct contact with other infested animals. A dog must spend time with another animal who has lice or be groomed with a contaminated brush or comb in order to be at risk.

If no fleas are present and you suspect lice, your dog must be bathed with an insecticide shampoo every week until the problem is taken care of. Lice live and breed exclusively on the dog herself, so it is not necessary to treat the dog's environment the way you must with fleas.

Ticks

If you live near a wooded area, you are bound to run across at least the occasional tick. In fact, your Rottie can pick up these parasites just by running through grass or brush. Ticks are bloodsucking parasites that bury their heads firmly into a dog's skin. The ticks gorge themselves on the dog's blood and then find a dark little corner to raise a family. And *family* is an understatement — tick offspring arrive by the thousands!

Ticks represent a serious health hazard to both humans and other animals. In some areas they carry Lyme disease and Rocky Mountain spotted fever. The entire area where the dog lives must be aggressively treated against ticks with sprays and dips made especially for that purpose.

To remove a tick, first soak it with a tick removal solution that can be purchased at most larger pet supply shops. When the tick releases its grip, you can remove it with a pair of tweezers. It is important to make the tick loosen its grip before you attempt to remove it. Otherwise, the head may break off and remain lodged in the dog's skin, where it could cause a severe infection. After the tick is removed, swab the area with alcohol to avoid infection.

Do not flush the tick down the toilet, because it may survive the swim! Also do not crush it between your fingers, because that will expose you to whatever diseases the tick is carrying. The best way to get rid of a tick is to put it in a jar with a bit of alcohol and then screw the lid on tight.

Always use latex gloves and tweezers to avoid the possibility of infecting yourself if the tick is a disease carrier. Wash your hands and clean with alcohol any instruments you've used as well. If you suspect your area to be infested with disease-carrying ticks, you can put the tick in a jar or plastic bag and take it to your vet to be tested.

Some of the same insect growth regulators that control fleas also do an excellent job of keeping ticks off your dog. I can attest to their effectiveness. We live at the edge of a huge forested track, and my dog and I take hikes through the woods all the time. He comes home tick-free, but more often than not, I end up picking the little varmints off myself.

Mange

There are two kinds of mange — demodectic and sarcoptic. Both are caused by mites and must be treated by your veterinarian.

Demodectic mange is believed to be present on practically all dogs, and it generally does no harm. However, some dogs just seem to be sensitive to the little creatures, and this sensitivity may be inherited. About 1 percent of all dogs have problems with demodectic mange. There are two forms of demodectic mange: local and general. Dogs affected locally may lose the hair around their eyes and in small patches on their chest and forelegs. This form of demodectic mange can be treated easily by a veterinarian. It must not be neglected, even if it seems very mild, because it can be uncomfortable for the dog and because, on rare occasions, the local form can develop into the more severe, generalized form.

Sarcoptic mange, also known as *scabies,* can be present over the entire dog. Symptoms include loss of hair on the legs and ears and often in patches over the entire body. Your veterinarian must do a skin scraping to identify the type of mange and prescribe treatment. Weekly bathing with medications especially formulated for this parasite can usually eliminate the problem. This type of mange is passed on by direct contact and is highly contagious.

Although the word *mange* may strike a note of terror in the hearts of most people, only sarcoptic mange is communicable to humans. And sarcoptic mange responds well to treatment.

Tapeworms

Tapeworms get into your dog when she swallows a flea. On an infested dog, you'll often see small, rice-like segments of the worm crawling around the dog's anus or in the stool just after the dog has relieved herself. Periodic stool examinations done by your veterinarian can detect tapeworms even though you may not observe the worm segments yourself. Your vet can administer an inoculation that quickly and completely eliminates the problem.

Heartworms

Heartworms are parasitic worms that take up residence in dogs' hearts, where they can do fatal damage. The worm is transmitted by mosquitoes that carry the worm larvae. Dogs are the mammals most commonly affected, and the condition is far more prevalent in warmer climates and areas with standing water. Blood tests can detect the presence of this worm, but it is difficult to treat.

Your veterinarian will know if heartworm is prevalent in your area. If it is, you can give your dog preventive medications, which are safe and effective.

Whipworms and hookworms

Whipworms and hookworms are shed in a dog's stool and can live for long periods in the soil. Both can attach themselves to the skin of humans as well as animals and eventually find their way to the lining of the intestines, where they burrow in. They are then seldom passed or seen. These two types of worms are only detected by microscopic examination of the stool, and each worm requires specific medication to ensure eradication.

Roundworms

Not an unusual condition, roundworms are seldom harmful to adult dogs. However, these parasites can be hazardous to the health of puppies if allowed to progress unchecked. Roundworms are transmitted from mother to puppies, so responsible breeders make sure their females are free of worms before they are ever bred. Roundworms can sometimes be visible in a dog's stool, but they are easily detected in a microscopic examination of a fresh stool sample. The coat of a puppy affected by roundworms is usually dull looking, and the puppy herself is thin but has a potbelly.

Grooming Your Rottweiler for Health and Beauty

Frequent grooming gives you a chance to inspect your Rottweiler's coat for the onset of any possible problems. Turn to Chapter 10 for a checklist of things to look for when grooming your dog.

A grooming table that puts your dog at a comfortable working level will save your back and keep your dog still while you attend to her. These tables can be purchased from any pet supply dealer or can be built at home. Trying to groom your dog while she is standing on the ground is difficult at best, because the dog will be inclined to pull away from what she doesn't like and you will have to hang on with one hand while you work with the other. Sometimes you need to use both hands, particularly when clipping nails or cleaning teeth. Having the dog on a grooming table will help.

Brushing

Frequent brushing removes the old dead hair, cleans and massages the skin, and allows the new hair to come in easily. A rubber curry comb is the ideal grooming aid for this project, and your Rottweiler will quickly learn to look forward to this regular "massage." A chamois cloth, which can be purchased at most hardware stores, can be used to finish off your brushing job and remove any stray, loose hairs. This final touch will produce a high luster on your dog's coat.

The Rottweiler sheds her coat just like the longhaired breeds do. The fallen hair is just far less noticeable. Allow your Rottweiler to sleep on a white or light-colored sofa or chair regularly and you will be amazed at the amount of hair that leaves the Rottweiler's body in just a few days' time.

Always brush in the same direction as the hair grows. Begin at the dog's head, brushing toward the tail and down the sides and legs. This procedure loosens the dead hair and brushes it off the dog.

Check the skin inside the thighs and armpits to see if those areas are dry or red. Artificial heat during winter months can dry out the skin and cause it to become chapped. Place a small amount of Vaseline or baby oil on the palms of your hands and rub your hands over the dry areas.

If you brush your Rottweiler regularly, bathing will seldom be necessary unless she has been off on a treasure hunt and found her way into something that leaves her coat with a nasty odor. Even then, many products (both dry and liquid) that eliminate odors and leave the coat shiny and clean are available at your local pet supply store.

A damp washcloth will put even the Rottweiler who has given herself a mud bath back in shape very quickly. If your Rottie's coat becomes wet in cold weather, be sure to towel dry the dog thoroughly.

Ears

The Rottweiler's ears are very sensitive, and a sore ear can make an otherwise happy dog cross and cranky. Keeping your dog's ears clean is a simple job, as long as you remember never to prod into the ear any farther than you can see. Dampen a cotton swab with warm water, squeeze out any excess liquid, and clean out all the areas inside the ear that you can see. When you do this, be careful not to injure any of the delicate ear tissue. If you ever smell a foul odor emanating from your Rottweiler's ear, schedule an appointment with your vet right away.

Teeth

If your Rottie has regularly been given those big hard dog biscuits or large knuckle bones to chew on, chances are her teeth are in great shape. Chewing helps keep tartar and plaque from forming. Buildup of either of these problems can cause extensive and permanent damage to the teeth and gums.

Regularly brushing your Rottie's teeth (as shown in Figure 12-1) can prevent tooth decay and the necessity of having your veterinarian take care of advanced cases under anesthesia.

Never use your own toothpaste on your dog. Dogs can't rinse and spit the way we do. Special dog toothpastes are available, but canine dentists say even more important than the toothpaste is the brushing action itself.

Figure 12-1: Brushing your Rottweiler's teeth regularly is the best way to keep them clean.

Eyes

If your Rottweiler's eyes appear red and inflamed, check for foreign bodies such as dirt or seeds. Flushing the eyes using a bit of cotton with cool water or a sterile saline solution will usually eliminate foreign matter.

If irritation persists and your dog's eyes remain red, or if off-colored mucous or a watery discharge is present, it could be a sign of entropion or conjunctivitis (both covered in more detail in Chapter 14). Both problems should be dealt with by your veterinarian.

Feet and nails

Always inspect your Rottie's feet for cracked pads. Check between the toes for splinters and thorns. Pay particular attention to any swollen or tender areas. In many sections of the country, there is a weed called a *fishtail* that has a barbed, hook-like end that carries its seed. This hook easily finds its way into a Rottie's foot or between her toes, and it very quickly works its way deep into the dog's flesh, which quickly causes soreness and infection. The hook is best removed by your veterinarian before serious problems result.

To keep your Rottie's feet compact and well arched, trim the nails regularly. Long nails can cause your Rottie's feet to become flat and spread. This is not only unattractive, but the long nails can also become deformed and cause a great deal of pain to the dog.

Do not allow your Rottie's nails to become overgrown and then expect to easily cut them back. Each nail has a blood vessel running through the center called the *quick,* shown in Figure 12-2. The quick grows close to the end of the nail and contains very sensitive nerve endings. If the nail is allowed to grow too long, you won't be able to cut it back to a proper length without cutting into the quick. Cutting the quick causes sharp pain for the dog and can result in a great deal of bleeding that can be very difficult to stop.

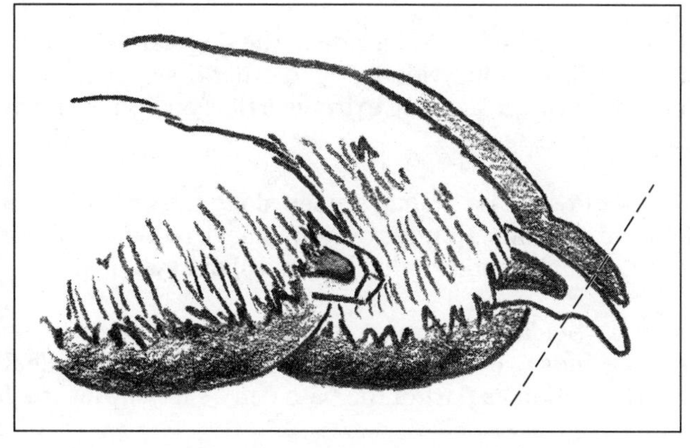

Figure 12-2: Avoid the quick when you trim your Rottweiler's nails.

If your Rottweiler is getting plenty of exercise on cement or rough hard pavement, her nails may be sufficiently worn down. However, if the dog spends most of her time indoors or on grass when outdoors, the nails can grow long very quickly. They must then be trimmed with canine nail clippers, an electric nail grinder (also called a *drumel*), or a coarse file made expressly for that purpose. All three of these items can be purchased at major pet emporiums.

I prefer the electric nail grinder because it is so easy to control and completely avoids cutting into the quick. If you want to use a drumel, you must introduce your puppy to it at an early age. The instrument has a whining sound not unlike a dentist's drill. The noise, combined with the vibration of the sanding head on the nail, can take some getting used to, but most dogs I have used it on eventually accept it as one of life's trials. My dogs have never liked having their nails trimmed, no matter what device I use.

The Rottweiler's dark nails make it practically impossible to see where the quick ends, so regardless of which nail trimming device you use, you must proceed with caution and remove only a small portion of the nail at time.

If you nip the quick in the trimming process, use any of the blood-clotting products available at pet supply shops, which will almost immediately stem the flow of blood. Have one of these products on hand in case you have a nail-trimming accident or your dog breaks a nail on her own. In a pinch, a bit of cornstarch will do.

Anal glands

The anal glands are located on each side of the dog's anus, and the scent they secrete identifies the individual dog to other dogs. These glands can become blocked, however, causing extreme irritation and even abscesses in the more advanced cases.

If you notice your Rottweiler pulling herself along the ground in a sitting position, check the anal glands. Contrary to popular belief, this habit is more apt to be the result of anal gland problems than a sign of worms.

Although not a particularly pleasant part of grooming your dog, if regularly attended to the glands will remain clear and relatively easy to deal with. Performing this function as part of the bath can be less awkward, for obvious reasons.

With one hand, place your thumb and forefinger on either side of the anal passage. Hold an absorbent cloth or a large wad of cotton over the anus with your other hand. Exert pressure to both sides of the anus with your thumb and forefinger, and allow the fluid to eject into the cloth you are holding. The glands will empty quickly, so be prepared.

If you're not comfortable performing this procedure, or if your Rottweiler seems unusually sensitive in this area, seek the assistance of your veterinarian or a professional groomer.

Keeping track of what you find

Keeping a notebook alongside your grooming table to record any problems you observe is a good idea. Just as soon as you note anything different in your Rottie's behavior or appearance, jot it down. If the situation develops into one that needs your vet's attention, record what the vet did and when. If veterinary care is necessary again at a later date, you may be able assist in the diagnosis with the notes you have made in your dog's medical book.

Your Rottie should definitely have an annual checkup at the vet's office, and taking your book along to scan while you're waiting could prove invaluable in avoiding any problems. This book is a good place to keep your dog's veterinary health and inoculation records, as well. It will remind you which inoculations are due and the dates they should be given.

Most veterinarians keep computer records of their patients and automatically notify owners of necessary follow-up treatment, but computers are computers, and even the best of them have occasional glitches. You should have your own record of when your dog needs heartworm and stool checks, or when booster inoculations are required.

Chapter 13

Being Prepared for Emergencies

In This Chapter

- Keeping a first aid kit handy in case emergency strikes
- Calling your vet when you need to
- Responding to emergency situations calmly and intelligently
- Administering medications to your Rottweiler when he is sick

No matter how careful you are about keeping your Rottweiler safe, dogs, like children, have an uncanny ability to get themselves into scrapes you can't possibly anticipate. And accidents do happen. You can be as careful as the day is long, but you can't protect your dog from the world at large. Although veterinarians are there to help you when there is an emergency, there are times when immediate care is critical and you need to know what to do *before* you can get your dog to the vet. I hope you will never have to use home emergency care, but if it is needed, your dog's life could depend on your level of preparedness.

Setting Up Your Own First Aid Kit

Here are the basics for a well stocked home first aid kit — for both you and your dog:

- Activated charcoal tablets
- Adhesive tape (1- and 2-inch widths)
- Antibacterial ointment (for skin and eyes)
- Antihistamine (approved by your vet for allergic reactions)
- Athletic sock (to slip over an injured paw)
- Bandages and dressing pads (gauze rolls, 1- and 2-inch widths)
- Blanket (for moving an injured dog or warming)
- Cotton balls
- Diarrhea medicine

- Dosing syringe
- Eyewash
- Emergency phone numbers (taped on the cover of the first aid kit)
- Hydrogen peroxide (3 percent solution)
- Ipecac syrup (to induce vomiting)
- Nylon stocking (to use as a muzzle)
- Petroleum jelly
- Pliers or tweezers (for removal of stings, barbs, and quills)
- Rectal thermometer
- Rubber gloves
- Rubbing alcohol
- Scissors (preferably with rounded tips)
- Tourniquet kit
- Syringe (without needle, for administering oral medications)
- Towel
- Tweezers

Ask your vet for any additional recommendations about what should be a part of your home first aid kit, because she may have a special device or product you may not have thought of. Check your first aid kit regularly to make sure that any liquids have not evaporated, medications have not expired, and materials that may have been used are replaced.

Make a list of emergency phone numbers to call if your dog needs help right away and put that list next to your phone. Include on the list your regular veterinarian's phone number, along with the number of the nearest 24-hour emergency veterinary hospital. The number of your local poison control center should be a part of this list as well. Another number you should have on hand is the one for the National Animal Poison Control Center. Call 800-548-2423 or 900-680-0000 for help.

Figuring Out When to Call the Vet

One bit of advice always applies in any case of your dog's illness or accident: If you aren't sure how to handle any health problem, do not hesitate to pick up the phone and consult your veterinarian. In most cases, your vet knows which questions to ask and will be able to determine whether she needs to see your dog.

If any of the following symptoms occur, get on the phone at once:

- Abscesses, lumps, or swellings
- Blood in the stool
- Chronic diarrhea
- Chronic vomiting
- Continued listlessness
- Dark or cloudy urine
- Deep red or white gums
- Difficult urination
- Discharge from eyes or ears
- Excessive thirst
- Gasping for breath
- Limping, trembling, or shaking
- Loss of appetite
- Loss of bowel or bladder control
- Loss or impairment of motor control
- Persistent coughing or sneezing
- Runny nose

Your veterinarian will be able to tell you what to watch for and whether you should bring the dog in. Sometimes these symptoms represent nothing more than minor ailments, but at other times they can mean your dog is at risk.

Almost all dogs ingest something at one time or another that can cause vomiting or diarrhea, but this does not necessarily mean your dog is seriously ill. Dogs often purge their digestive tracts by eating grass to induce vomiting. Puppies often vomit when they have eaten too much or too fast. Mother dogs who are attempting to wean their puppies will often eat and then regurgitate their food for the puppies to eat. These are all common and harmless behaviors. But if vomiting or diarrhea persist, don't hesitate to call your veterinarian.

Nervousness or fright can cause vomiting in some dogs and diarrhea in others. None of this is cause for alarm unless it occurs repeatedly. Occasional diarrhea is best treated by switching your dog's regular diet to thoroughly cooked rice with a very small amount of boiled chicken. Keep your dog on this diet until the condition improves, and then switch back to your dog's regular food over a period of several days.

When in doubt, *always* call your vet. Waiting to see if symptoms get worse can be a very dangerous practice.

Knowing What to Do When You Need to Do It

You aren't a veterinarian, and the information in the following sections is not meant to be a substitute for the knowledge and experience your own vet has spent a lifetime accumulating. There will be times, though, when know-how on your part can help prevent serious complications. There are also situations in which your intervention will keep your dog alive until you can get to your veterinary hospital.

These are basic life-saving techniques every dog owner should know. Always exercise extreme care in dealing with very ill or injured animals. Don't forget that where you and I use our hands in an automatic response to pain, a dog uses his mouth.

Canine health insurance is offered to help owners with the cost of the new and expensive advances in veterinary procedures. The policies range from excellent to practically useless. As the Romans used to say, "caveat emptor" (let the buyer beware). Read the policies carefully and find out if your veterinarian honors such policies.

Muzzling an injured dog

Of course your Rottie loves you beyond all reason and would never think of biting you (on purpose!), but any animal can snap in reaction to pain. So muzzling your dog is a smart idea when administering medical treatment. Get your Rottie accustomed to being muzzled now. You both could use the practice, and it will not make your dog think you are trying to kill him when and if the time comes that a muzzle is really needed.

I use a discarded women's nylon stocking for this purpose, because it is strong and will not cut or irritate the dog's muzzle. Snugly tie the center section of the stocking around the dog's muzzle. Do not tie it so tight that you make the dog uncomfortable, but make it firm enough so that the dog cannot use his jaws to bite. Tie the two ends again, under the jaw, then draw them back behind the dog's ears and tie them there. Check out Figure 13-1 for illustrated instructions.

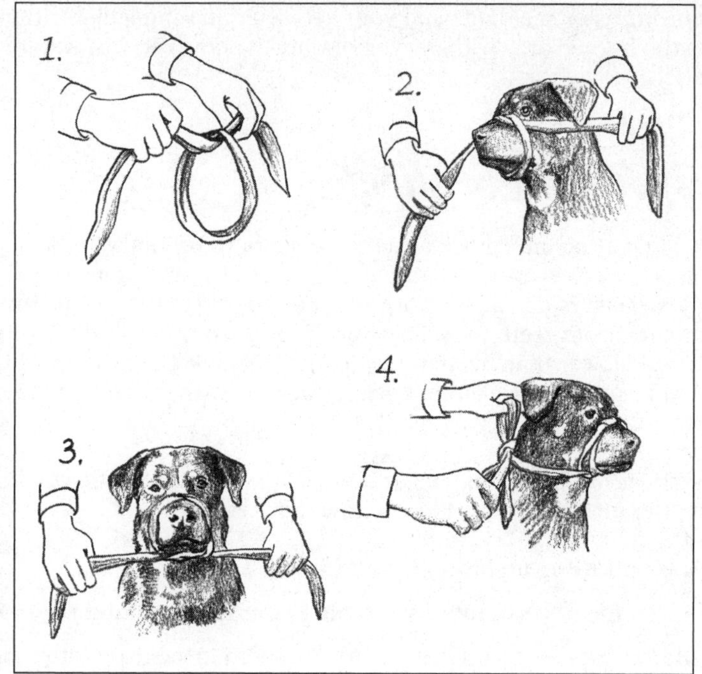

Figure 13-1: Muzzling an injured dog keeps both you and the dog safe and allows you to get him the help he needs.

Moving an injured dog

Moving an injured dog the size of an adult Rottweiler can be a challenge, especially if you are alone. So start by trying to get someone to assist you. Lay the injured dog on a large bath towel or blanket. Then open the car doors; you and your helper can then lift the blanket by the edges and transport the dog to the car.

If you are alone and cannot lift your dog by yourself, move the dog onto the blanket and drag the blanket along the ground until the dog is out of harm's way or until you reach your waiting vehicle. Hopefully, you will be able to attract someone's attention to assist you in lifting the dog into the car. If not, do your best to move the dog into the car with as little disturbance as possible.

Treating burns

Minor burns can be treated by applying cold water or a cold compress. Use gauze pads to apply an antibiotic cream. Cover the burn with a gauze pad that can be held in place with an elastic bandage.

Serious burns or scalding need your veterinarian's immediate attention. Cool down the burned area with very cool water or cover it with water-soaked towels.

Responding to shock

Your dog may go into shock as a result of a burn or injury. If the dog is unconscious, check to be sure his airway is open. Clear secretions from his mouth with your fingers and a piece of cloth. Pull the tip of the tongue forward beyond the front teeth to make it easier for the dog to breathe. Keep the dog's head lower than his body by placing a blanket beneath his hindquarters, and use another blanket to keep the dog warm on the way to the vet's office.

If the dog is not breathing, begin artificial respiration right away. To give a Rottweiler artificial respiration, follow these steps:

1. **Place the dog on his side with his head low.**
2. **Close the dog's mouth by clasping your hand around the muzzle.**

   Be careful that you do not cause the teeth to close over the tongue.
3. **Place your mouth over the dog's nose, and blow into the dog's nostrils.**

   The chest should expand.
4. **Release your mouth to let the dog exhale.**
5. **Repeat so the dog gets 20 breaths per minute (one breath every 3 seconds).**
6. **Continue until the dog breathes on his own, or as long as the heart beats.**

Never practice artificial respiration on a dog who is already breathing. You can hurt the dog by doing this.

Attending to bites and bleeding wounds

If your Rottie is bleeding, you must attend to the wounds at once. If the flow of blood is not stemmed, your dog could bleed to death. Apply pressure directly to the bleeding point with a cotton pad or compress soaked in cold water. If bleeding continues, you must seek your veterinarian's advice by phone before transporting the dog.

If your Rottweiler is bitten by another dog, get your dog to the vet immediately. Even the most minor bite wounds can get infected and should receive antibiotic treatment without delay.

Responding to poisoning

Always keep the telephone numbers of the local or national poison control center and the local 24-hour emergency veterinary hospital current and easily available. If you know or suspect what kind of poison your dog has ingested, give this information to the poison control center — they may be able to prescribe an immediate antidote. When you speak to your vet, pass on any information the poison control center gives you.

If you are not sure if your dog has been poisoned or do not know which poison he has ingested, be prepared to describe the symptoms you are observing to the poison control center or your veterinarian. Common symptoms of poisoning include paralysis, convulsions, tremors, diarrhea, vomiting, and stomach cramps, accompanied by howling, heavy breathing, and whimpering.

Many apparently harmless substances can be extremely toxic to dogs. Chocolate, coffee, and many decorative plants, including the ones in the following list, could easily take your dog's life. Read labels and discuss potentially harmful household items with your veterinarian.

- Airplane plant
- Azalea
- Caladium
- Cyclamen
- Diffenbachia
- Foxglove
- Holly
- Jerusalem cherry
- Mistletoe
- Mother-in-law's tongue
- Philodendron
- Poinsettia
- Rhododendron
- Spider plant
- Yew

Handling broken bones

If you suspect your dog has broken a bone, remaining calm is extremely important. If not handled correctly and immediately, broken bones can cause fatal injuries. Panic on your part can upset your Rottweiler even further and cause him to thrash about, making matters even worse.

If your Rottie is unable to stand or if one of his legs is held at an unnatural angle, or if he reacts painfully to being touched, try to obtain assistance in moving the dog. This is particularly important if the dog was injured on the road. Make every effort to support the dog's body as much as possible. If a blanket or coat is available, slip this under the dog and move the injured animal.

You can create a temporary cast by forming a tube around the injured Rottie's leg with a magazine or a substantial section of the newspaper. Then wrap the tube with gauze bandage or adhesive tape.

Do not attempt to determine how serious the injuries may be. Often there is internal bleeding and damage that you are unable to detect. Get your dog to the veterinarian's office immediately. If there is someone available to drive you and your dog to the veterinary hospital, all the better. That way you can devote your attention to keeping the dog as calm and immobile as possible.

Removing foreign objects and responding to the choking dog

All puppies and even adult dogs have a need to vacuum up every little object they find on the floor or out in the yard. It isn't the least bit unusual for all kinds of objects to get lodged or trapped across a dog's teeth, usually halfway back in the mouth or even where the two jaws hinge. If you see your Rottweiler pawing at his mouth or rubbing his jaws along the ground, check to see if there is something lodged in the dog's mouth.

If something is stuck there, grasp the object firmly between your fingers and push firmly toward the *back* of the mouth where the teeth are wider apart. This normally dislodges the object. *Be sure to have a firm grip on the object so the dog does not swallow it!* If the object does not come loose immediately, get your Rottweiler to the veterinarian at once.

If the object is not visible in the mouth, it may have already been swallowed. If it is still present in the dog's throat, the dog may be choking. Wedge something like a screwdriver handle or similar object in the dog's mouth to keep the jaws open. Pulling the tongue out should reveal any objects lodged at the back of the throat. If you see something, grasp the object firmly and pull it out (needlenose pliers may be of use here). If the dog seems to be having trouble breathing, the object could be lodged in the windpipe. Sharp blows to the ribcage can help make the dog expel air from the lungs and expel the object as well.

Whenever any small object is missing in the home and you suspect your Rottweiler has swallowed it, do not hesitate to consult your veterinarian. X-rays can normally reveal the object and save your dog's life.

Responding quickly to bloat

Gastric torsion or bloat can be fatal if it's not treated quickly. Drooling, pacing, panting, and abdominal swelling are all signs of bloat. Do not attempt any home remedy without your veterinarian's immediate advice. In this situation, minutes count. Get on the phone at once. If you get a busy signal, call the operator and tell her you have an emergency call to put through.

Dealing with heatstroke

The temperature of a dog in heatstroke soars above the normal 100 degrees to 102.5 degrees and breathing is very rapid but shallow. Cooling the dog down right away, either in a tub of cool water or with a garden hose, is critical. Place ice packs on the dog's abdomen, head, neck, and body. Cover the dog's body with water-cooled towels. Call your vet right away.

The easiest way for a Rottie to get heatstroke is for the dog to be left in a car in hot weather. Anyone who is guilty of this should not have a dog!

Responding to hypothermia

In northern climates, a Rottweiler may be in danger of *hypothermia,* in which the dog's body temperature drops below normal. Even a few degrees could spell danger. With hypothermia, a dog's heart rate increases significantly and shivering sets in. Immersing the dog in warm water or wrapping him in warmed blankets or heating pads will bring his temperature back up to normal.

If the dog's mouth and tongue begin to turn blue, this is a sign that circulation is closing down. Warm the dog as much as possible and call your vet!

Attending to stings and bites

Rottweilers are forever curious and will give crawling and flying insects more attention than is wise, which often results in potentially harmful stings and bites around the feet or, even worse, around the mouth and nose.

Visible stingers can be removed with a pair of tweezers. When the stingers are removed, apply a saline solution or a mild antiseptic to the site of the sting. If the swelling is severe, particularly inside the mouth, or if the dog appears to be in shock, consult your veterinarian at once.

Snake bites from poisonous snakes necessitate immediate action, because snake venom travels to the nerve centers very quickly. *Keep the dog quiet.* Venom spreads rapidly if the dog is active. Excitement, exercise, and struggling increase the rate of absorption. If possible, carry the dog. Do not wash the wound, because this increases venom absorption. Do not apply ice, because this does nothing to slow absorption and can damage tissue.

Because different snake venom requires different anti-venom, try to get a very good look at the snake and describe it to your vet in as much detail as you can.

Removing porcupine quills

If your Rottie's nose has come up against the porcupine's defense system and you are unable to get your dog to a veterinarian, do your best to muzzle the dog before attempting to do anything else. Then cut the quills back to 1 or 2 inches and remove them with pliers, pulling them out with a straight, outward motion. A vet's attention is important, even after you've removed the quills.

Responding to the dog who has come across a skunk

If your suburban or country Rottweiler fashions himself a hunter, he can easily come in contact with skunks. Your dog will probably not particularly enjoy his encounter with a skunk, but you will *hate* it! The odor is not exactly the latest scent to hit Fifth Avenue.

Even though a skunk encounter is not a *medical* emergency, it is a situation that requires immediate action. Many commercial products sold by pet emporiums will eliminate the odor quickly and thoroughly. If you are unable to obtain one of these products when you need it, tomato juice is a handy and effective remedy. Spray the dog thoroughly with the juice, allowing the juice to remain on the coat for about 20 minutes. Then rinse it off and, if possible, allow the dog to dry in the sun.

Odor is not the only problem resulting from an encounter with a skunk. Reports of rabid skunks are alarmingly high, and skunks are not the least bit timid about defending themselves. If skunks are present in your area, or if you plan to take your dog to an area where skunks may be found, be sure your Rottie's rabies shots are up to date.

Giving Your Rottie the Medicine He Needs

Follow-up care often requires giving your dog some sort of medicine. If you think it's hard to get your 60-pound child to take her medicine, wait until you try it with your 100-pound Rottweiler! A few tricks are handy to know, and I cover them in the following sections.

Medications and ointments

If possible, ask for medications and ointments in tubes with nozzle applicators. These special applicators help in aiming the medication exactly where you want it to go, so you can make sure it finds its way into the eye or down the ear canal. This type of tube also helps get ointments into punctures or cuts.

Muzzling your Rottweiler if you're applying an ointment that may sting or burn is always wise. The inside of a Rottweiler's ear is particularly sensitive, and applying medication there can sometimes be startling to the dog.

Pills

Although you can get a pill down your dog's throat in a number of different ways, I have found the fine art of deception works best. I disguise the pill in a bit of the dog's favorite food or snack. Although I certainly do not recommend sweets as a mainstay in your Rottie's diet, Mary Poppins's advice that "a spoonful of sugar helps the medicine go down" can be taken literally here: Rolling the pill up in a bit of soft candy or peanut butter can get the pill over the tongue and down the throat in a second and certainly beats trying to wrestle your friend into submission.

Cheese or tuna work equally well if they are on your Rottweiler's list of favorite treats. I usually give my dogs a pill-free sample of the snack first to whet their appetite; this ensures the second treat containing the pill will be wolfed down in a second.

Putting medication in a dog's food dish and assuming it has been eaten is not a good idea. Many dogs have built-in detectors that can find a pill the size of a pinhead. These same clever detectives also know just where to hide the pill so you won't find it for at least a week or two!

If trickery doesn't work, you may have to resort to manual insertion (see Figure 13-2). Do this gently and whisper sweet nothings to your dog while you do so. Simply open your dog's mouth and place the pill at the back of the tongue. Close the mouth and tilt the dog's head upward until the pill is swallowed. To encourage swallowing, gently stroke your Rottie's throat. When you see a gulp, you will know the pill is on its way to doing some good. Again, some dogs are very clever about this and have a way of swallowing without the pill going down. So watch your patient for a few minutes afterward to make sure the pill doesn't wind up on the floor.

Liquid medicines

Trying to put a spoonful of medicine into your Rottie's mouth can be a bigger chore than you may imagine, especially if the medicine has a taste your dog dislikes. A turkey baster (or a syringe minus the needle if there is only a small amount of liquid) can help you solve the problem easily.

Aim the medication into the side of the dog's mouth or under the tongue. Don't shoot any liquids directly into the throat, because the dog could easily choke. And if you are giving a large dose, administer it slowly and make sure you give your dog enough time to swallow.

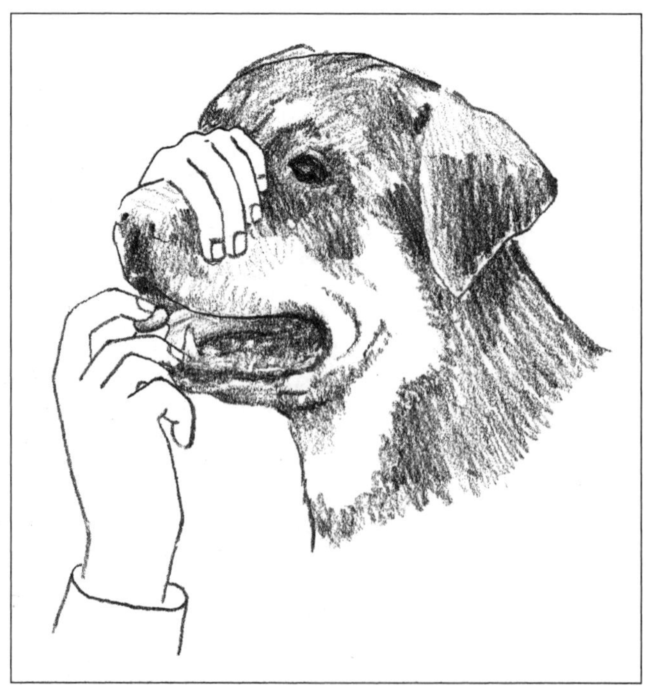

Figure 13-2: If your Rottie is too smart for tactics of trickery, you can help him swallow a pill by placing it at the back of his tongue, tilting his head up, and stroking his throat.

Chapter 14

Knowing What to Do When Your Dog Gets Sick

In This Chapter

- Helping your Rottweiler live with chronic conditions
- Looking seriously at alternative approaches to medicine, such as homeopathy, acupuncture, and massage

Responsible breeders do everything in their power to purge their breeding stock of genetic disorders. Concerned buyers seek out these breeders to avoid these problems. And yet, through no one's fault, dogs from the very best of bloodlines can develop chronic health problems.

When that happens, finding someone to blame is not the point. You must find a way to either correct the problem or learn how to deal with it so that the dog can enjoy a long life that is as pain-free as you can possibly make it. In this chapter, I show you how to do exactly that.

Living with Chronic Conditions

Many dogs with chronic health problems can still live long, happy lives. A little bit of work and a lot of patience on your part will go a long way toward making sure your dog has the best life possible. Sometimes it's just a matter of adjusting the dog's diet or exercise regime, or finding the dog a softer or warmer spot to be comfortable. Sometimes you'll be called upon to do some medical management as well, but this is often simple stuff: using a cream or ointment, or giving your dog her medication regularly.

Having a good relationship with a veterinarian you know and trust is always important. But that's especially true when you have a dog with a chronic health problem, like the ones covered in the following sections.

Hip dysplasia

As I discuss in Chapter 10, hip dysplasia is of such a complicated genetic nature that even the most discriminating breeder has to deal with it on occasion. The problem cannot be detected in very young puppies, but as a puppy grows, particularly during the accelerated growth period that takes place between three and nine months of age, the condition begins to manifest itself.

Symptoms can be so minor as to be undetectable without an x-ray examination. On the other hand, hip dysplasia can affect movement from a mild degree on through to crippling the dog. If any problem is suspected, the dog should be x-rayed and the results interpreted by a veterinarian who is trained in identifying this problem.

In some cases, symptoms seem more apparent while the dog is growing and may diminish upon maturity. The degree of dysplasia and how much it affects the dog will determine what must be done to keep the dog from unnecessary discomfort. Mild cases may only require rest, restricting high-intensity exercise, and weight control. Serious and debilitating cases may require surgery. Only your veterinarian can make this determination, but rest assured, there are ways of coping with hip dysplasia.

Bone disorders

Many large and giant breeds, including Rottweilers, are susceptible to bone and joint diseases that can be traced to nutritional, environmental, or hereditary factors. Still others are brought about by physical stress or accident.

Because these bone and joint disorders can stem from such a wide range of causes, limping or painful areas should be observed closely. If they persist for more than a day, confine your dog and consult your veterinarian at once. A veterinarian's diagnosis is critical, because treatment — ranging from prescribed medication to physical therapy — could prevent permanent damage.

Although we want our puppies to be suitably plump, they should never be fat. You are not being cruel by controlling the amount of food you give your Rottie. Excess poundage weighs heavily on the muscles and skeleton of your dog and can lead to serious chronic conditions.

Eye problems

Eye problems can affect any dog, and they range from the easily curable to the more serious. I cover the more common eye problems in the following sections.

Cataracts

Cataracts are a degenerative condition of the part of the eye directly behind the pupil. The pupil becomes either fully or partially opaque, giving it a milky white or blue color. The condition is not at all uncommon among older dogs, and it can also be caused by an injury to the eye. In advanced cases, cataracts can cause blindness.

Cataracts normally progress very slowly, so if they first appear in an elderly dog, the dog may live out his entire life with only a minimal loss of vision. A form called *juvenile cataracts* is hereditary, but it is seldom found in Rottweilers. When juvenile cataracts are present, the problem can be observed in puppies often immediately after the eyes first open. There is little that can be done for cataracts other than highly skilled and expensive surgery.

Conjunctivitis

Conjunctivitis occurs when airborne debris such as pollen and dust, and even smoke and bacteria, create an inflammation of the membrane that covers the inner surface of the eyelid — the *conjunctiva.* The condition causes inflammation and tearing, and, in advanced cases, a sensitivity to light. Conjunctivitis can normally be cleared up by removing the airborne cause of the infection and medicating the eye. One particular type called *follicular conjunctivitis* can be resistant to medication and may require surgery.

Entropion and ectropion

Entropion and *ectropion* are best dealt with by corrective eye surgery. Veterinarians experienced in dealing surgically with these problems can entirely eliminate the conditions.

Be aware that surgery to correct entropion and ectropion prohibits the dog from being shown in AKC conformation dog shows (the rules bar any dog who has had surgery that has altered the dog's appearance). However, these are painful eye conditions, and there should be no question that a humane owner would choose corrective surgery over a show career. The AKC's stipulation applies only to conformation show events and does not restrict the dog from competing in any AKC performance events.

Skin disorders

The causes of skin disorders can run the gamut, from hereditary allergies to infections, parasites and hormonal imbalances. Veterinarians have done extensive research into all of these areas, and although control can be involved and expensive, advances are made each year that can relieve your suffering Rottie from having a skin disorder that runs rampant with no hope of cure.

An ounce of prevention

What you've been doing with your Rottie thus far is exactly what will help stave off infectious diseases and parasitic conditions that drain your pal's immune system. Regular visits to your vet from the first days your pup becomes a member of your family can help preclude the possibility of minor ailments becoming major illnesses.

Vaccinations in their proper doses and frequency will protect your Rottie against canine distemper, parvovirus, hepatitis, leptospirosis, and rabies. Medications and other products can help your dog ward off kennel cough and parasitic complications.

Spaying and neutering also help keep your Rottweiler healthy. A spayed female has a much lower risk of tumors and vaginal infections, and no risk of uterine infection. Male dogs benefit by a reduction of prostate problems as they grow older.

Even though your Rottie appears to be fit as a fiddle, don't neglect those semiannual health checks by your vet. It may seem like an unnecessary expense when there doesn't appear to be any problem, but rest assured that preventing the onset of problems is incredibly less expensive than curing them.

Usually the first time you suspect a skin disorder is when your Rottweiler starts scratching. Within days the dog may be scratching so often and so severely that parts of her coat will be scratched away. Check the skin in the area that is being scratched and in the areas that are harder for the dog to reach as well. Any signs of skin eruptions, puffiness, or irritation should be cause for concern. Turn to the following sections for more information on specific skin disorders.

Aging changes the quality and texture of the geriatric dog's skin. The skin of an older dog is far more sensitive to attacks from fleas, lice, and ticks. Be even more judicious about keeping your older Rottie's coat clean and well brushed. Your veterinarian may recommend a change in diet or adding diet supplements to help keep the aging Rottie's skin and coat healthy.

Chronic flea dermatitis

Some dogs are extremely sensitive to fleas, and at the first flea bite the dog will begin scratching so furiously that the skin will be damaged, bringing about the onset of *chronic flea dermatitis.* If your Rottie has this extreme sensitivity, it is absolutely essential to be especially diligent about keeping your home and property free of fleas. Your veterinarian will be able to recommend the products best suited to the flea-sensitive Rottie.

Lice

Lice, covered in more detail in Chapter 12, can cause skin problems for Rottweilers. Actually, lice infestation is far easier to deal with than is commonly believed. Because lice only exist on your dog, you don't have the problem of reinfestation from insects in the environment unless there is actual contact with another host animal.

Mange

Demodectic mange is usually relatively mild, with minor hair loss only in isolated spots. There is a slightly rarer and more severe form of demodectic mange, but only your vet can determine the difference through microscopic examination of a skin scraping.

Sarcoptic mange is easier to recognize because it is extremely irritating to the dog and usually causes severe scratching. In some cases, the scratching is so extreme that bloody lesions appear. These lesions form scabs and large areas of the dog's coat are shed. In extreme cases of this nature the skin can be permanently damaged. Sarcoptic mange is highly contagious and can infect both humans and other dogs. Like demodectic mange, it can only be diagnosed by microscopic examination of a skin scraping. Medicated baths, orally administered medications, or injections may be prescribed.

Bloat

Most large dog breeds are susceptible to *gastric torsion* (commonly referred to as *bloat*), a condition in which the stomach twists and closes off, filling with gas. If not treated by a veterinarian right away, bloat is nearly always fatal. In many cases, surgery can save the dog's life. Surgeons can also reduce the possibility of the condition reoccurring by securing the stomach in a safe position.

Signs of bloat vary, but any rapid distension of the stomach should be looked on with suspicion. If your Rottie appears extremely restless and unable to settle down and get comfortable, or attempts to vomit and cannot, call your vet at once! Bloat gets very serious very quickly.

Dogs who have had bloat once are susceptible to it again. Although the causes of bloat are poorly understood, it is generally accepted that feeding a dog more frequent, smaller meals helps. Avoid feeding right after the dog has exercised, and avoid strenuous exercise after eating as well. And do not allow your dog to drink water after eating a large meal of dry food.

Considering Alternative Therapies for Your Ailing Rottie

It only makes sense that our interest in a natural way to maintain health through diet and exercise would be accompanied by a fascination with nature's own way to restore fading health with natural remedies. A realization that many of modern science's drugs are derivatives or chemical simulations of plants and herbs found in nature created interest in the fields known as *herbal* and *homeopathic* medicine.

Conventional medicine is not the only way to ward off chronic problems. Natural medication, as practiced by people all over the world for many centuries, and in many cases by our own grandparents, was found to have many of the healing properties and with fewer of the side effects of artificially created medications.

Several organizations are now devoted to holistic veterinary medicine. If you contact them, they will be happy to help you find a practitioner in your area.

- Academy of Veterinary Homeopathy, 305-652-1590
- American Holistic Veterinary Medical Association, 410-569-0795
- American Veterinary Chiropractic Association, 309-658-2920
- International Association for Veterinary Homeopathy, 770-516-5954
- International Veterinary Acupuncture Society, 303-682-1167

Herbal therapy

Herbs have been used effectively for centuries and are now the basis for what is popularly referred to as *herbal therapy.* Scientific research has revealed there is certainly no mystery involved in their effectiveness and, *when properly prescribed and administered,* there is no risk involved.

With herbal remedies, do not assume that what works for humans will also work for dogs. This is not always the case. Even though your Rottie may weigh as much as you do and may be suffering from the same or a similar malady as you are, the canine system operates much differently than that of a human.

If you have found herbal remedies effective for yourself and wish to consider this alternative approach for your dog, consult a trained and experienced herbalist. Be careful here, however. This person is probably not a veterinarian. More and more veterinarians are using herbal remedies in their practices, but if you cannot find a veterinarian who does, I strongly suggest that you consider working with an herbalist and a veterinarian in tandem. Most vets are willing to work along with an herbalist. If, on the other hand, your Rottie has been under treatment with a veterinarian who does not feel comfortable with the use of herbs, it will be up to you to decide what the next step should be.

At the very least, only work with an herbalist who has extensive experience treating dogs. An herbalist trained to treat humans will be able to suggest what works best for the problem at hand, but only a practitioner who knows dogs can ascertain whether the herb is safe for canines. Your Rottie may already be on a prescription medication, and a veterinarian's scientific knowledge can assist you in deciding if the herbal recommendation and the prescription medication are safe to be used together. If they're not, it is up to you to decide which approach to use.

More and more reports are being published of the successful use of herbal therapy in treating chronic skin conditions that were totally resistant to all other approaches. Owners whose dogs were suffering from rheumatoid arthritis report significant results through herbal therapy, as well. Holistic veterinarians are rapidly dispelling the belief that canine arthritis is only treatable and not curable. Changes in diet and the use of natural nutritional supplements are proving safe and effective and are allowing dogs to return to the natural flexibility and athleticism of their younger days. Recent studies have also revealed there are herbs that offer marked improvement in a dog's memory, in scent work, and in reducing stress. Herbs are also being credited with improving general health and well-being.

Because there are no regulatory controls placed on herbs and herbal remedies, strengths and required dosages vary from product to product. Be extremely careful in this respect, and never administer any herbal treatment that does not have the product's strength clearly printed on the container.

Herbal teas are excellent for dogs because they are quickly and easily assimilated into the system and they can be added to a dog's food or, in some cases, to a dog's drinking water.

Homeopathy

Although homeopathy may appear to be a product of New Age thought, it is far from being news. The basic principles of homeopathy can be traced to the ancient Greeks, but it is Dr. Samuel Hahnemann (1755–1843) who is credited as the father of the modern homeopathic approach to health care. Treatment in Hahnemann's day was absolutely barbaric, using cutting, hacking, bloodletting, and violent poisons, even when the patient was doing all he could to cling to life.

Medicine in those days dealt solely with the symptoms of a disease. Even if the patient survived the often savage treatment of those symptoms, the cause remained untreated and reoccurrence was almost assured. Hahnemann believed symptoms are simply a sign that something is not working properly within the person's system. He set about trying to find a more sensible approach to dealing with the symptoms by seeking the source of the problem. Hahnemann also felt that the best healer is the person's own system. It was his belief that if he could encourage the body to heal itself, permanent cures were possible.

To better understand how homeopathic medicine differs from conventional (or *allopathic*) medicine, a skin rash can be used as an example. The homeopathic approach would consider Bruno's skin rash as a manifestation of a much deeper problem. Thus, finding the internal cause and treating it would be the homeopathic practitioner's approach. Perhaps the underlying cause is an unhealthy immune system (allergies, for example). The homeopath would then seek to help the body heal its inappropriate immune response. The allopathic or conventional practitioner, on the other hand, would determine what kind of rash Bruno was suffering from and prescribe treatment to eliminate the rash. If the prescribed ointment or pill did not eliminate the rash, tests would be conducted to determine what external substances were causing the rash. Attempts would then be made to eliminate the substance from Bruno's environment. The two approaches do not necessarily conflict. In fact, they move closer together as the years pass and as modern medicine more fully understands the value of the holistic approach. There is little doubt that in the future both views will be able to modify and assist each other in bringing about what is referred to as *complementary* medicine, and thereby bring about even greater medical advances.

Be very careful in seeking out a homeopathic practitioner. Anyone can call himself a *homeopath,* but not anyone can call himself a *homeopathic veterinarian.* To call himself a veterinarian of any kind, the person must have a proper degree: Doctor of Veterinary Medicine (D.V.M.) or Veterinary Medical Doctor (V.M.D.).

Bodywork therapies

Acupuncture, acupressure, chiropractic therapy, and massage for dogs? Am I serious? You bet! These bodywork therapies are becoming increasingly popular with pet owners, and more and more practitioners are available across the country. In fact, therapies like acupuncture work especially well for chronic conditions (where conventional medicine works less well).

Acupuncture and acupressure

The ancient Chinese practices of *acupuncture* and *acupressure* are proven methods of relieving pain and eliminating chronic conditions by using very thin needles or the fingers to stimulate specific points of the body.

Modern science has found that needles or pressure applied help release corrective biochemicals within the system and also help realign the body's natural energy flows. When the channels are open, the corrective substances are able to reach the injured or ailing points.

Chiropractic therapy

An alternative approach to injury relief, chiropractic therapy has been effectively used on human patients for many years, but only recently has it been found to be an effective and valuable tool in veterinary medicine. In this therapy, the careful manipulation of joints, bones, and the surrounding tissues realigns the body and releases energy flows through the nerves and spinal cord to the affected areas.

Massage

Our dogs may take on a great deal of their owners' tension, creating stress that leads to abnormal tightness and makes a dog prone to injury. Massage therapy is aimed at relieving tension in your dog's muscles and soft tissues.

Part V
The Part of Tens

In this part . . .

This is the place to turn if you want a lot of information but only have a few minutes to spare. Here you can find reasons to get a Rottweiler as well as reasons *not* to get one. I give you quick tips for training your new friend, suggestions for traveling with your dog, and important questions to ask of kennels or pet sitters for those times when you can't take your Rottie with you.

Chapter 15

Ten Reasons to Own a Rottweiler

In This Chapter

- Knowing all the reasons Rottweilers make great pets
- Getting excited about owning a Rottweiler

Rottweilers make fantastic friends. If you're considering getting a Rottweiler, you'll find some great reasons to get one in this chapter. (Turn to Chapter 16 for some reasons *not* to get a Rottweiler.)

You Know What You're Getting

Any dog of any breed can be a loving companion. He doesn't even have to be purebred to fulfill that role. However, just how that dog loves you can be an entirely different matter! The little ball of fluff you bring home from the animal shelter can grow up to be the biggest, shaggiest, most hyperactive and neurotic beast who has ever crossed your threshold. Bringing a well bred Rottweiler into your life eliminates all this uncertainty and lack of predictability. For the last century, all efforts of those responsible for the breed's development have been aimed at producing a breed whose physical and mental characteristics live up to rigid standards of perfection. When you buy a Rottie puppy from an accredited and responsible breeder, you can rest assured he will grow up to look very much like his mother and father and his brothers and sisters. Long-time selective breeding assures you of this defining "look." But even more important, this concentrated focus has produced a dog who has a mental capacity that few other breeds have achieved. Buying a well bred and properly raised young Rottie is not buying a "pig in a poke," as the old saying goes. If you live up to your part of the relationship, you can bank on the quality of the dog you raise.

You Can Find Out Anything You Want to Know about the Breed

In some breeds, finding out where you can go to locate a representative specimen, or, just as important, where you can find out what you want to know about a breed's specific care and training, can be a time-consuming process of trial and error. The prospective buyer can only hope what he or she is being told is actually fact and not fiction. With Rottweilers, you will find an entirely different story. Many wonderful books have been written on the breed; these books equip owners to deal with the breed properly in order for their dogs to achieve their greatest potential. In addition, seminars are held throughout the country on Rottweiler training, breeding, and showing. The resources for educating yourself on the breed are vast.

Rottweilers Have Good Temperaments

Since the first standard of the Rottweiler breed was written over a century ago, demand for a sound and stable temperament has been considered the most important characteristic of the breed. Responsible breeders through the years have been aware that as high as 95 percent of the dogs they breed will spend their lives as family companions. Therefore, no effort is ever spared in maintaining the "calm, confident, and courageous" temperament of the Rottweiler — the hallmark of the breed. The Rottweiler has earned his reputation as the finest example of devotion and reliability, because the standards that must be achieved in this area have not been compromised among responsible breeders.

Rottweilers Are Highly Trainable

Careful selectivity has produced a dog who ranks at the top of the breeds with training capacity. The well bred Rottweiler's soundness of mind and body along with his strong nerves and strong desire to work did not come about by accident. Those who formed the breed had a highly restricted breeding program and only those dogs and bitches who were able to pass the tests devised to determine suitability for breeding were permitted to be used to perpetuate the breed. Conformation and freedom from inherited problems and diseases that may restrict a Rottie's ability to perform his assigned duties were assessed, as were character and responsiveness. This is the breed's unique foundation, and dedicated breeders have worked diligently to maintain these important characteristics. Purchasing a Rottweiler from a breeder who has kept the original concept of the breed foremost in mind ensures the buyer of a dog who is born with the capacity to learn almost anything the trainer is able to teach.

Rottweilers Are Easy to Care For

The grooming needs of the Rottweiler can best be described as accomplished with "a lick and a promise." No fancy clipping, no mats to untangle — all the Rottweiler needs is a thorough brushing once or twice a week to make sure the coat and skin are kept free of debris, and dog and owner can be on their way. With a regular inspection and maintenance program for teeth, nails, and inside the ears, the Rottweiler will lead a happy, healthy life. Nor does the breed require exotic diets or supplements. A high-quality, animal-protein-based dry dog food (and perhaps the addition of a suitable meat product), combined with sufficient exercise, will keep your Rottie fit as a fiddle.

Rottweilers Are Protective

Several years ago, we attended a Neighborhood Watch seminar conducted by the police department in Beverly Hills, California, in which the officer in charge described the many kinds of burglar alarms and how thieves had learned to disengage them. "The best alarm and safety device we know of," said the officer, "is a well bred Rottweiler. Most would-be thieves strike homes guarded by a Rottie off their 'easy mark' list almost immediately," he said. The officer went on to explain, "Thieves have no way of knowing if your Rottweiler is as friendly as a kitten or if he's a raging tyrant — and they aren't about to find out with so many other homes on the block that do not have the potential problem of dealing with a Rottweiler."

Rottweilers Do Good Work

You name it and the Rottweiler can probably do it. Rotties can be found anywhere from entertaining in circus acts to herding the farmer's cattle. Don't forget, the Rottweiler was originally a herding dog back in the early days of the breed, and few have lost that ability. The Rottie's protective instincts are legendary and the breed can achieve superstar status in the obedience ring with dazzling scores in every level from the basic Companion Dog (CD) level on through all the advanced degrees. The Rottie has proven outstanding in search and rescue work and just as adaptable to therapy dog work in hospitals, orphanages, and homes for the elderly.

Rottweilers Know How to Have Fun

If you're an athlete, your Rottweiler can be your best workout buddy. A Rottie can jog, hike, swim, or walk just as far as the average person, if not a lot farther, and love every minute of it. And don't underestimate the breed's ability to just have some good old fun! Rotties love flyball, agility competition, Frisbee, hide-and-seek, and just about any other game you may be able to think up for your four-footed friend.

Responsible Breeders Are Everywhere

Although there are always the unscrupulous who will exploit any breed of dog that becomes popular, with some care the prospective Rottie buyer will be able to find responsible breeders throughout the country who have dedicated their lives to breeding dogs that live up to the high expectations and standards set for the breed by the founding fathers. The prospective Rottweiler buyer has the advantage of an entire network of information sources that can lead to the purchase of a stable and healthy member of the breed. The American Rottweiler Club (ARC) can provide interested parties with the names and contact information of individuals and local organizations that can be used as resources in learning about and purchasing a Rottweiler. (Turn to Appendix B for contact information for the ARC.)

Rottweilers Give a Lifetime of Friendship

Of all the countless breeds of dogs available to the dog lover, there are probably none that can offer more love and devotion than the well bred and well cared for Rottweiler. As far as a Rottie is concerned, there is nothing more important than his human family and the home in which they live. Strangers are tolerated if so instructed by the Rottie's owner, and the well mannered Rottie will endure the attention of strangers. The Rottie has just one purpose in mind, and that is giving you the best days of his life.

Chapter 16

Ten Reasons *Not* to Own a Rottweiler

In This Chapter

- Taking a look at some common misconceptions about dog ownership
- Being honest with yourself about what you are (and are not) willing to give

Rottweilers are wonderful dogs, but they're certainly aren't for everyone. In this chapter, I give you some things to consider if you're thinking about getting a Rottweiler. If you read this chapter and remain convinced that a Rottweiler is the dog for you, you're well on your way to being your dog's best friend.

The Neighbor Down the Street Is Selling Rottweilers for Next to Nothing

Don't even think about buying a Rottweiler if you aren't going to take the time and make the effort to locate a responsible and experienced breeder to purchase your puppy from. Buying a Rottie puppy from a pet shop or from the people down the block who decided their dog should have a litter just for the fun of it can prove to be extremely costly — and, in some cases, it can even create dangerous situations for dog and humans alike. Why? All dogs of any breed can carry undesirable recessive traits in their genetic makeup that they may not exhibit themselves. However, bred to another dog carrying that recessive trait, a resulting puppy may well manifest the undesirable trait, and that trait may not be detectable in puppyhood. The problem may be a genetic disorder causing physical impairment or it may be an overly aggressive temperament, neither of which are situations that you would want to be faced with. Inexperienced breeders or pet shops that purchase dogs from faraway sources are usually totally unaware of genetic disorders or temperament problems in the puppies' backgrounds. This lack of knowledge is definitely *not* what you want as part of the package when you bring a Rottie into your home.

You Think Having a Dog to Pet Every Once in a While Would Be Fun

Do you resent giving up your footloose and fancy-free lifestyle? Think about Rottie ownership carefully! Dogs aren't a once-in-a-while job.

Prior to your arrival, your puppy's life was just a bowl of cherries, or in this case, a whelping box full of Rotties. Day in and day out, there was nothing for the pup to do but dine at mama Rottweiler's milk bar and play with her brothers and sisters. Now, you come along and all those happy days are over — no mama, no brothers and sisters, and none of those smells the pup has known since birth. Even the bravest member of the Rottie litter will be bewildered when all that ends and she's thrown into an entirely new environment, one where everything is strange and there is no one around to turn to for a confidence booster. From that moment on, you are your puppy's mom, brother and sister, psychologist, nutritionist, and confidant. All that, and disciplinarian, too.

You Want to Feel Needed

Some people get pets because they want to feel needed. They like the thought of someone depending upon them. But these people are usually the same ones who don't stop to think what's involved with being responsible for a living being other than themselves. As the owner of a dog, you have to fulfill every single one of your puppy's needs 24 hours a day, 7 days a week. A puppy cannot open the refrigerator when she's hungry, nor can she turn on the tap when she wants a drink of water. You have to be there to open the door when she needs to go out and when she wants to come back in. A few of your dog's needs end in puppyhood, but by and large, you will be her significant other and sole provider for the rest of her life. If you live alone with your Rottie pup, your days of leaving home "for an hour or two" and having that stretch into an overnighter are over. You now have a very dependent baby waiting for you. Granted, she's a canine baby, but a baby nevertheless, and you are the responsible provider. Owning and caring for a dog is similar to raising a child. But one important difference is that, with a child, you arrive at the point where you can wipe your hands and say, "Well, I've done a good job and now you are on your own." That day never comes with a dog. As smart as the Rottweiler is, there are many things she will not be physically capable of doing for herself, and even those things that she is capable of accomplishing must be taught by — you guessed it — *you!* Think of it this way: Your Rottie puppy arrives at your home with an absolutely clean slate, and anything you want written on it will have to be put there by you. If this seems like a bit too much trouble to go to just to feel important, it is.

Getting a Rottweiler isn't all about what the dog gives to you; it's also about what you give to the dog.

You're Not Prepared to Be the Leader of the Pack

Don't consider being a Rottweiler owner unless you are prepared to be the leader of the pack. No, you won't have to dress in leather and buy a motorcycle in order to properly supervise your Rottie, but you are definitely going to have to be the leader. You have to be in charge — and there are no *ifs, ands,* or *buts* about that fact. You can love your Rottie and be fair and kind, but you must never forget that a Rottweiler needs direction and guidance and a leader who can provide both. If she doesn't have that kind of leader, the Rottweiler will assume that role herself and start making decisions on her own. Considering the fact that a Rottie has a century-old history of fearlessness and determination behind her, this could quickly prove to be a very real — and perhaps dangerous — problem.

You Lack Physical Strength

Don't even *think* about owning a Rottie unless you're strong enough to handle one. The Rottweiler is not a breed for the proverbial 90-pound weakling, I assure you. Some males of the breed approach 100 pounds, and their female counterparts aren't far behind. And we're not talking about 100 shy and retiring pounds; this is all muscle and bone. An untrained and unresponsive Rottie can flatten the average man or woman without batting an eye. Think about that oversexed and uncontrollable male spotting the dog of his dreams on the opposite side of four lanes of rush-hour traffic. You won't think long if you haven't trained your Rottie to respond without hesitation or if you aren't physically able to restrain your dog under all circumstances. All this may sound like a joke, but I could not possibly be more serious in advising you to assess your own physical capabilities if you plan to own a Rottweiler.

You Tend to Procrastinate

If you live life by a motto that dictates, "Never do today what you can put off until tomorrow," the Rottweiler is not the breed for you. Correcting those cute little puppy growls and play attacks "later," teaching her the basic obedience commands next summer "when you have more time," or building a fence around the backyard "when he starts thinking about girls," is just not going to cut it with a Rottweiler. Stalling on things that need to be done today — those potential problem areas — could easily prove to be too late.

Even if you're not entirely too late, you may need at least two or three times the time and effort to correct a problem after it's developed than you would have needed to train your Rottie the right way in the first place. Teaching your Rottie the rules of life in the beginning will *always* take far less time than asking her to unlearn the bad habit so that you can set about teaching the good one. If procrastination is your middle name, buy a goldfish.

Your Living Space Is Restricted

A Rottie is not for you if she isn't going to fit into the environment in which you live. A growing Rottweiler needs space in which to stretch those rapidly developing muscles — to stretch out full tilt at a gallop. Obviously, a small apartment is not going to allow that possibility, so you will have to be prepared to get out with your dog two or three times a day a do some *vigorous* exercise. And do understand that exercise will not be confined to the days when the weather is just right; it means every day and not just for 5 minutes at a time.

Trying to housebreak a Rottie pup when you're living on the 22nd floor of an apartment building may be more than you bargained for as well. This is not to say your problems are over if you decide to move into a private dwelling. On the contrary, if you do not have a securely fenced yard or a dog run that permits your Rottie to be outdoors on her own, you have exactly the same situation to contend with that you had when you were an apartment dweller. The Rottweiler, whether puppy or adult, needs room to stretch out and move in. You have to provide that space — and it must be a space that is safe for both man and dog.

You're Not Sure How You're Going to Pay Your Next Credit Card Bill

Don't think about buying a Rottweiler if you can't afford to own one. First of all, people who breed top-quality Rottweilers and who guarantee health and temperament do not have "bargain sales." Breeding good dogs is extremely costly and breeders seldom come anywhere near making a profit even when selling their dogs at a sensible price. And it is highly unlikely that any of these breeders would ever have to offer puppies at a discounted price in the first place. They probably have a waiting list for their puppies; most good breeders do. Quite frankly, when you see Rottweiler puppies advertised at "reduced prices," it usually means someone is trying to unload his puppies because he isn't able to care for them properly — a dangerous place for your puppy to have begun her life.

And don't think costs end with the purchase of a dog. Ordinary health care and inoculations all require trips to the vet. Spaying, neutering, licensing, accidents, toys, boarding while you're away — none of these things are free. If you resent or are reluctant to spend money on the health and upkeep of your Rottie, you should not own one.

Patience Is Not Your Virtue

Just because the Rottweiler is known to be a smart breed doesn't mean she will arrive at your home with her Ph.D. diploma tucked under her arm. Your Rottie will have her instinctive behaviors all neatly in place, but even a lot of those will have to be channeled in directions other than those she would chose for herself. Just because the Rottie is a smart breed doesn't mean yours (or any of them for that matter) will jump to respond. Your directions may be questioned.

Rotties are very intelligent dogs, so don't expect your Rottie to respond blindly and stupidly to your commands. It may take any number of serious discussions and many, many repetitions before your Rottie decides she is ready to respond right away. And then there are those days when she may decide to see if you really meant all those training sessions or if they were just for your own amusement. Rottweilers are smart, but they aren't pushovers. They need a consistent, firm, and, above all, *patient* hand.

You're a Loner

A Rottie can't survive and be well adjusted without a person to be devoted to and without someone who can give them a great deal of love in return. All dogs need the care and companionship of their humans, and Rotties especially so. They're people dogs, and they always have been, which is what brings a Rottie to the breed's full potential. Don't waste a perfectly wonderful companion by bringing a dog like this into a sterile environment that lacks the very essence of a Rottie's needs — to love and protect the home and hearth of her very own.

Chapter 17

Ten Tips for Training Your Rottweiler

In This Chapter

- Being a good trainer for your Rottweiler
- Knowing what to train your dog to do

Training is an important part of owning a dog, no matter what the breed. But when you own a Rottweiler, training is paramount. To help you get a jump start on training — or to give you a quick refresher course if you've already starting working with your dog — this chapter points out ten important steps to training your Rottie.

Remember That Training Is Something Your Rottie Needs

Be aware that Rottweilers have been selectively bred for many generations to be receptive to training. Denying your dog training leaves him unfulfilled and victim to making random decisions based on needs that are entirely different, perhaps in opposition, to those of the humans around him.

Teach Your Rottie Your Rules

Even the smartest, most perfectly trained Rottweiler in the world entering your home for the first time has no idea what your household rules may be. Consider the position of the new puppy or even young dog who has had little or no training at all. The fact that you believe a dog's relieving himself in the home or chewing on furniture are unacceptable means little to an untrained dog. Your ideas about right and wrong are totally foreign to the beginning house dog. You need to introduce all these lessons — the behaviors that are important to you and the manners that will make your dog a good canine citizen — to your Rottie.

Give Positive Reinforcement

A Rottweiler does not comprehend violent treatment and violence is completely unnecessary with this highly trainable breed. A pleasant but firm approach to new lessons with a reward for compliance are what work best in training your Rottie. He must understand that you mean business when a command is given and that it not only pleases you for him to respond correctly but your pleasure will be shared with him in the way of lavish praise or even with a food treat.

Be Consistent

Always be consistent with your Rottie in regard to both what is permissible and what is not. Allowing him to sleep on the sofa one day and then not the next is very confusing for a dog. The fact that you've just vacuumed and want to keep that sofa hairless for company means absolutely nothing to your dog. "Sometimes" is an extremely difficult concept for any dog, even the brilliant Rottie, to master.

Dogs respond to a command *word* and not the *meaning* of the word. Your Rottie may readily respond to the command "sit" but would have absolutely no idea what you were talking about if you were to tell him to "be seated." So, a word like *down* has to mean either "get down off the sofa" or "lie down," but it can't mean both. Your dog will have no idea what to do if you use the word interchangeably.

Use the "down" command when you want your Rottie to lie down and "off" when you want him to get off the sofa.

Start Training Right Away

The minute your Rottie puppy enters your home, his training begins. Do not let your Rottweiler do anything today that you do not want him to do tomorrow or at any time in the future. A Rottie puppy's natural instinct is to bite and growl when playing. Biting and growling is what your pup did when he was roughhousing with his brothers and sisters in the nest. But this behavior is not something you can permit when he is dealing with humans. It may be cute when an 8-week-old puppy growls and grabs at your hand, but it is not at all cute when an adult dog tries the same thing.

Rotties have an inherent desire to guard and protect, and you must never allow that urge to be directed at you. If a Rottie puppy learns that aggressive behavior pays off, you will have difficulty in convincing him that it does not.

"No!" Means "No!"

No Rottie puppy is too young to understand the meaning of the word *no.* But he will only understand the word if it *always* means no. Don't give the "no" command (or any command for that matter) unless you are prepared to follow up on it. Understand that your puppy would rather chew on the lamp cord than respond to your command for him to stop. Your job, however, is to make the puppy understand that he may not chew on the cord. Your only task is to make sure your young Rottie quickly learns that "no" means "cease and desist immediately."

Keep Your Lessons Short and Sweet

Always make initial lessons quick and fun. You can tell if your Rottie is looking forward to his training time by his reaction to the rattle of his training collar. If he greets the appearance of his training color with enthusiasm, you will know that your approach is a good one. A dejected, hangdog look says just the opposite. And no matter how the training session goes, *always* end it on a happy note with a lot of praise and your Rottie's favorite treat.

Curb Certain Instinctive Behaviors

All of your Rottie's behavioral traits have been passed down generation after generation, tracing all the way back to the time when dogs were still in the wolf stage of their development. Through the ages, however, man has intervened and redirected some of these instinctive behaviors and all but eliminated others. Some of those instinctive behaviors retained may be appropriate in one area but not in another.

The Rottweiler still retains his ability and desire to herd. This is all well and good out on the range or on a cattle ranch, but it's completely unacceptable when your Rottie spies something moving through the bushes and wants to bring it down or even control it. That moving object could be a child or someone else's small cat or dog. The chase instinct still lives on in your Rottweiler, but you must be very careful to ensure that it remains curbed.

Be in the Right Frame of Mind for Training

Never attempt to train your Rottweiler if you feel upset or irritable. Trust me, your dog will sense your frustration and the session will never be what it could be if you were in a better frame of mind. Taking a couple of hours to put yourself in the proper mood or, in extreme cases, postponing training until the following day, is better than trying to train your dog when you're just not in the mood to do so.

Laziness is not a valid excuse for neglecting training.

Do the Minimum in Basic Training

There is a certain basic minimum for every mature Rottweiler in the training department. The following checklist contains the basics that not only make your Rottie a good canine citizen but also provide the framework for everything else you may want to teach him. Your Rottie should do the following:

- Come immediately when called.
- Walk on a leash quietly at your side, even on a crowded street.
- Allow any stranger to pet him when you give the okay.
- Sit and lie down on command and remain in position until you say otherwise.
- Be tolerant of other dogs.
- Show no unprovoked aggressiveness toward any person.

Chapter 18

Ten Tips for Traveling with (Or without) Your Dog

In This Chapter

- Traveling by car or plane with your Rottweiler
- Finding accomodations and travel destinations that you and your dog can both enjoy
- Leaving your Rottweiler in good hands when she can't come with you

To be or not to be . . . alone, that is. Long road trips, back and forth to the office, to and from vacations — all those trips can be extremely boring after a while, and you can only listen to the top 40 hits from the 1980s just so many times before you start thinking about pulling the stereo system out by its roots!

Why not take your Rottweiler along with you for company? She's grown up, completely house-trained, car savvy, and loves to be with you regardless of where you're going. Another thing you can rely on is that she will never, ever ask, "Are we there yet?" In fact, she won't ask you anything. No backseat drivers, no needing to stop a million times to look at this, that, and the other thing. Dogs somehow manage to be great company without saying a word. Nor do they complain if you choose to talk — or even sing! — your head off.

But it's not simply a question of whether your pal should hop in the back seat. Taking your dog along when you shop, go out of town on a business trip, or take a vacation involves some forethought, and the longer you are gone the more considerable the preparation. If there's an airplane flight involved in your plan, there are a number of legal requirements that must be met as well.

Even if you decide the answer must be no this time and your precious pooch will have to stay behind, there are questions to be answered if there isn't someone at home to take over. Where will your buddy stay while you are gone? Will she shrivel up and wither away if she's sent to a boarding kennel? Are there places where you can check out a boarding kennel's reputation?

Perhaps a pet sitter is a better answer. Do you know of anyone who is willing to come in several times a day to check on your Rottie, or to move in for the week you're gone? Where do you find that kind of person?

Sooner or later, every dog owner I've known, married or single, family person or not, has had to answer all these questions. And because you didn't buy this guide just to occupy space on your bookshelf, in this chapter I do everything I can to point you in the right direction for the ten most important issues surrounding traveling with (or without) your dog.

Get the Right Car for Your Rottweiler

If you're like most of us, shopping for a new car that will best suit your dog probably isn't realistic. But if you have a new Rottweiler and it's also time to shop for a new car, keep in mind a few important issues. Although you may look like you've just driven off the cover of *GQ* with your Rottie pup sitting in the passenger seat of your Ferrari, it won't work for very long. Large Rottweilers from little Rottie pups grow, and the two of you will soon be wedging yourselves into a space that wasn't made to accommodate all that mass.

Plus, on a warm day, your full-grown Rottie will use up the available oxygen in a closed sports car at a rate that may surprise you. And who in this day and age is going to leave their nifty little sports car sitting there open to the world? Your dog will guard the car with her life, you think. Sure she will! Unless someone is clever enough to waltz a handsome male dog by the car or a cat goes streaking by. And who's to prevent that nasty car thief from streaking down the highway with your prized possession? There you will be — sans car, sans Rottweiler.

Think about space and what you will be transporting when you buy your next car. Consider the safety of both your dog and your valuables. The larger the car, the easier it will be to safely accommodate your pal. SUVs and minivans are extremely popular and are actually far more useful to you and your Rottie than a passenger car.

Who would have thought you would one day be buying a car for your Rottweiler? But haven't I always said that there was no such thing as a cheap Rottweiler? See what I mean?

Think about the Weather Before You Leave

If you're planning stops in hot weather, will your Rottweiler be able to accompany you indoors or to a shaded spot? When you stop, the car's air-conditioning is turned off, and on a sunny day the temperature inside the car can soar to a dangerous level in minutes. You may find that those gourmet restaurants you are accustomed to dining in along the way will have to be relinquished for drive-thrus so you can keep the air-conditioning going or sit outside in the grass with your dog.

Although most people don't think of temperatures in the 80s as unbearable, on a sunny day the temperature inside a car, even one with the windows partially rolled down, can soar up to over 100 degrees in just a few minutes. No dog is able to sustain these temperatures without suffering permanent brain damage or death. Do not take chances with your dog in a car on warm days!

Leaving windows open really doesn't help much on a hot day, either. The sun shining through the front and rear windows sends temperatures up at an alarming rate, and the metal of the vehicle seems to trap the heat inside. When it's just 80 degrees outside, it can reach 120 degrees in 20 minutes inside your car — even with the windows partially rolled down. The safest rule on a hot day is never to leave your pet in a vehicle unless the vehicle can be parked in a completely shaded area and you can leave the windows rolled down all the way.

If you do leave the windows down, you must be able to keep the vehicle in view at all times. Regardless of how well trained your Rottweiler is, if she gets too hot inside the car, good sense is going to make the dog try to escape. My advice: If it's very hot and you know you will have to make prolonged stops and are not sure of available shade, leave your dog at home in a cool room!

Buckle Up for Safety

All the reasons we are given for buckling up with seat belts when we drive apply to our pets as well. Canine seat belts are now available that can be adapted to just about any make of car and size of dog. They provide the safety and restraint that can ensure both you and your pet have a comfortable and safe trip.

Although having your Rottweiler loose right next to you so she can get the full impact of your words of wisdom may be nice, she can be injured or killed by being thrown against the windshield in a sudden stop or collision. Then, too, if she were to spot the dog of her dreams through the driver's-side window, she could leap onto your lap, interfering with your sight or controls and possibly causing an accident.

A dog is safest confined to the rear seat of a passenger car or behind a barrier in a van. Whether with seat belts or in a crate, all dogs should be restrained for safety's sake. Even though riding in a solid crate may rob your dog of the opportunity to see all the sights as you travel, that's better than being hurled out of the back seat or along the full length of a van. This problem can be solved by purchasing one of the wire collapsible crates that can be firmly secured in the back of your wagon or van.

A travel crate can give you a little peace of mind if you do have an accident. Aside from the physical protection it affords your dog, imagine being in a wreck where your car is damaged badly enough that the doors pop open. Your Rottie could jump out to go find help for you (or simply out of fear), run across a busy highway, and never be seen again. If you know your dog is in a crate, you know this won't happen.

Another reason for a travel crate exists if the hosts at your destination also have a dog. Most dogs are not particularly happy about another pooch invading their home territory, and some can be downright hostile about it. Thinking they'll work it out between themselves may be just fine for a couple of Chihuahuas, but when you are talking about dogs the size of a Rottweiler, working it out is not really an option.

When you hit country roads, you will probably see ranch and farm dogs in the back of pick-up trucks. Nothing could be more dangerous! A sudden stop could send the dog catapulting through the air, and if the dog is tethered in the truck, the sudden stop could easily break the dog's neck.

Remember Your Rottweiler's ID and Medication

Most states throughout the country, as well as the governments of Canada and Mexico, require up-to-date vaccination against rabies. Be sure your rabies inoculations are current and that your Rottweiler is wearing the tag your veterinarian issues when you have that taken care of. Crossing the border to Canada and Mexico will also require health certificates validated by your veterinarian — yearly for some, every three years for others.

Your vet will also be able to advise you of any special precautions you may have to take, depending upon the area you are traveling to. Certain sections of the United States present an increased risk of tick-borne diseases such as Lyme disease, and heartworm, which is spread by mosquitoes.

Bring Along Your Travel Necessities

If you plan ahead, even the longest trip with your Rottweiler can be a totally pleasant experience. Think about what you need when you and your dog are at home, and that will help create your list for what you need when you're on the road.

Professional dog show handlers are on the road a good part of every week, and experience has taught them to carry everything their dogs may need both for their daily routine and in case of an emergency. Your traveling companion probably has no need for all the cosmetic equipment that a show dog requires, but there are a number of doggie items that you should definitely stow in your Rottie's steamer trunk:

- **Enough food for the length of the trip, plus a bit more.** Changing food suddenly can cause diarrhea.
- **Regular drinking water in 1-gallon plastic containers.** Changing water suddenly can cause stomach upset.
- **Food and water dishes.**
- **Leash and collar, with clearly marked ID and rabies tags.**
- **First aid kit.** See Chapter 13 for information on what you need to include in it.
- **Current medications, if any, including flea and tick controls and heartworm preventives.**
- **Solid or collapsible crate.**
- **List of parks and rest stops along the way that welcome dogs.**
- **Pooper-scooper and plastic bags for disposal.**
- **Paper and terrycloth towels for cleanup and drying.**
- **Appropriate bedding for the season of the year.**
- **Favorite toys.**
- **Brush and comb.**
- **Grooming tools, including nail clippers and toothbrush.**

Plan a Vacation for the Whole Family to Enjoy

There is no doubt about it: Your Rottweiler is just as much a part of the family as you and the kids. So why shouldn't she share in the fun you will be having on that vacation you have planned? You've done your job well, and she is well trained and well socialized. So reap some of the rewards of all your effort and have this well-behaved family member join you.

Granted, you may not find New York City or the Champs Elysées an entirely appropriate place for your Rottie, but there are all kinds of vacation plans that can easily accommodate you and your pal. Take a tip from the singles crowd and think of your Rottweiler as an icebreaker. You will be amazed at how many people find it much easier to strike up a conversation with you when they can start with comments on your pooch. (I know several young men who borrow friend's dogs to take to the dog park, with nothing but socialization in mind!)

On the other hand, those with less than honorable intentions are inclined to shy away from a child or family being watched over by a Rottweiler. You can always feel confident that you and yours are relatively safe with your Rottie standing by.

Taking a vacation with your dog is simply a matter of planning and knowing which destinations offer the most pleasure and convenience for all of you. Lakeside cottages and mountain cabins provide a degree of privacy yet plenty of opportunity for family fun and social events in nearby towns. Look into beach houses, as well, because Rotties love to swim. A good friend of ours spends a couple of weeks each year on a houseboat with wife, daughter, and the family pooch. A hiking/camping trip provides lots of fun and adventure, to say nothing of the excellent exercise in the great outdoors.

Find Dog-Friendly Lodgings

Not all hotels and motels accept dogs. Even though you may not be the type of person who likes to have his travel plans so structured that every stop is reserved ahead of time, do give this some serious thought. Driving until you are totally exhausted and then starting a search for dog-friendly accommodations will not be a very attractive option.

You'll find your traveling more relaxed when you know for sure that you have accommodations waiting at a specific location. Speak directly to the hotel or motel beforehand. Even though some establishments advertise the fact that they accept dogs, this may mean only small dogs or that all dogs must be confined to their travel crates.

The Automobile Club of America publishes catalogs listing accommodations throughout the nation, and most indicate whether they accept dogs. Travel agents are also able to make reserved bookings and will be able to find accommodations that will accept your Rottie. Or check out the series of dog-friendly travel guides written by Dawn and Robert Habgood called *On the Road Again with Man's Best Friend.*

If you will be spending much time in a specific city or town, the local Chamber of Commerce can be very helpful as well. Chambers of Commerce can usually provide a list of hotels and motels that accept dogs and may also be able to provide a list of local veterinarians. Vet's offices are usually aware of which local accommodations will accept dogs, and having quick reference to a veterinarian isn't a bad idea either.

Fly Well with Your Rottweiler

If your plans include traveling by air, the whole picture becomes a bit more complicated. Not impossible mind you, but certainly not as easy as having your Rottie safely secured in the back of your SUV. The fact that your Rottweilers won't fit under the seat in front of you on an airplane means you don't have the option of carrying her on board.

If your Rottie is going to travel with you by air, the dog must fly as excess baggage in the cargo hold of the plane at a cost of about $50 or more each way. Air travel for dogs is no longer unusual — hundreds of dogs accompany their owners back and forth across the country each day. The Department of Agriculture estimates that approximately 600,000 animals travel by air every year. A good percentage of them are dogs and cats. The Air Transport Association reports that 99 percent of all animals shipped in the U.S. reach their destination without incident. Of course, that remaining 1 percent includes everything from minor complaints to the death of the animal.

You *can* have your Rottie travel on the same plane as you are on with more than reasonable expectations that the two of you will reach your destination safely. However, because dogs travel in the cargo area of the plane, keep in mind that even though this area is pressurized, there are no air-conditioning or heat controls. Because of this, federal regulations require that no animal be shipped by air if the ground temperature at either end of the flight is above 85 degrees or below 45 degrees.

Obviously, air travel for pets is not entirely risk-free. Whenever travel by air is necessary, keep in mind the following safety measures that will help increase your dog's odds of a safe arrival:

- **Check out the airlines.** Call the airlines you prefer and ask about their policies regarding shipping dogs. Select the airline that offers the greatest safety assurances.
- **Make sure you understand the rules.** Airlines have all kinds of rules about what kind of crate they'll accept, what identification needs to be on it, where and when you drop off and pick up your dog, and everything else related to your trip. And each airline has different rules. Make sure you understand exactly what you must do, well in advance of your trip.
- **Make an advance reservation.** Most airlines will only accept a limited number of dogs per flight. Your travel agent is able to do this for you when making your own reservation. However, reconfirm (and then reconfirm again) before flight time.
- **Schedule a direct, nonstop flight.** Making connections, changing planes, and having long stopovers are just some of the ways you increase the risk of loss and fatalities. Overnight and very early morning flights are least crowded and offer better temperatures for your dog.
- **Talk to your vet.** Many states require a health certificate signed by a veterinarian, and nearly all airlines will require one whether your destination does or not. Discuss your travel plans with your vet. He or she may advise against shipping geriatric dogs, pregnant females, and any puppy less than 8 weeks old. Trust me, take this advice! Should your vet give you the okay, discuss whether you should tranquilize your dog before shipping. When it comes to sedatives, my advice is always this: Don't, if you don't have to.
- **Take a last-minute potty break.** Exercise your Rottweiler at the very last minute to make sure she has relieved herself.
- **Use an airline-approved shipping crate.** The crate you ship your dog in must be airline-approved or purchased directly from the airline. It must be large enough for your dog to stand up and turn around in. This does not mean the crate should be the size of the Taj Mahal. Just enough room protects your dog from being jostled about.
- **Prepare the crate well.** Federal law requires absorbent bedding on the bottom of the crate. You must also supply food and water in dishes that are attached to the inside of the crate's wire door. Fill one of the water bowls from the shipping crate and put it in your freezer the night before you ship your Rottie. Just before you leave home, take out the frozen bowl and place it in the crate. The ice will melt gradually and provide water for your Rottie for a longer period of time and with less spillage. Tape a small bag of food to the top of the crate along with food and water instructions for the next 24 hours, in case of delays. You are not allowed to put a lock on the crate door. However, you can offer double security with bungee cords or tape.

- **Mark the crate.** You must include a "live animal" sticker on the crate. Airlines have these stickers available at the point of departure. Tape a sign giving full information regarding contact persons at the points of departure and destination, with phone numbers and addresses.
- **Make sure your dog is wearing a collar and ID tags.** Regardless of how careful everyone may be, accidents do happen and a dog can manage to escape from her crate. If your Rottie should elude officials and get beyond the airport, there will be no way for anyone to contact you unless the dog carries identification. There are cases in which owners have opened the crates at arrival only to have their dogs bolt out in panic. Include a telephone number on the tag where someone can be reached 24 hours a day. And remember, only use buckle collars whenever your dog is in a crate. Training collars (also known as *chain collars* or *choke collars*) can get caught on crate wires and hang your dog.
- **Arrive at the airport early.** Get to the airport a minimum of 1½ hours before flight time, and go directly to the passenger check-in counter. Make sure the dog is fully checked in and insist that you stay where you can see the dog until it is time to transport the crate to the loading area. At that point, make a headlong dash for the gate and watch to see that your dog is loaded on the plane. When you get on board, have the flight attendant check to make sure the dog is on board, too. Will this make you seem like a bit of a nuisance? Perhaps. But better that than you ending up in one city and your Rottweiler in another.

When you arrive at your destination, your Rottweiler will be ecstatic to see you again after all those hours away from you. However, leave your dog in the crate until you get to a place that is less frantic and a bit safer than the airline terminal. Have a good sturdy leash with you in your carry-on bag and snap the leash on while your pal is still in her crate so she can't get away from you.

Find a Good Kennel If Your Pal Can't Go

Although having your Rottie along may be great fun, it just may not be practical. What then? Cancel the trip? Well, you could. Or as an alternative, you could find a good boarding kennel that will take super care of your pal while you're gone.

Don't just drop your dog off at the closest kennel. The only way you can find a great kennel is by doing a lot of checking. To help steer you in the right direction, your vet can offer local recommendations, and there is an American Boarding Kennel Association (ABKA) that can do the same. You can contact the ABKA by logging on to its Web site at `www.abka.com` or by calling 719-591-1113. Your dog's breeder may also have recommendations, and so may your neighbors.

Even with recommendations, no kennel is adequate for your Rottie unless it meets your approval. When you have found several kennels that sound like possibilities, drop by during business hours and ask if you can have a tour. Understand that few kennels are going to be as neat and spiffy as your kitchen or living room. (Imagine your own home with a couple of dozen dogs in it.) But this doesn't mean the kennel should give you a sense of unsanitary conditions and neglect. It's hard to keep any kennel smelling as sweet as a meadow in springtime, but bad smells and smells that linger in the air no matter where you go don't offer much promise of sanitary conditions.

Any kennel that will not allow you to look around definitely should *not* get your business! Accept no excuses.

Check to see whether the food and water containers are kept clean. Do the runs show signs of regular care and cleaning? Look at what the surface of the runs is made of. Do the surfaces provide good footing and easy cleanup and sanitizing? Is the run your dog will be kept in big enough? If not, what provisions are made for exercise? What about security? Are the runs escape-proof?

Even though your practically perfect Rottweiler may not be a fighter, the dog in the next run at a boarding kennel just may be, and he could encourage your pacifist to do battle. So look at the fencing and make sure it provides safety without making the dog feel totally cut off from the world. Metal mesh between runs keeps ears and paws attached to the proper owner but still allows the dogs to see each other.

Discuss your dog's attitude toward strangers and ask the kennel employees what their views of Rottweilers are. Understanding the breed is very important, and Rotties seem to sense those who can relate to them. The owner of the kennel I use thoroughly understands the Rottie psyche and gets on famously with even the toughest visitors.

If your Rottie wants and needs attention, make sure the kennel attendants will be able to provide this. Many kennels provide what they call *playtime,* in which the dog is given time in a large paddock and someone to play catch with. They may charge a few dollars extra per day for this service, but it can mean a big difference in your pal's stay.

Ask the manager what inoculations and health precautions boarders are required to have when they check in. Every kennel I have ever used demands proof of current rabies inoculations and protection against bordatella (also known as *kennel cough*). Are incoming dogs screened for fleas, ticks, and other parasites? If there are no requirements regarding health safeguards, look elsewhere.

When you check your pal in to the kennel, be sure to leave your veterinarian's name, address, and phone number in case of emergency, and leave a contact number where you can be reached while you're gone. Bring your Rottie's blanket and plenty of her favorite toys. Check on the food the kennel feeds before you arrive, and if you do not feel that it is suitable for your dog, bring enough of the food your Rottie is accustomed to for the duration of your absence.

Fear not, your Rottweiler will probably have just as good a time as you do on your vacation. Well-run kennels are managed by people who love dogs, and they do their best to return Bruno to you in as good shape (or better) as when she checked in.

Consider Getting a Pet Sitter

Even with all my praise of well-run boarding kennels, you still may feel there is absolutely no way you would even consider abandoning your buddy to the kennel life. In that case, think about a *pet sitter,* someone who will come to your home at regular intervals during the day to feed your dog and provide time for exercise and those calls of nature. Although you won't be home to hold your Rottie's paw, with a pet sitter everything else remains the same. If your Rottie isn't happier about this, at least *you* will be.

You undoubtedly have a friend or relative who gets along well with your Rottie (an important factor!) who will happy to do this for a day, or perhaps even two days. But if your absence is going to extend beyond that, consider paying someone to come in to take care of everything. Your vet may be able to recommend someone, and there are national organizations dedicated to making recommendations for qualified pet sitters, including the following:

- **National Association of Professional Pet Sitters,** 1030 15th Street NW, Suite 870, Washington, DC 20005; telephone: 800-296-7387; Web site: `www.petsitters.org`
- **Pet Sitters International,** 418 East King Street, King, NC 27021; telephone: 800-268-7487; Web site: `www.petsit.com`

Hiring a professional pet sitter is best. Most professionals provide credentials and written agreements as to what they will and will not do, and what they agree to be responsible for. Of course, in your case, you want a sitter who knows and understands the Rottweiler and who your Rottie agrees to get along with.

A professional pet sitter who is a member of a national pet-sitting organization is usually bonded and insured. This is very important, because any dog lover can advertise that he or she is a professional. You don't want to come home to find your Rottie is sitting there waiting for you in a home stripped of every valuable possession you ever had.

Although a pet sitter may seem like a simple alternative to a boarding kennel, it is a bit more complicated. Just because the sitter and your dog hit it off like long lost friends doesn't mean the sitter is honest, nor does the bonded and insured sitter guarantee he or she knows what to do with your canine treasure in case of emergency.

Entrusting your pal and your entire household to someone who may well be a perfect stranger is a serious step. Consider the following bottom-line requirements:

- **Is the person a member of a bona fide professional pet-sitter organization?**
- **Have you spoken directly to an official of the organization about the individual you are considering and determined that the person is bonded and insured?**
- **Have you checked a realistic number of the person's references?**
- **What kind of experience has the person had with Rottweilers?**
- **Does what is included in the sitter's agreement cover everything you feel is important?**
- **Has the sitter provided you with a complete list of questions concerning what he or she needs to know about your dog and your home?**
- **Does the sitter have a 24-hour pager or cell phone?**
- **Is the sitter familiar with the local laws and regulations that govern animal care?**
- **Is there an alternate who can step in for the sitter in case of illness or accident?**
- **Have you and the sitter completely agreed upon the charges for everything you wish to have taken care of?**

These items can start you off in the right direction. There are undoubtedly other items specifically relevant to your situation that should be included on this list as well.

Appendix A
Glossary

American Kennel Club (AKC): The organization that registers purebred dogs and sanctions dog shows and other competitions.

angulation: The angles formed by the meeting of the dog's bones. The term is usually used in respect to the bones of the forequarters and hindquarters.

balanced: A term used to signify that a dog is a symmetrically and proportionally correct.

bitch: A female dog.

Best in Show (BIS): The designation for the best dog at an all-breed show.

Best in Specialty Show (BISS): The designation for the best dog at a Rottweiler-only show.

Best of Breed (BOB): The designation for the best Rottweiler at an all-breed show.

Best of Opposite Sex (BOS): After the Best of Breed (BOB) is awarded, the best individual of the opposite sex receives this award.

Best of Winners (BOW): Winners Dog (WD) and Winners Bitch (WB) compete to see which is the best of the two, and the winner is given this designation.

Bitter Apple: A commercially available liquid used to discourage dogs from licking or chewing on themselves or household objects.

body language: A dog's method of communicating his feelings and reactions.

breed standard: A written description of the ideal specimen of a breed.

Canine Good Citizen (CGC): A basic test of a dog's good manners and stability. Passing the test earns an official CGC designation, which can be added to the dog's name.

castration: Surgical removal of the testicles of the male dog. Also known as *neutering.*

Canine Eye Registration Foundation (CERF): Tests and certifies eyes against genetic diseases.

character: The general appearance and/or expression that is considered typical of the breed.

condition: A dog's overall appearance of health or lack thereof.

conformation: The form and structure of a dog, as required by the breed standard.

Champion (CH): The winner of 15 American Kennel Club (AKC) championship points under three different judges. Two of the wins must be *majors* (where three or more points are available).

cryptorchid: A male dog whose testicles have not properly descended.

dentition: The arrangement of a dog's teeth.

down: The command used to instruct a dog to lie down.

estrus: The stage of the reproductive cycle in which the female will stand willing for mating.

Federacion Cynologique Internationale (FCI): The controlling body of pedigreed dogs in most of the European and Latin American countries.

heartworm: A parasitic worm that invades the heart and lungs of a dog and can so affect those organs as to become fatal. Veterinary treatment is required, and preventive treatment is recommended for all dogs to avoid the problem.

heel: The command given to a dog so that he will walk along at the handler's left side with his shoulder in line with the handler's knee.

herding trials: Trials designed to test a dog's ability to control livestock.

hip dysplasia: Abnormal development of the hip, affecting dogs in varying degrees of intensity.

hookworm: An internal parasite of the dog that can create an anemic condition.

incisors: The teeth located between the fangs in the front of the upper and lower jaws.

International Championship (Int.Ch.): A designation which can only be awarded by the Federacion Cynologique Internationale (FCI).

level bite: When the front or incisor teeth meet exactly top to bottom.

Lyme disease: A tick-borne disease that can create joint and neurological problems in both dogs and humans.

molars: Rear teeth that are used for chewing.

monorchid: A male dog who has only one testicle descended.

neutering: Surgical removal of the testicles of the male dog. Also known as *castration.*

Orthopedic Foundation for Animals (OFA): Certifies x-rays of hips and elbows.

overshot: When the front or incisor teeth of the top jaw overlap the front or incisor teeth of the lower jaw.

Schutzhund: A German dog sport that tests a dog's excellence in obedience, protection, and tracking.

scissors bite: A bite in which the front upper teeth or incisors just barely overlap the lower front or incisor teeth of the lower jaw.

Sieger: Best male in a German Rottweiler show.

Siegerin: Best female in a German Rottweiler show.

sound: A term used to signify that a dog has an overall good construction and good health.

spaying: Surgically removing the ovaries of the female dog.

specialty show: A show restricted to only one breed of dog.

stay: Command given to a dog that requires remaining in one place until a release command is given.

stop: The juncture at which there is a step-up from the muzzle to the skull.

therapy dogs: Well-trained dogs who bring comfort and companionship to hospitalized and elderly people.

tracking trials: Trials that test a dog's ability to track humans or lost articles.

type: The distinguishing characteristics of a breed, as called for in the breed standard.

undershot: When the front or incisor teeth of the lower jaw extend beyond the front or incisor teeth of the upper jaw.

withers: The top of the first dorsal vertebra, or the highest part of the body just behind the neck. Often referred to as the top of the shoulders. A dog's height is measured from the ground to the withers.

Appendix B
Resources

Books

The Complete Puppy and Dog Book, New Revised Edition, by Norman H. Johnson, D.V.M. (published by Galahad Books, 2000)

The Complete Rottweiler, by Muriel Freeman (published by IDG Books Worldwide, Inc., 1984)

A Dog Owner's Guide to the Rottweiler, by Joan Blackmore (published by Tetra Press, 1995)

Dr. Pitcairn's Complete Guide to Natural Health for Dogs and Cats, by Richard H. Pitcairn, D.V.M., Ph.D., and Susan Hubble Pitcairn (published by Rodale Press, 1995)

How to Be Your Dog's Best Friend: A Training Manual for Dog Owners, by The Monks of New Skete (published by Little, Brown and Company, 1978)

The Rottweiler: Centuries of Service, by Linda Michels and Catherine Thompson (published by IDG Books Worldwide, Inc., 1998)

The Rottweiler, An International Study of the Breed, by Dagmar Hodinar (published by Von Palisaden Publications, 1985)

Schutzhund Theory and Training Methods, by Susan Barwig and Stewart Hilliard (Published by IDG Books Worldwide, Inc., 1991)

Superdog: Raising the Perfect Canine Companion, by Michael W. Fox (published by IDG Books Worldwide, Inc., 1996)

The Ultimate Rottweiler, edited by Andrew H. Brace (published by IDG Books Worldwide, Inc., 1995)

Magazines

Journal of Veterinary Medical Education
Richard B. Talbot, D.V.M., Ph.D., Editor
VA-MD, College of Veterinary Medicine
Virginia Polytechnic Institute and State University
Blacksburg, VA 24061
Web site: scholar.lib.vt.edu/ejournals/JVME/V21-1/tofc.html

Rottweiler Quarterly
GPQ Publications
P.O. Box 900
Aromas, CA 95004
Telephone: 408-728-8461

Videos

Competitive Agility Training, Canine Training Systems.

Dog Steps, Rachel Page Elliot, American Kennel Club.

In the Ribbons, Rottweiler, Canine Training Systems.

Let's Talk About Rottweilers, Joan R. Klem, JRK Videos.

The Rottweiler, American Kennel Club.

CD-ROMs

The Rottweiler CD
Sherluck MultiMedia
29001 176th Avenue SE
Kent, WA 98042

Web Sites

AltVetMed: Complementary and Alternative Veterinary Medicine, www.altvetmed.com

American Kennel Club, www.akc.org

American Rottweiler Club, www.amrottclub.org

The American Veterinary Medical Association, www.avma.org

National Animal Poison Control Center, www.napcc.aspca.org

Organizations

American Kennel Club
5580 Centerview Drive
Raleigh, NC 27606-3390
telephone: 919-233-9767
Web site: www.akc.org

United Kennel Club, Inc.
100 East Kilgore Road
Kalamazoo, MI 49002-5584
telephone: 616-343-7037
Web site: www.ukcdogs.com

American Rottweiler Club
Pamela J. Grant, Secretary
45 Erika Lane
Belen, NM 87002-0000
telephone: 505-864-2070
Web site: www.amrottclub.org

Index

• A •

• B •

• C •

• D •

• E •

• H •

• I •

• O •

• P •

• R •

• S •

• T •

• U •

• V •

• W •

Notes

Notes

Notes

Notes

Notes

Notes

Notes

FREE
RECIPE
"for the"
Perfect
ROTTWEILER
1 HAPPY DOG

KONG
company